THE HARROWING OF HELL

by Evan Dahm

IRON CIRCUS COMICS

strange and amazing

inquiry@ironcircus.com   www.ironcircus.com

THE HARRO

OWING
OF HELL

Christianity in its true sense puts an end to government. So it was understood at its very commencement; it was for this cause that Christ was crucified.

Leo Tolstoy
The Kingdom of God is Within You

He saw with his own eyes the trophy of a cross of light in the heavens, above the sun, and bearing the inscription,

CONQUER BY THIS.

Eusebius Pamphilus
The Life of the Blessed Emperor Constantine

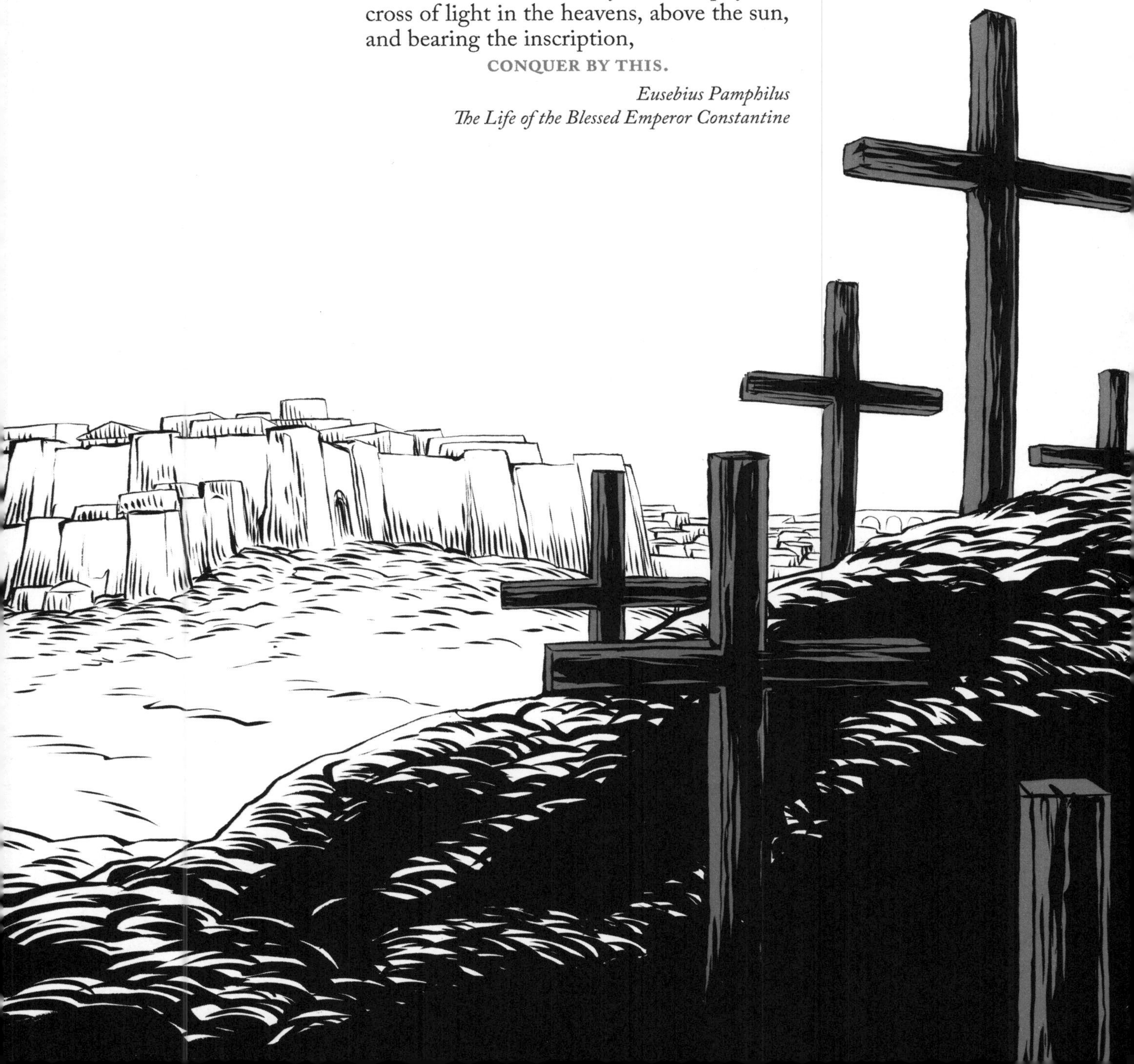

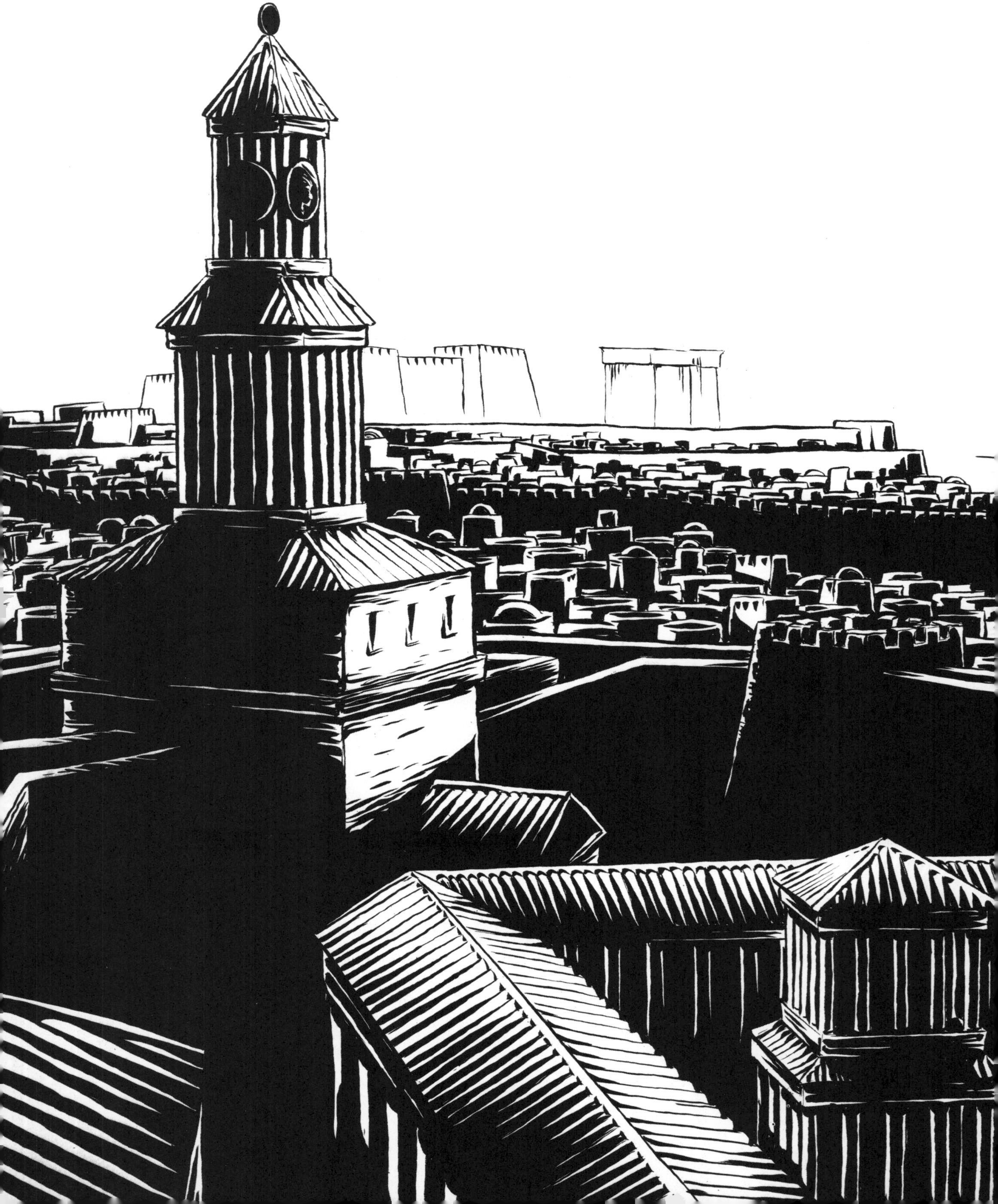

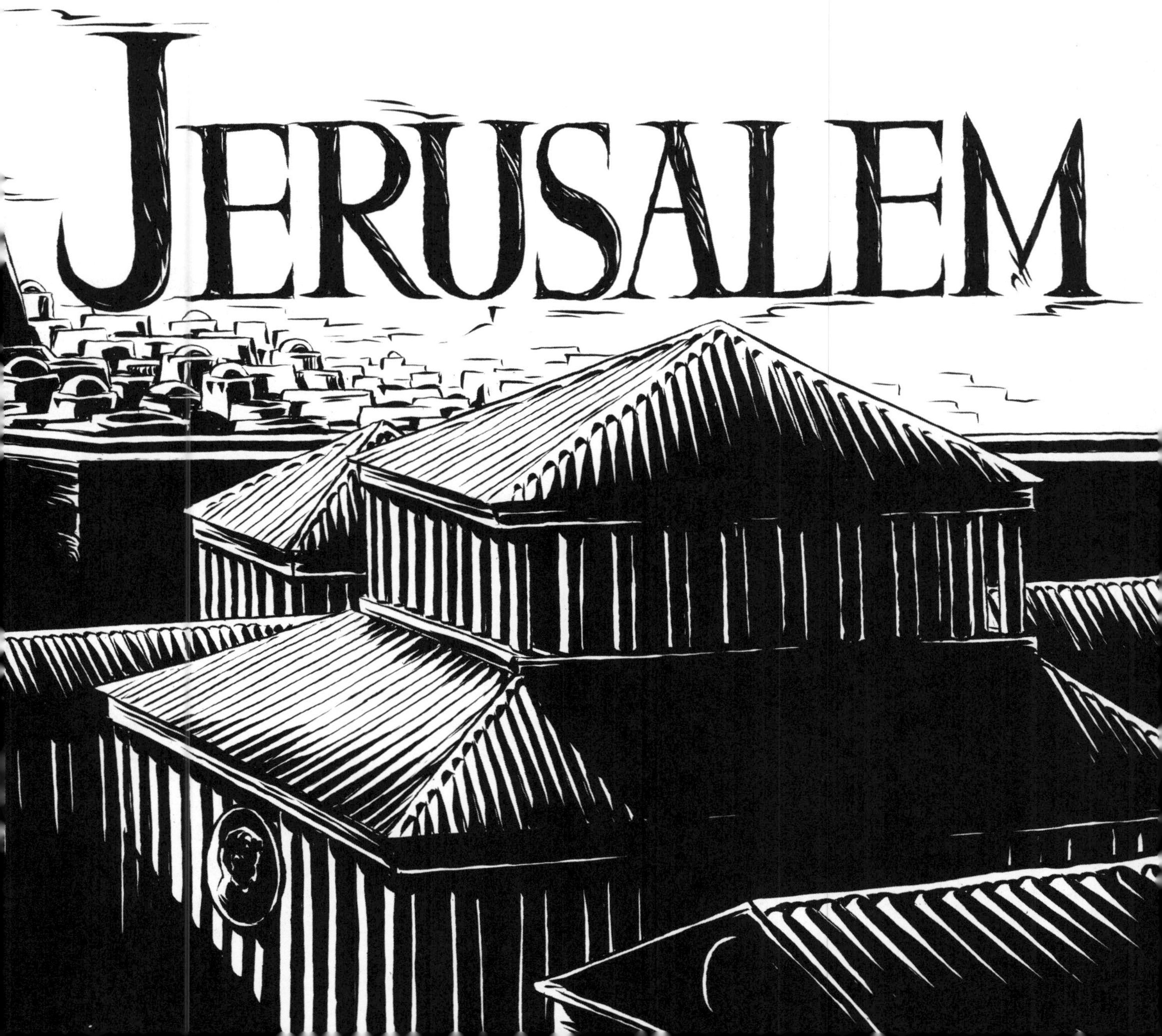
JERUSALEM

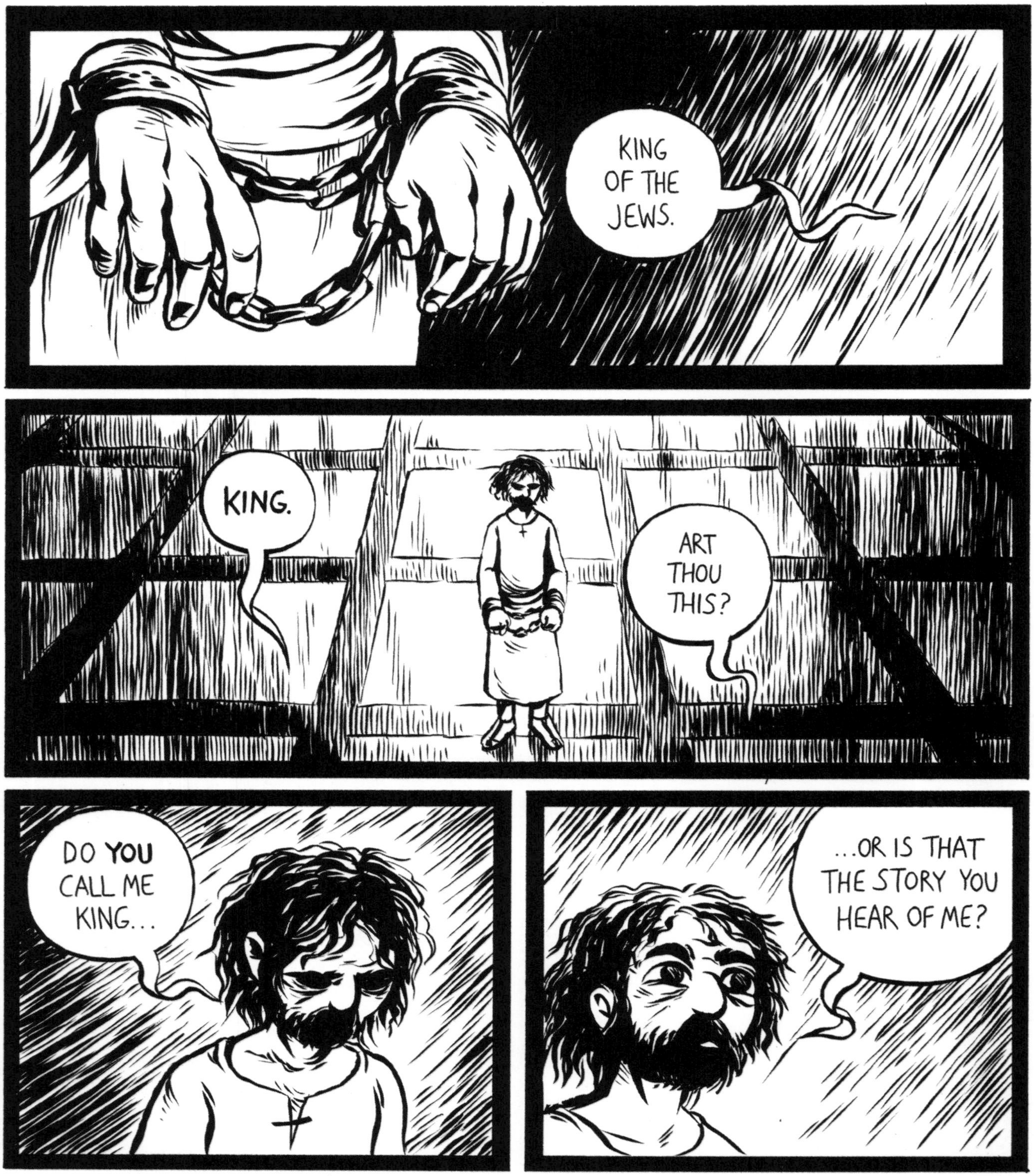
KING OF THE JEWS.
KING.
ART THOU THIS?
DO **YOU** CALL ME KING...
...OR IS THAT THE STORY YOU HEAR OF ME?

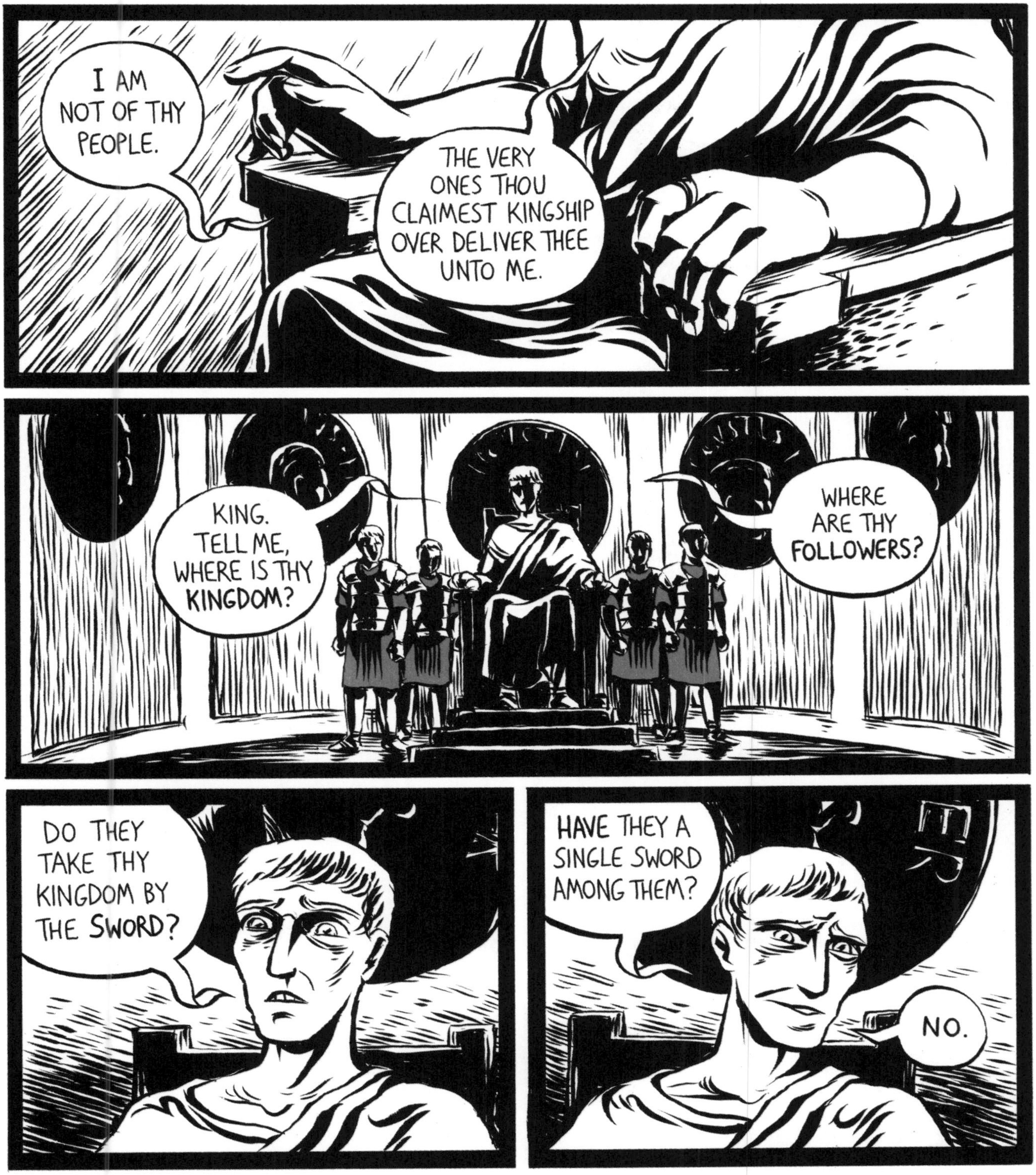
I AM NOT OF THY PEOPLE.
THE VERY ONES THOU CLAIMEST KINGSHIP OVER DELIVER THEE UNTO ME.
KING. TELL ME, WHERE IS THY KINGDOM?
WHERE ARE THY FOLLOWERS?
DO THEY TAKE THY KINGDOM BY THE SWORD?
HAVE THEY A SINGLE SWORD AMONG THEM?
NO.

PEASANTS AND FISHERMEN.
NO ONE NAMES THEE KING.
THEY HAVE NO KING BUT CAESAR.
THOU ANSWEREST NOTHING?

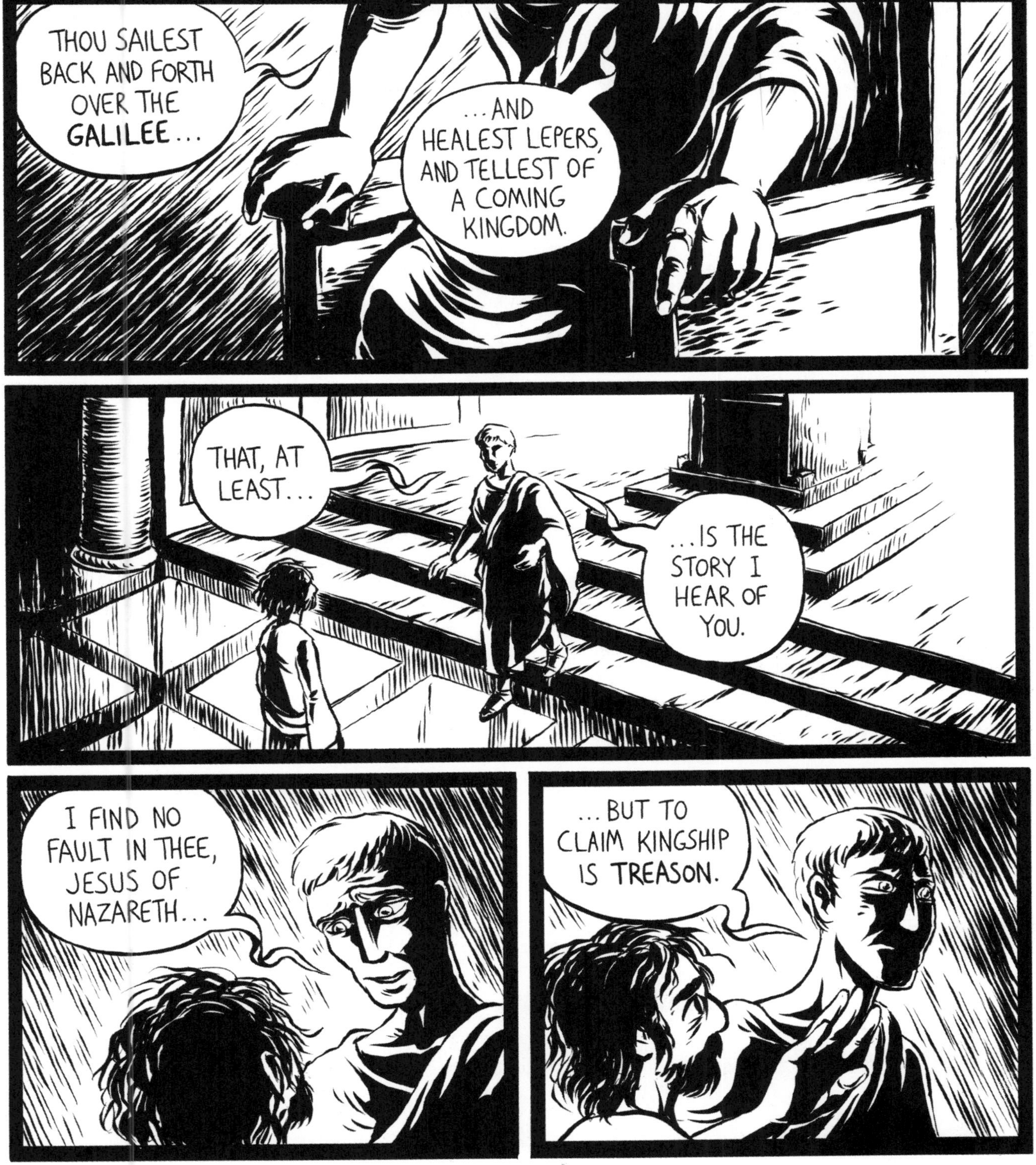
THOU SAILEST BACK AND FORTH OVER THE GALILEE...
...AND HEALEST LEPERS, AND TELLEST OF A COMING KINGDOM.
THAT, AT LEAST...
...IS THE STORY I HEAR OF YOU.
I FIND NO FAULT IN THEE, JESUS OF NAZARETH...
...BUT TO CLAIM KINGSHIP IS TREASON.

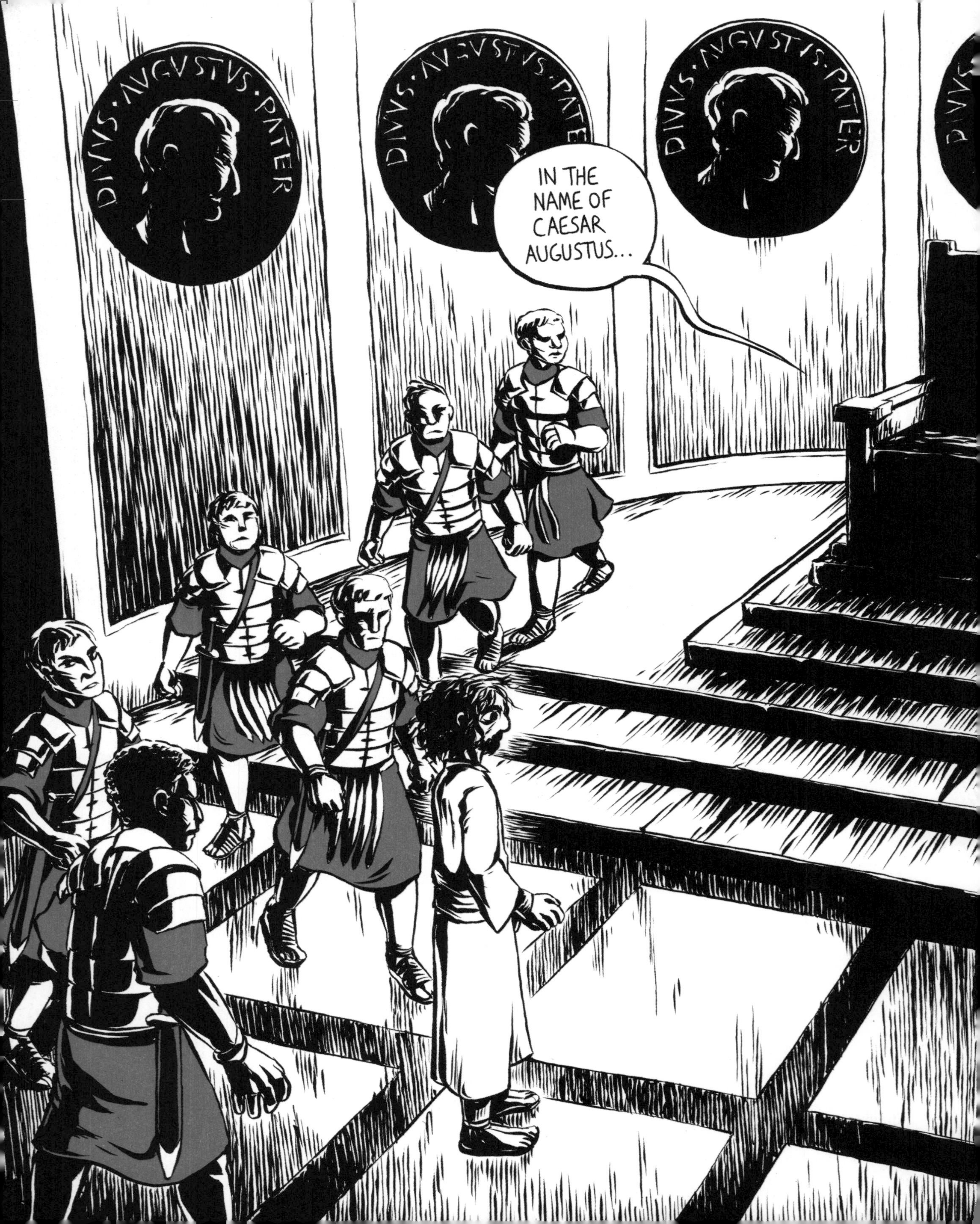
DIVVS·AVGVSTVS·PATER
DIVVS·AVGVSTVS·PATER
DIVVS·AVGVSTVS·PATER
IN THE NAME OF CAESAR AUGUSTUS...

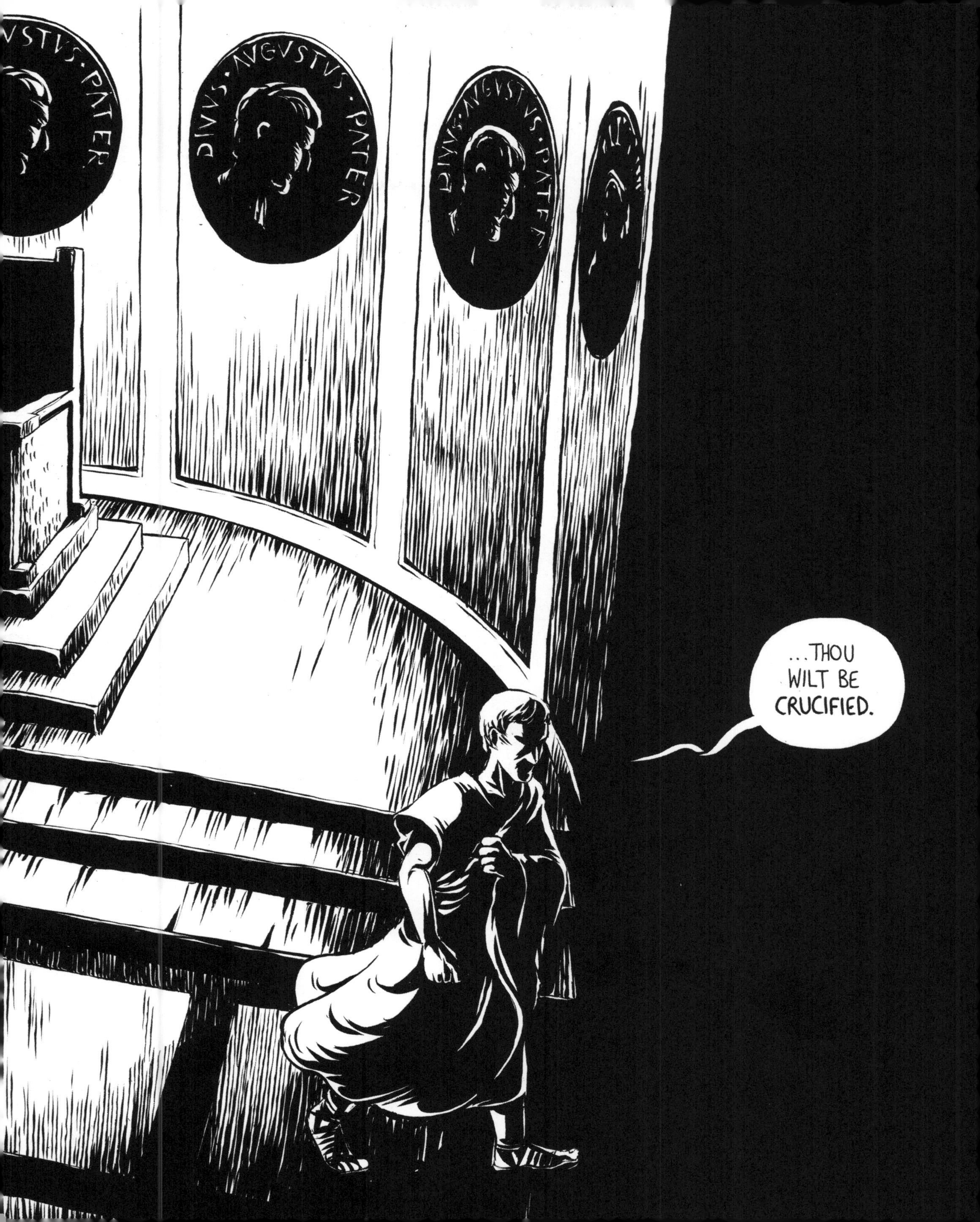
DIVVS·AVGVSTVS·PATER
DIVVS·AVGVSTVS·PATER
...THOU WILT BE CRUCIFIED.

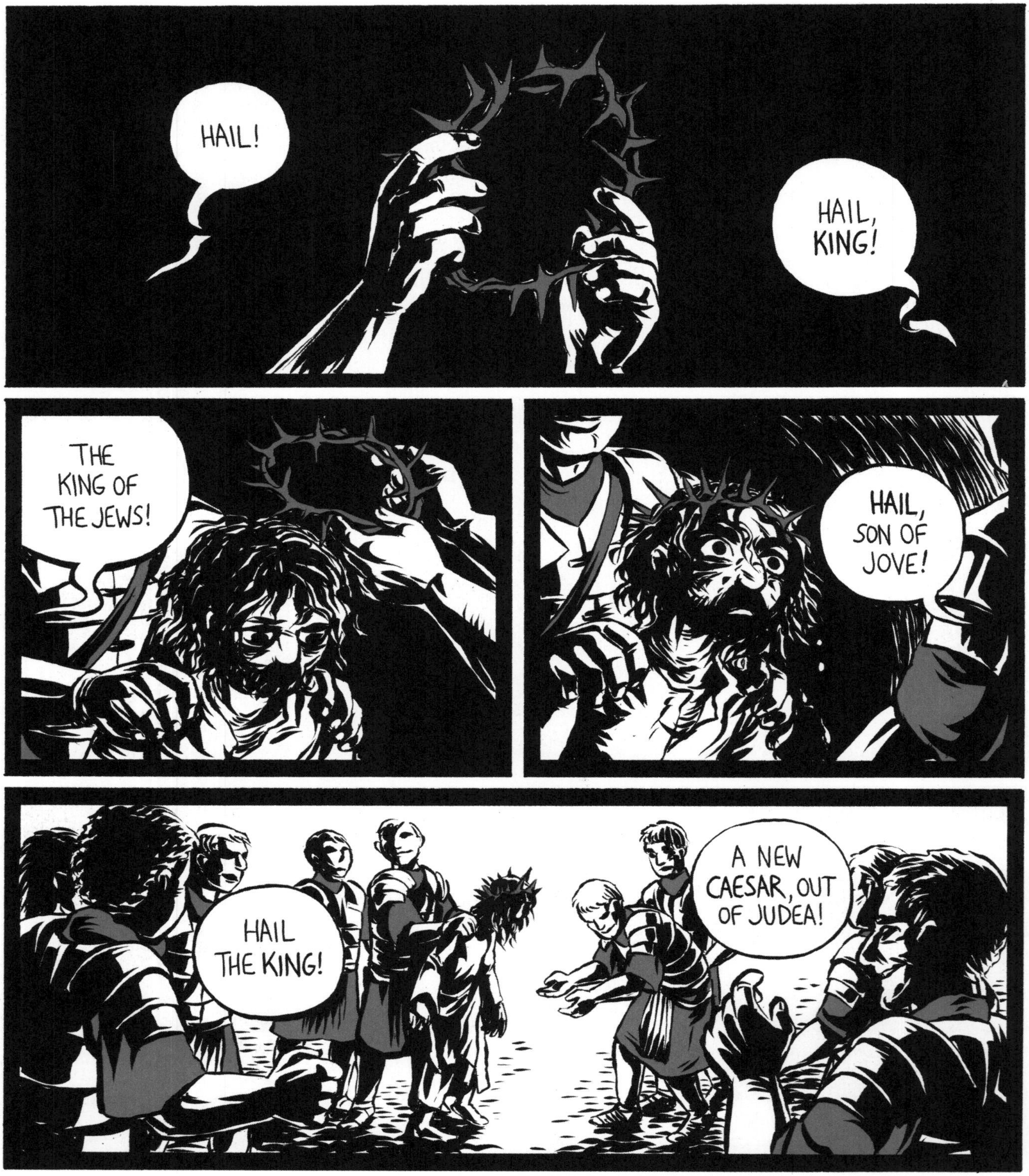
HAIL!
HAIL, KING!
THE KING OF THE JEWS!
HAIL, SON OF JOVE!
HAIL THE KING!
A NEW CAESAR, OUT OF JUDEA!

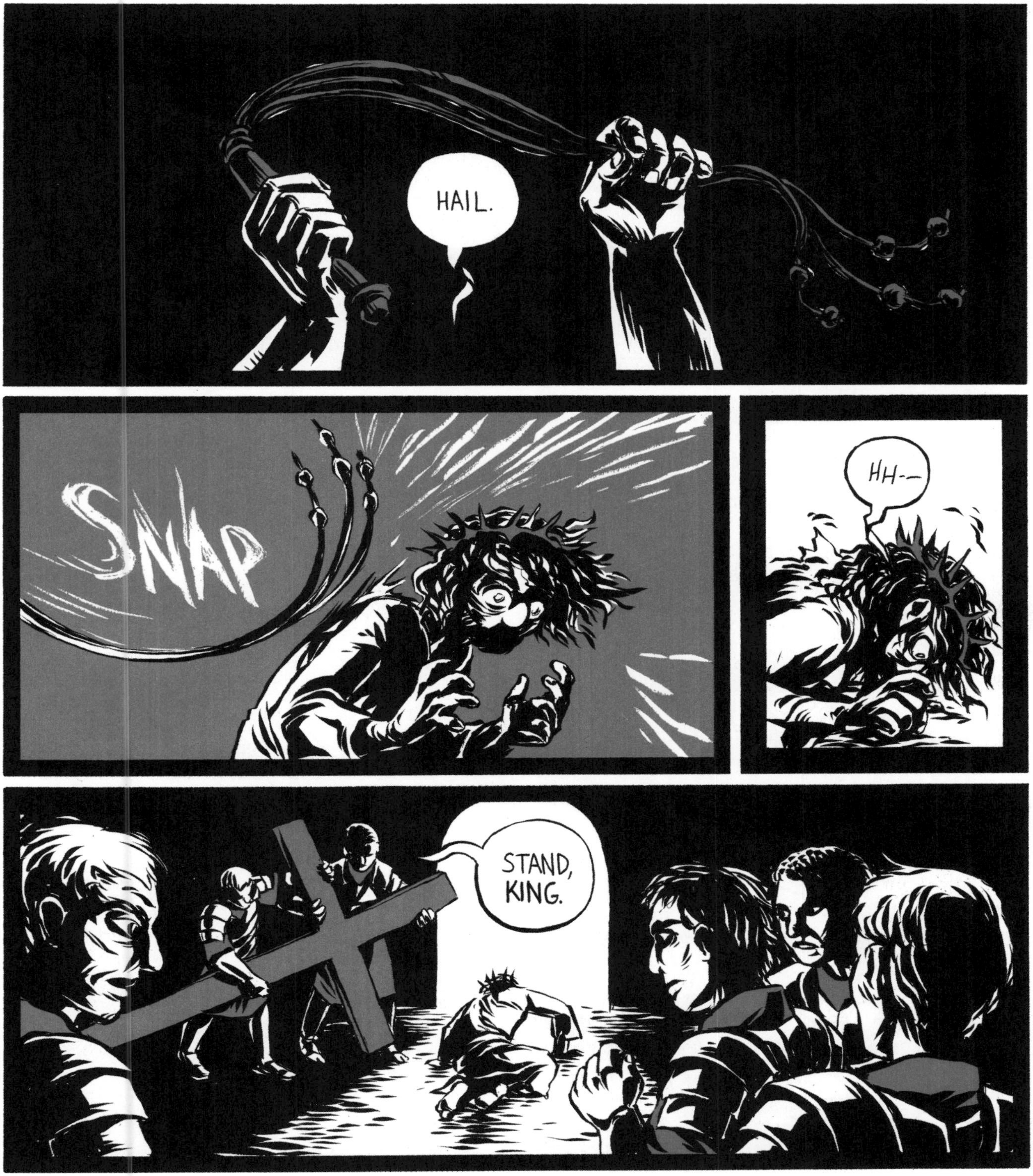
HAIL.
SNAP
HH--
STAND, KING.

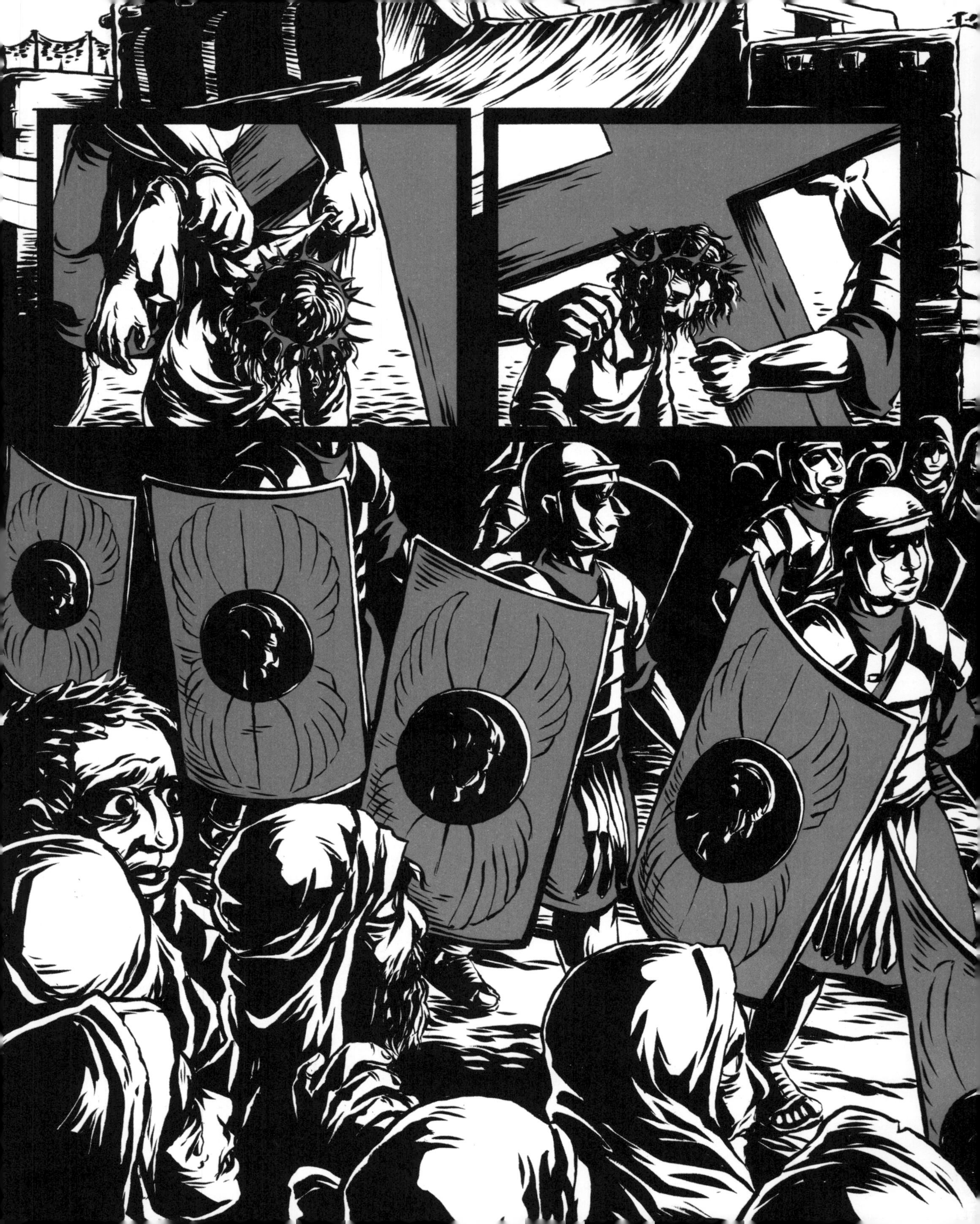

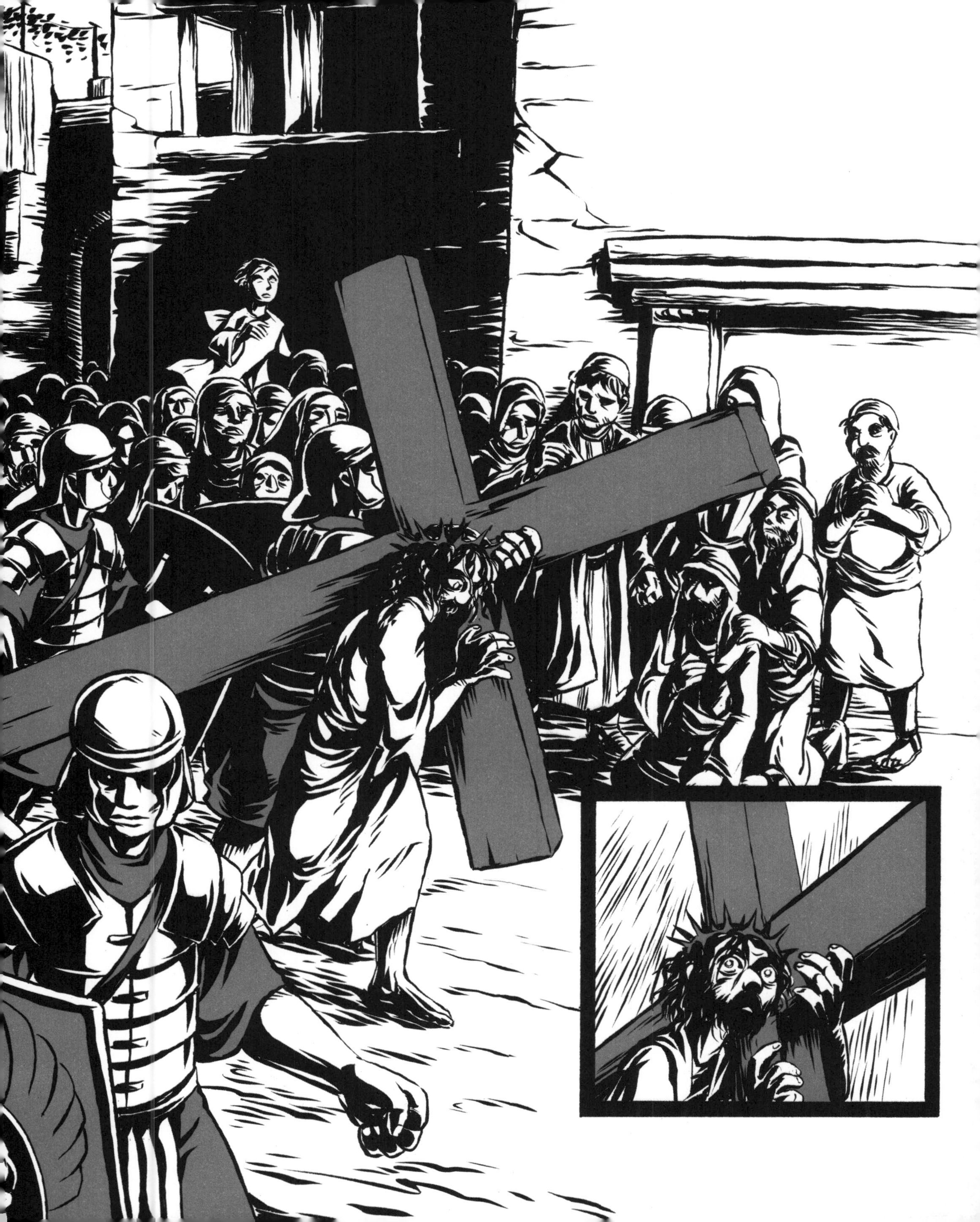

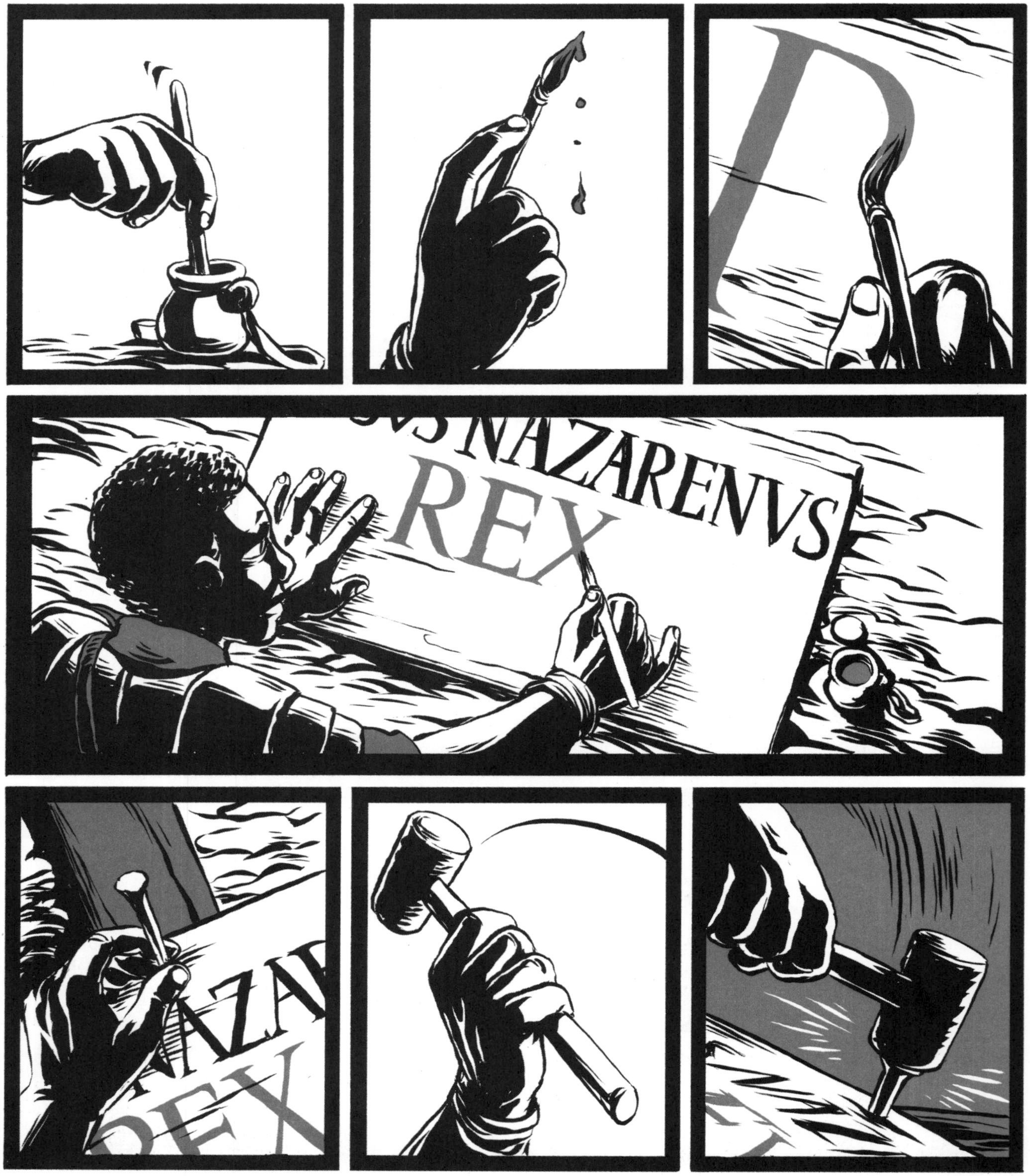
NAZARENVS
REX

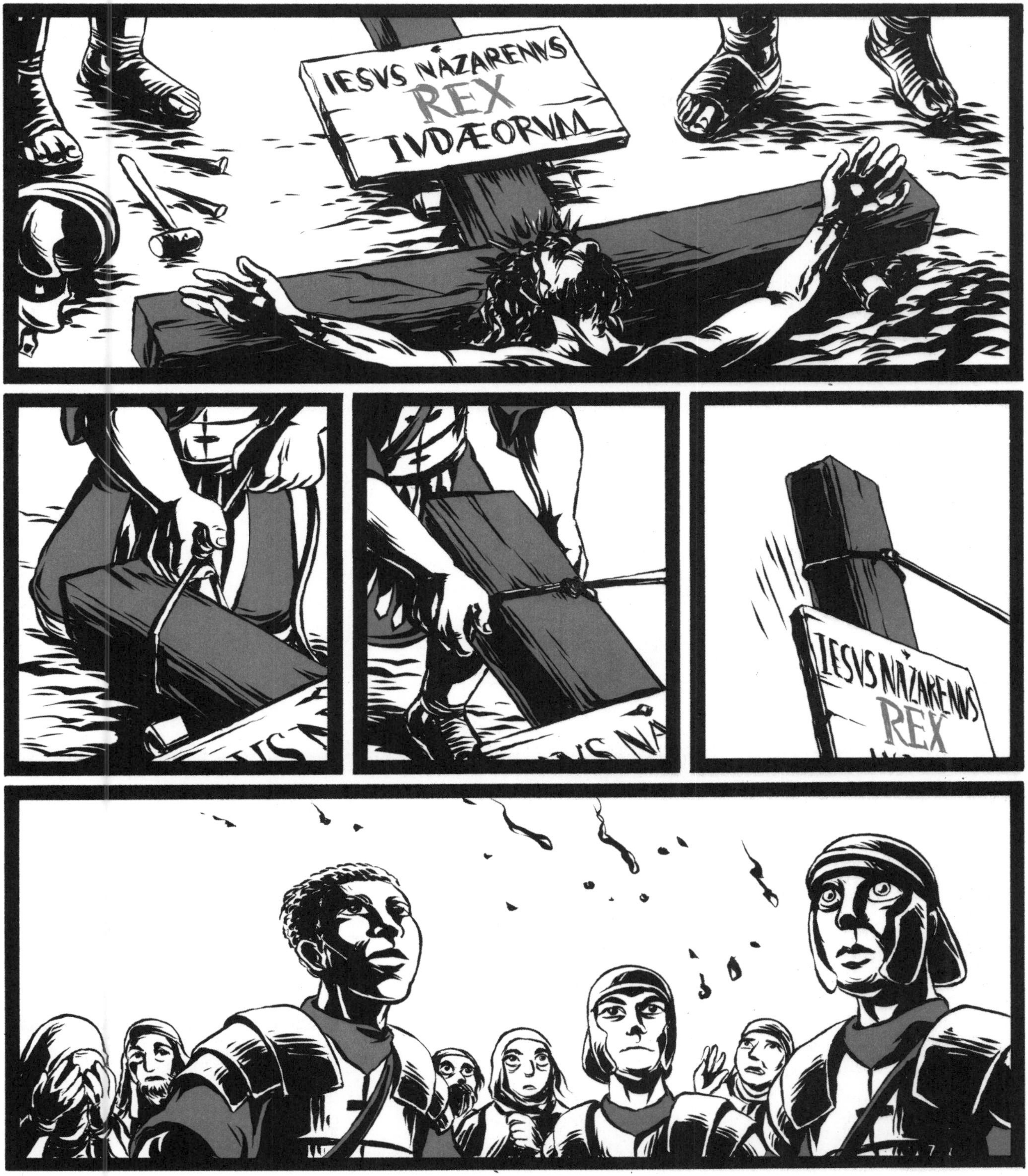
IESVS NAZARENVS
REX
IVDÆORVM
IESVS NAZARENVS
REX

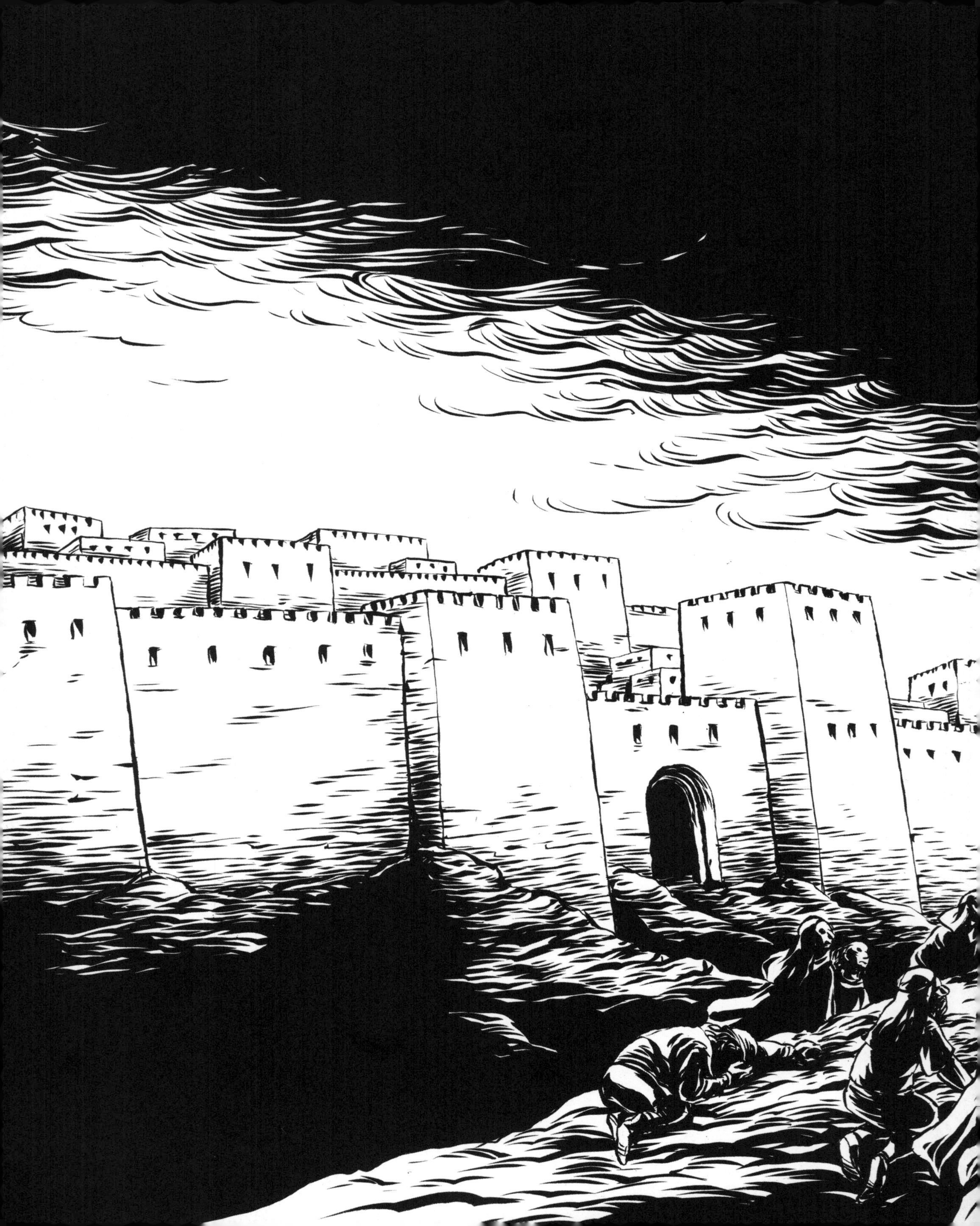

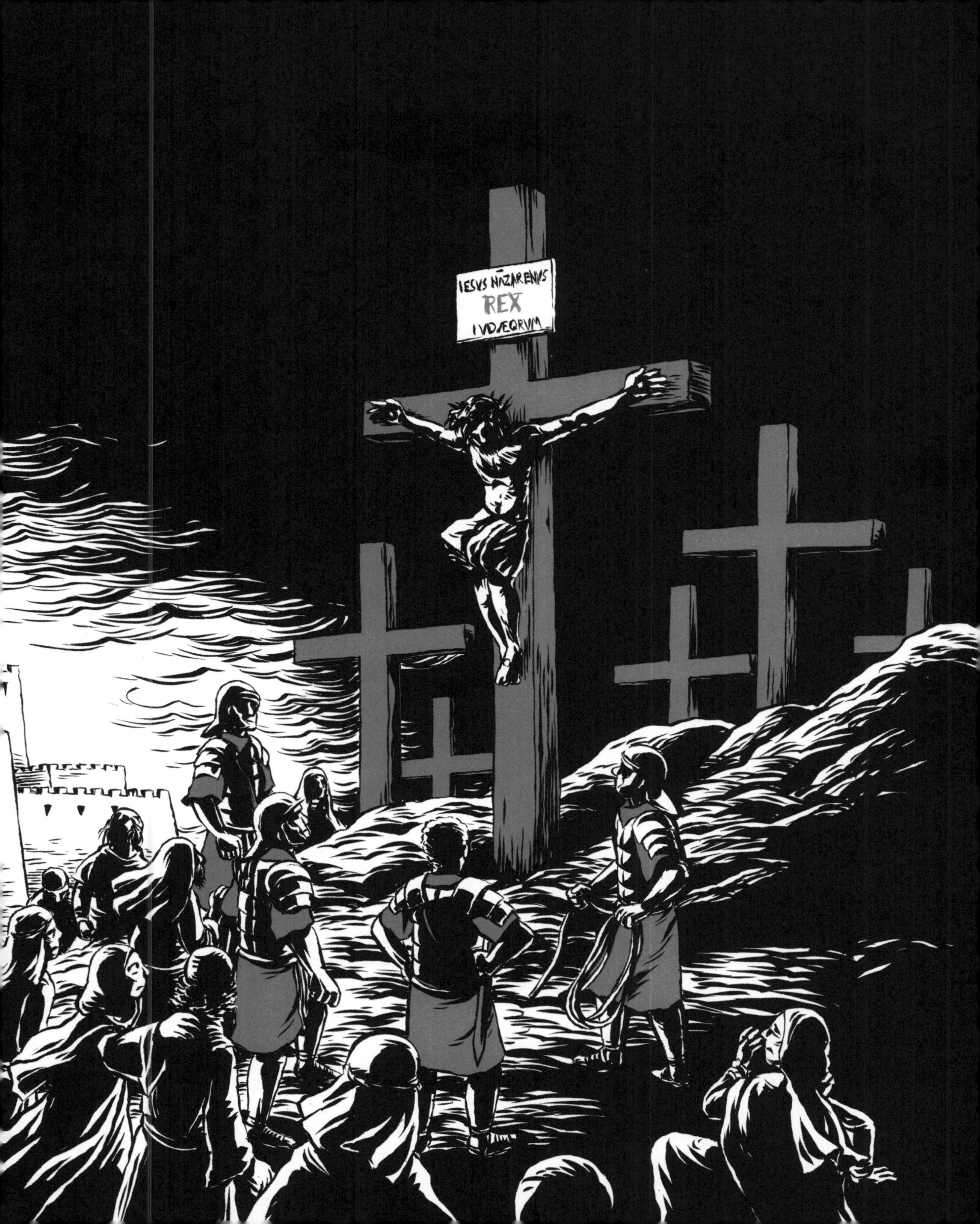
IESVS NAZARENVS
REX
IVDÆORVM

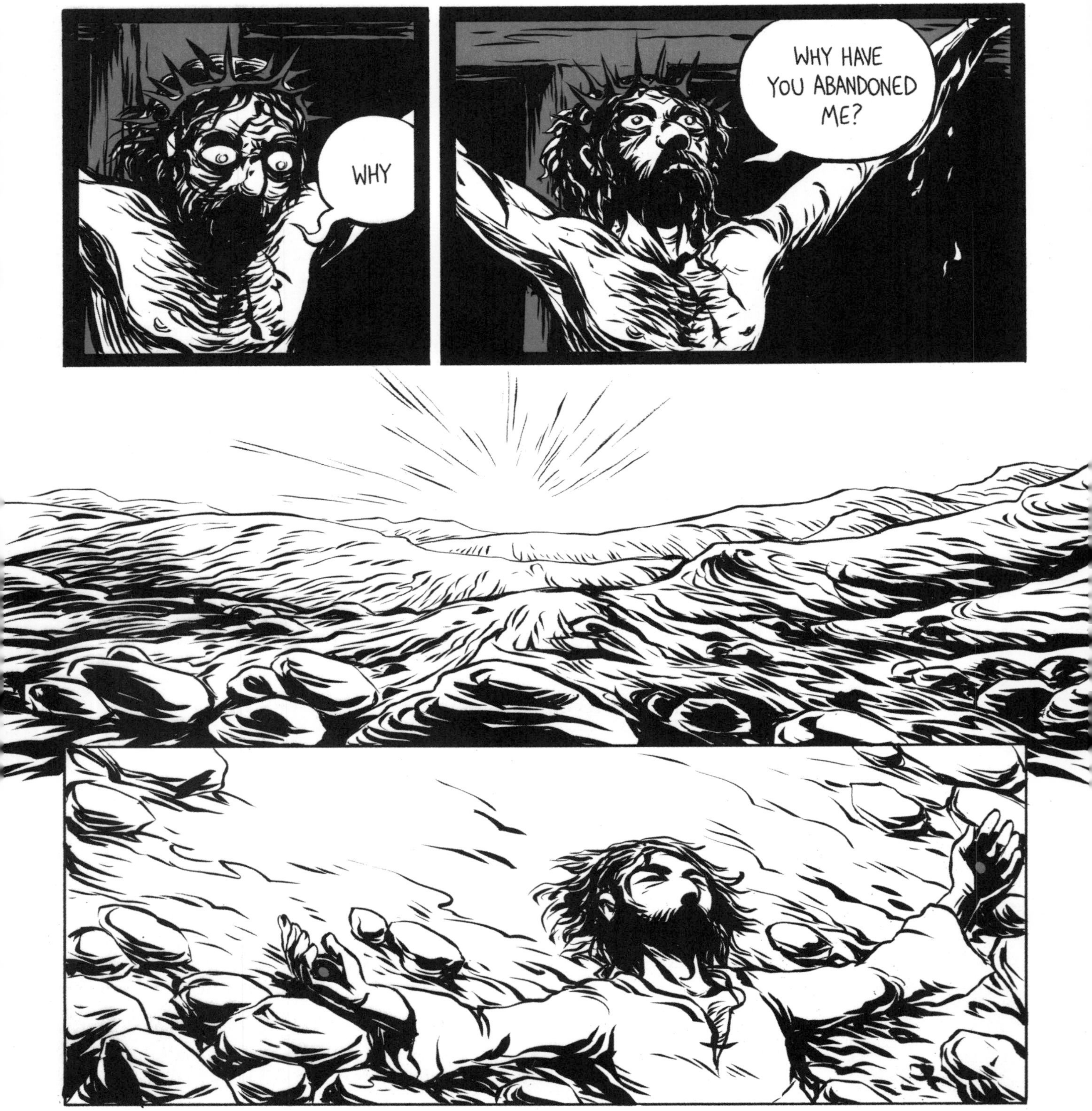
WHY
WHY HAVE YOU ABANDONED ME?

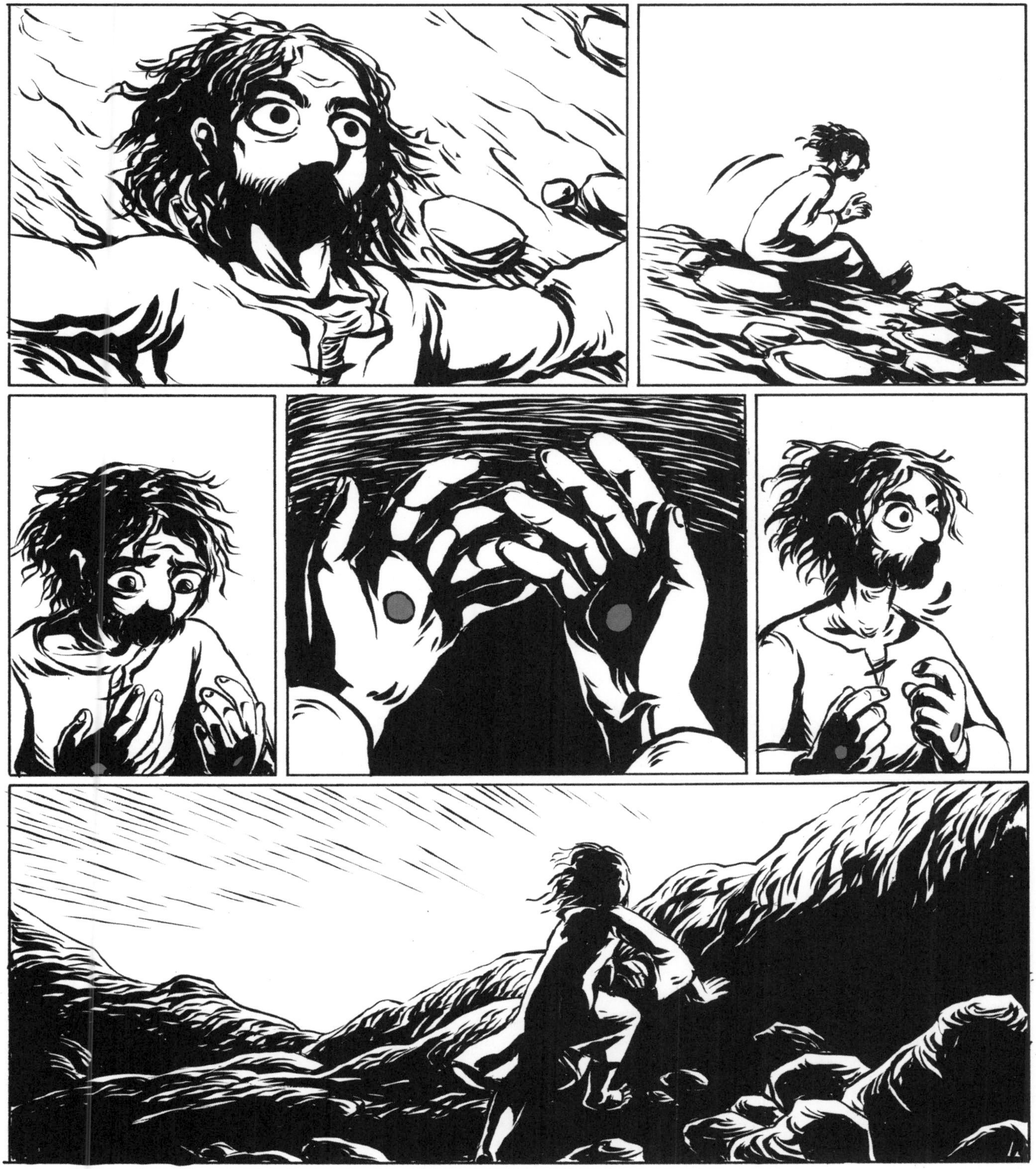

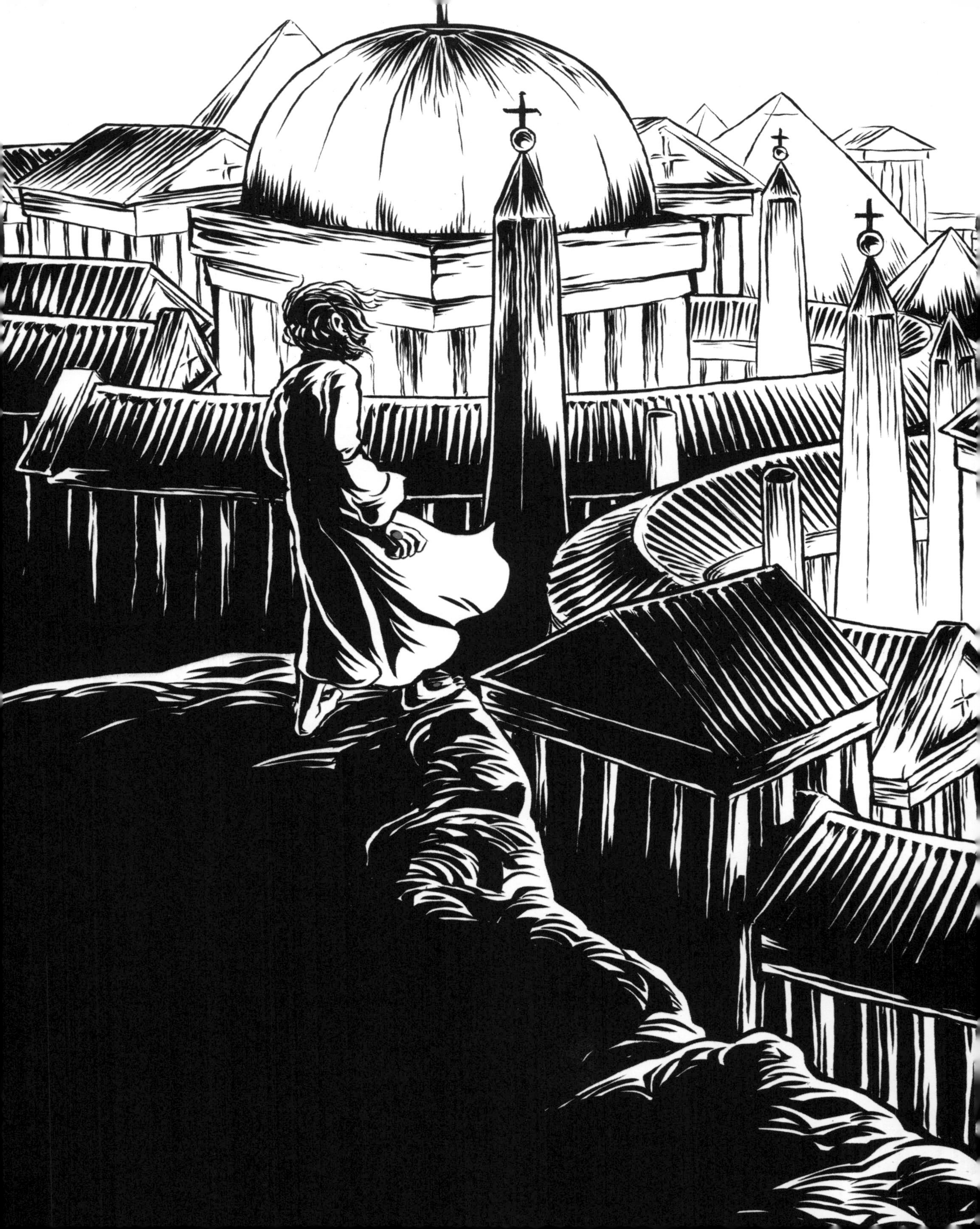

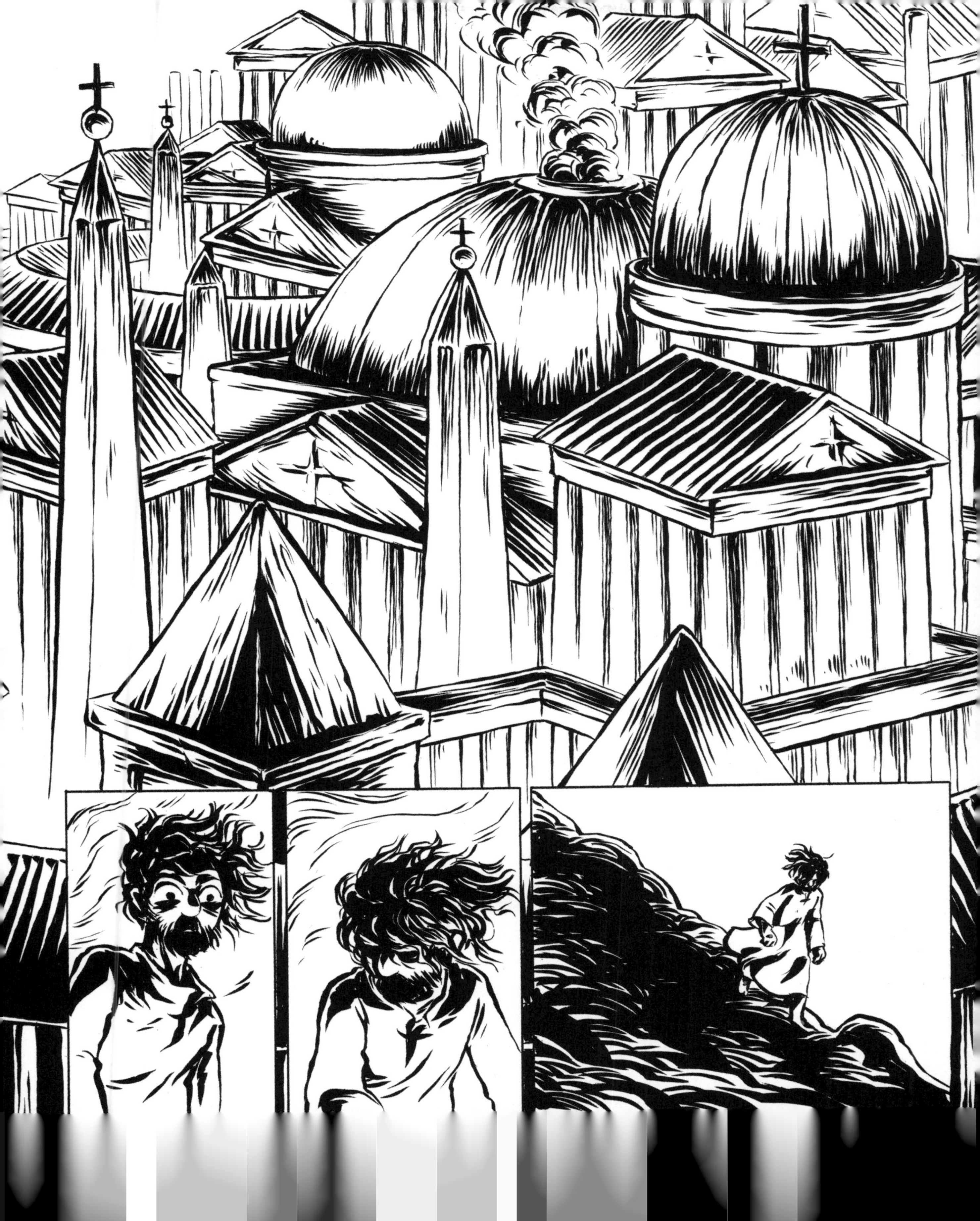

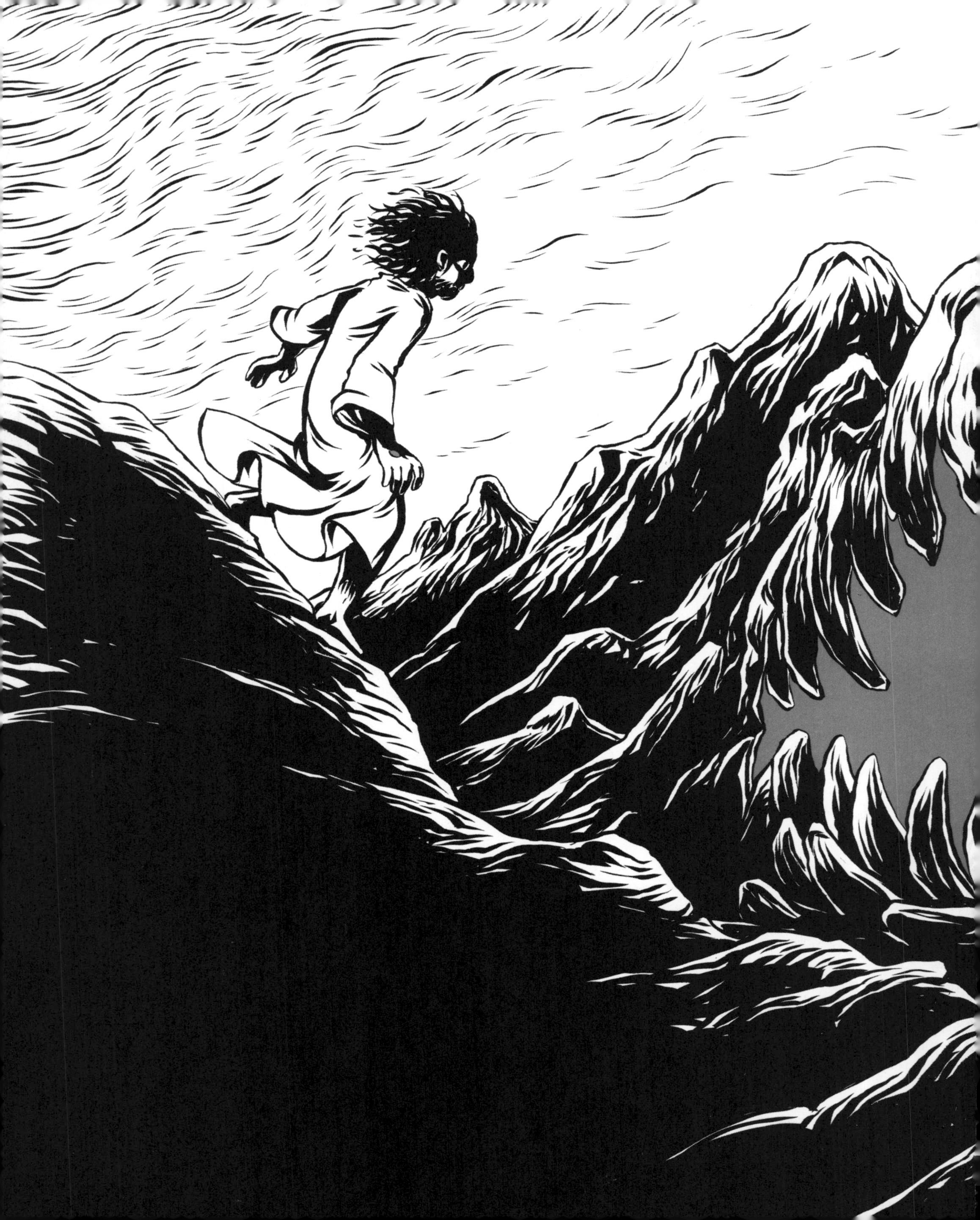

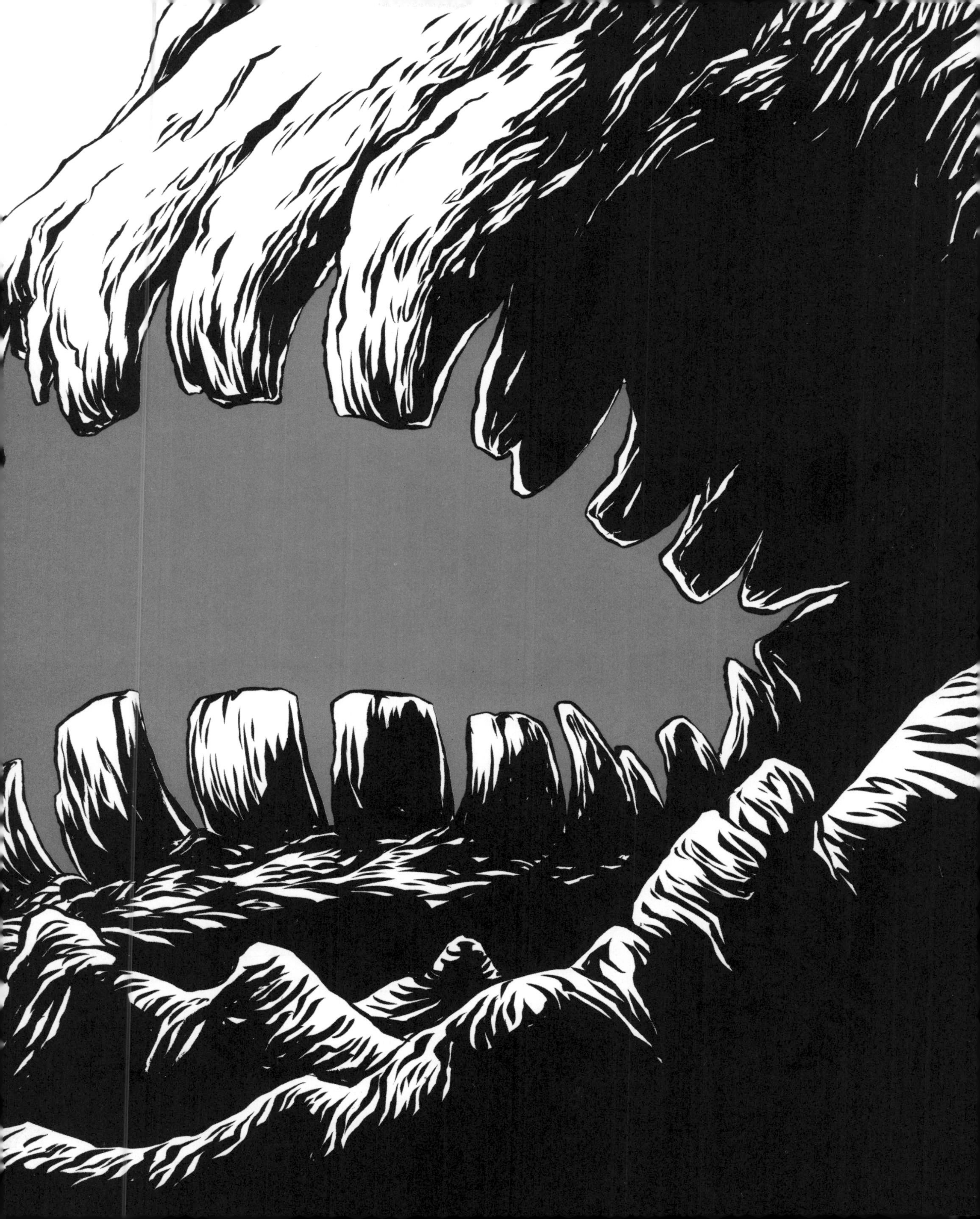

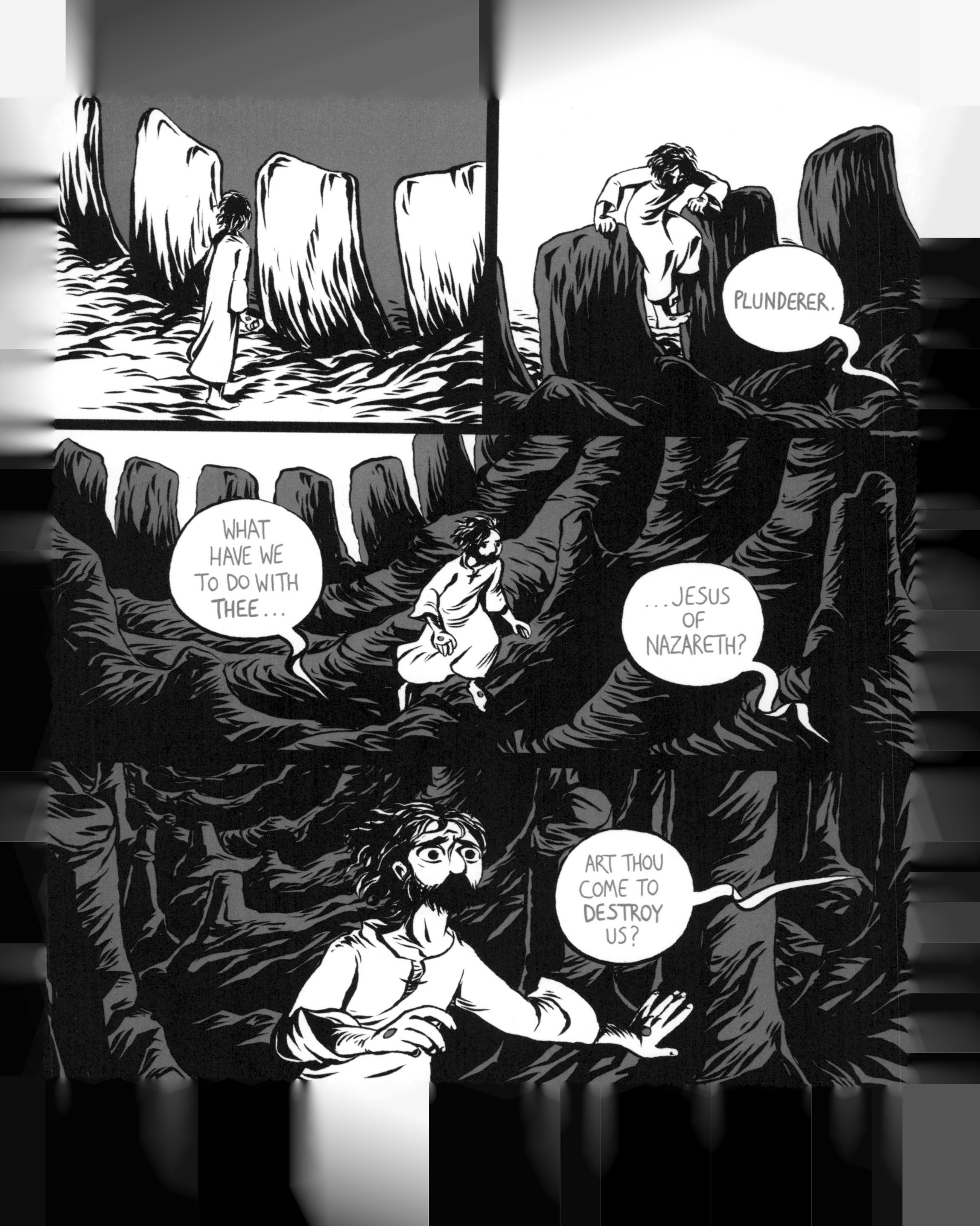
PLUNDERER.
WHAT HAVE WE TO DO WITH THEE...
...JESUS OF NAZARETH?
ART THOU COME TO DESTROY US?

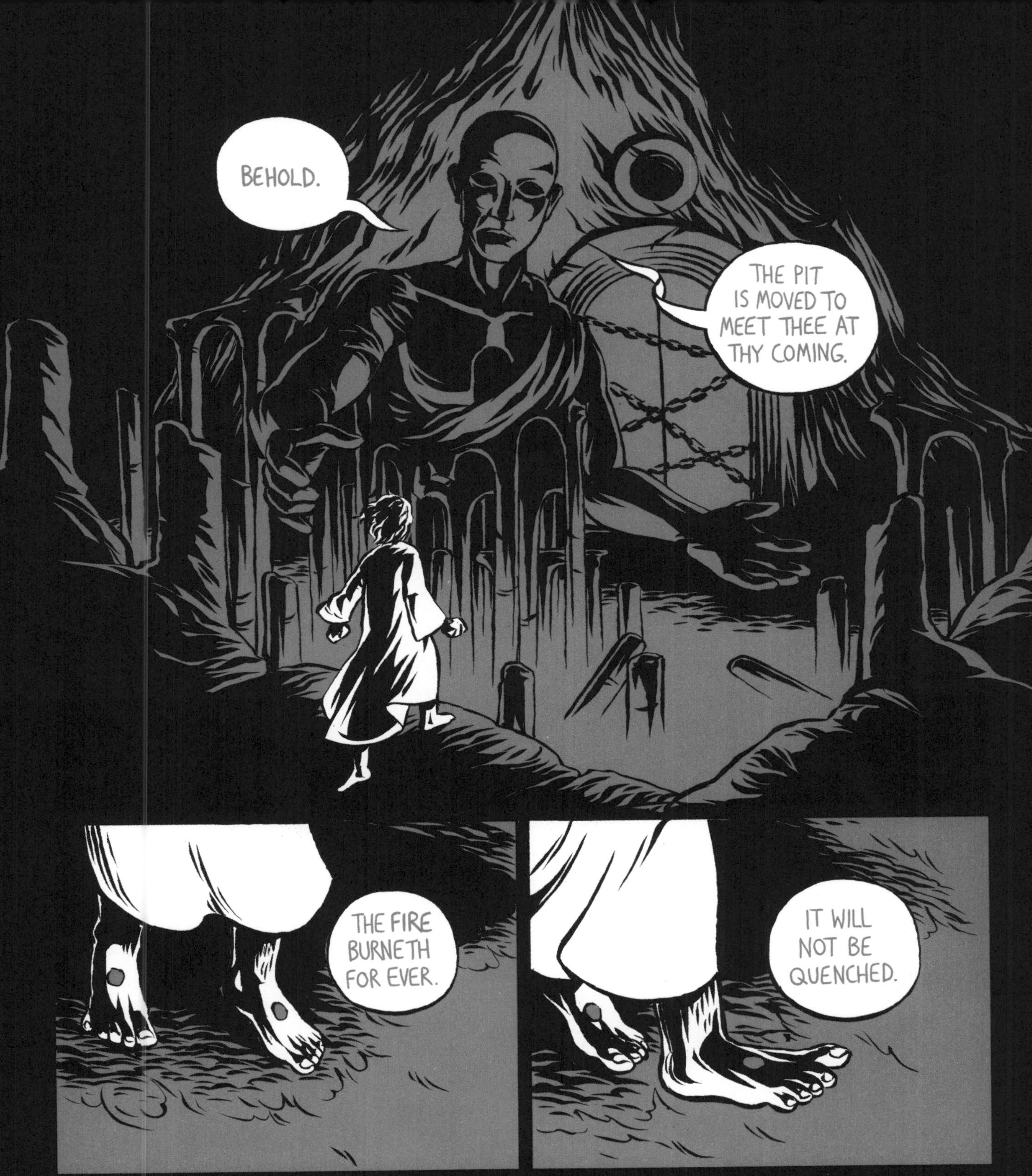
BEHOLD.
THE PIT IS MOVED TO MEET THEE AT THY COMING.
THE FIRE BURNETH FOR EVER.
IT WILL NOT BE QUENCHED.

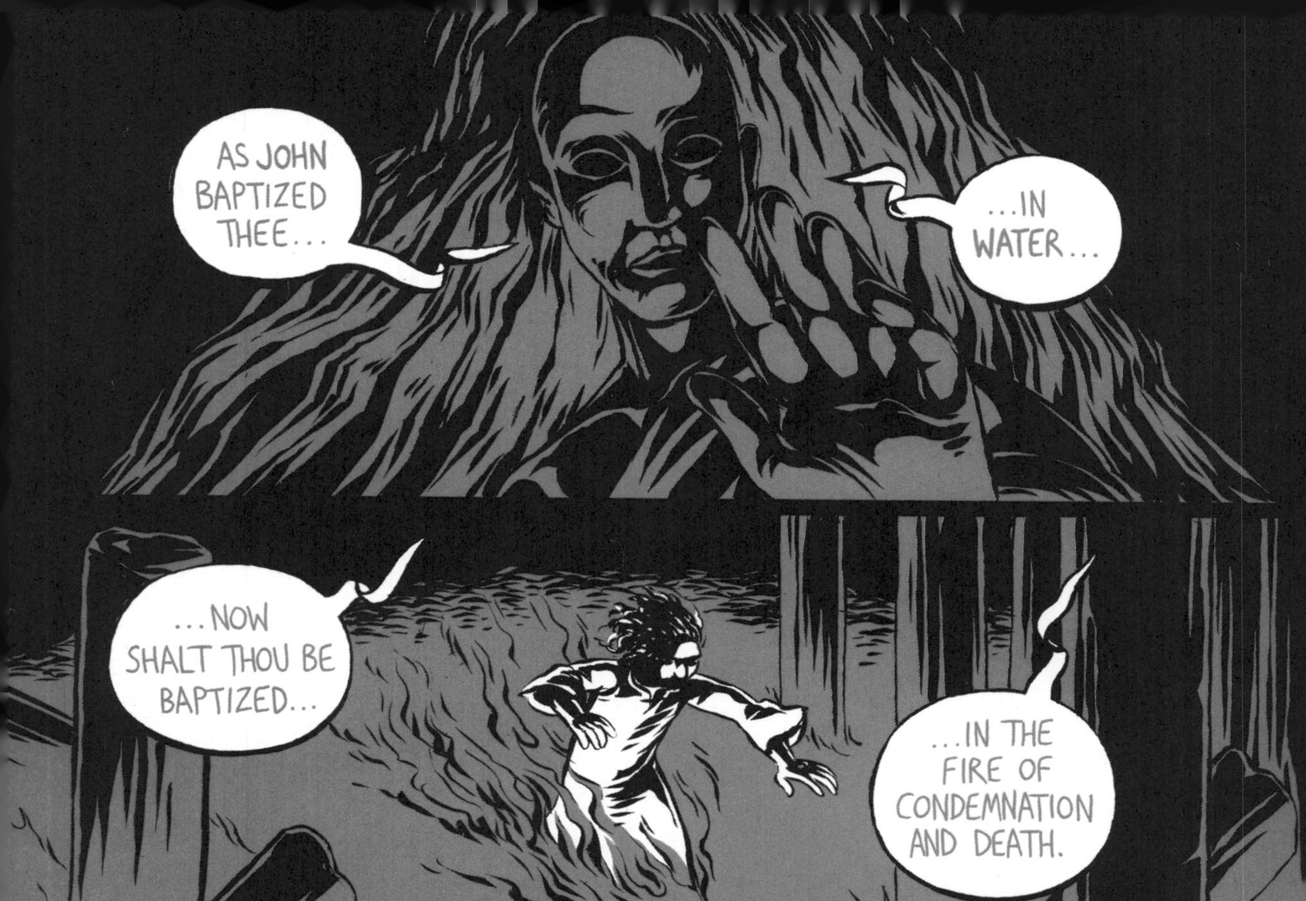
AS JOHN BAPTIZED THEE...
...IN WATER...
...NOW SHALT THOU BE BAPTIZED...
...IN THE FIRE OF CONDEMNATION AND DEATH.
THOU WILT NOT CAST US OUT,
HOLY ONE OF GOD.

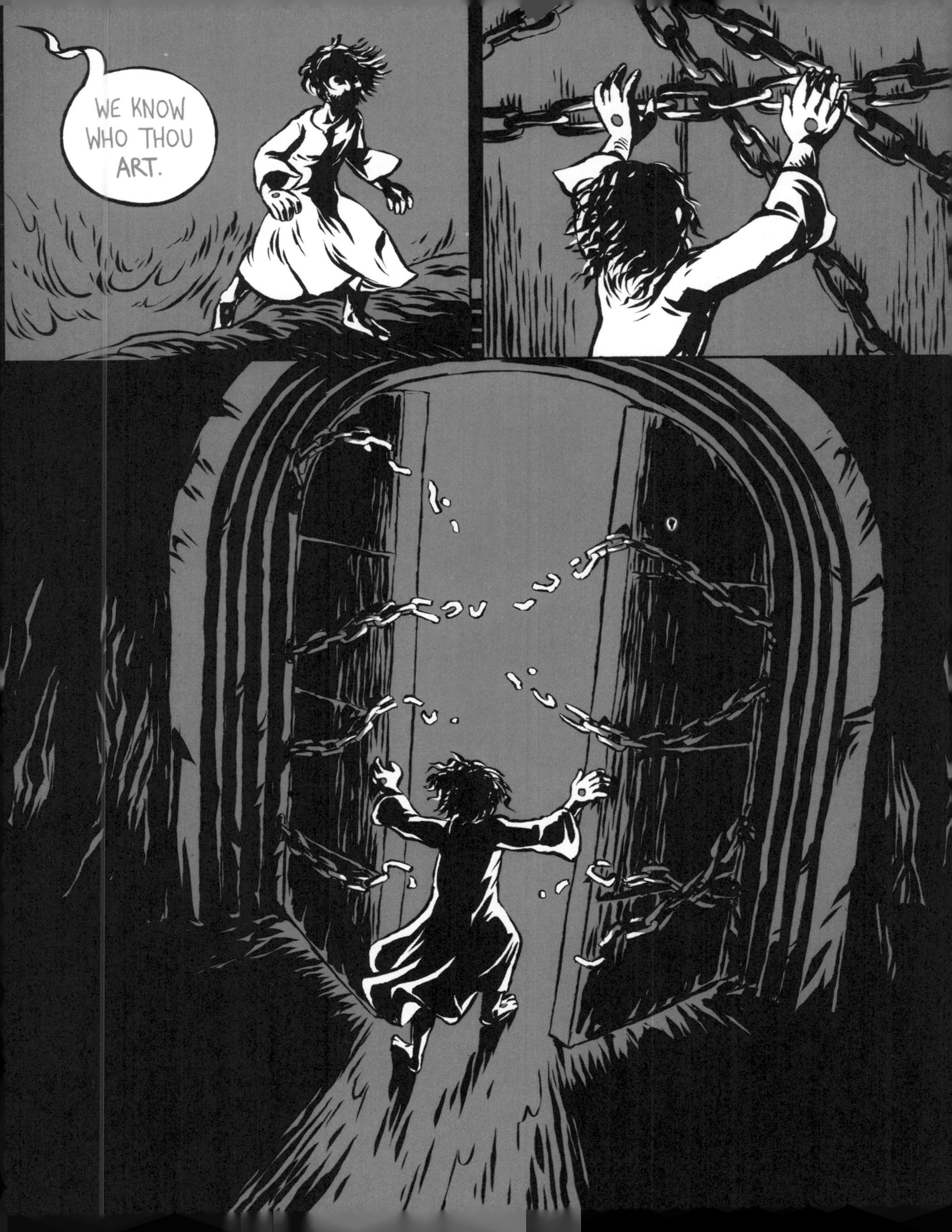
WE KNOW WHO THOU ART.

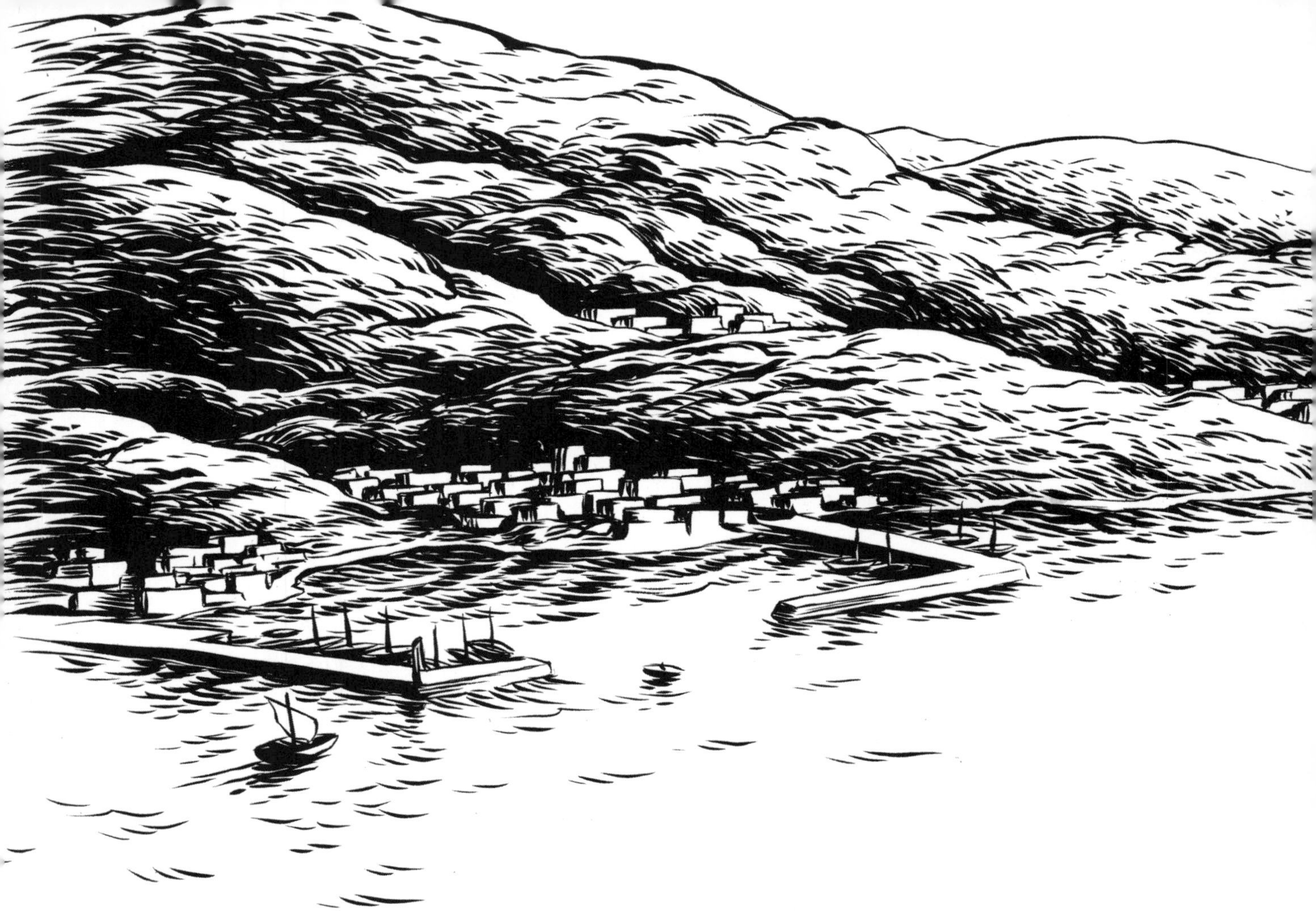

GALILEE

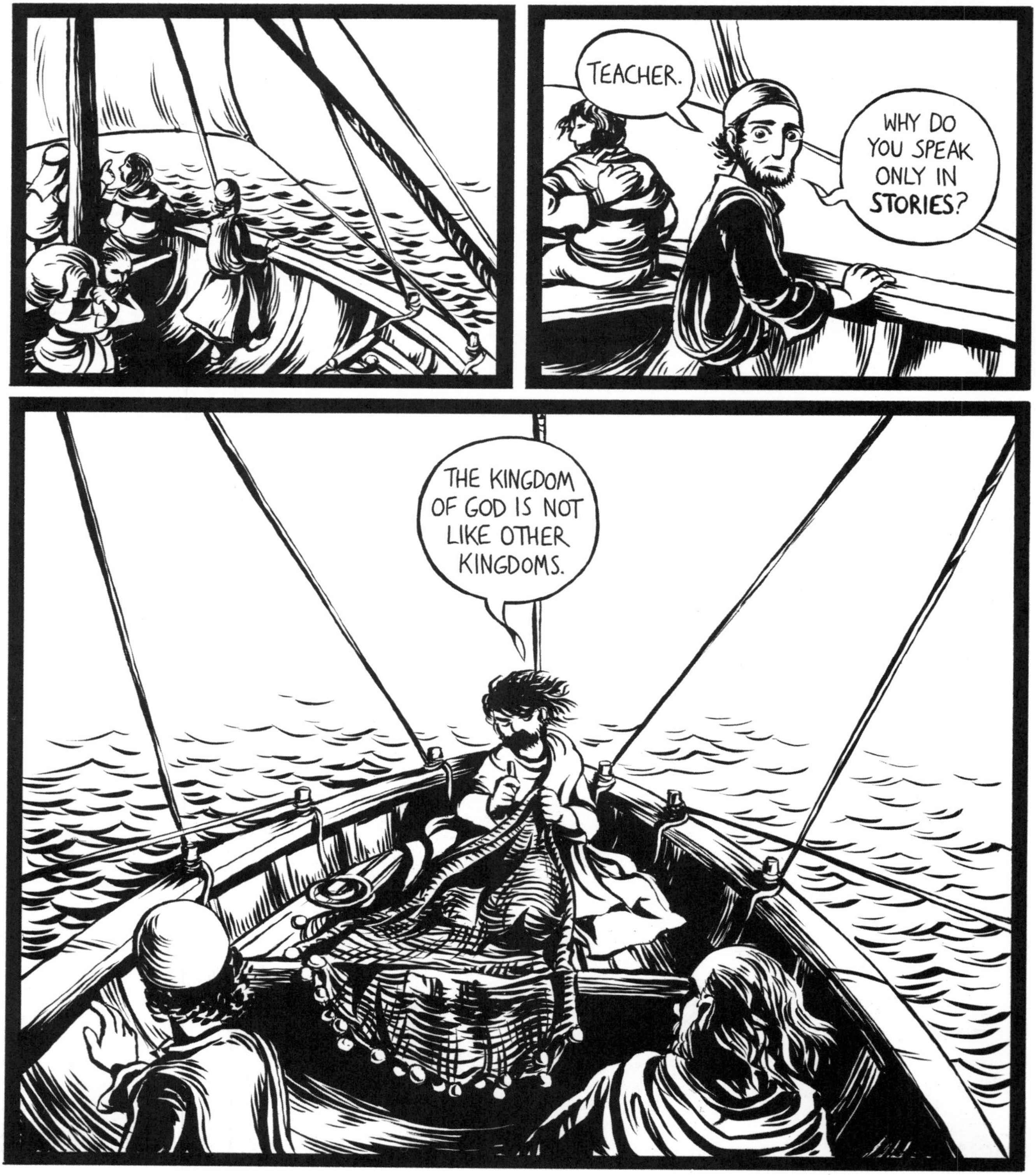
TEACHER.
WHY DO YOU SPEAK ONLY IN STORIES?
THE KINGDOM OF GOD IS NOT LIKE OTHER KINGDOMS.

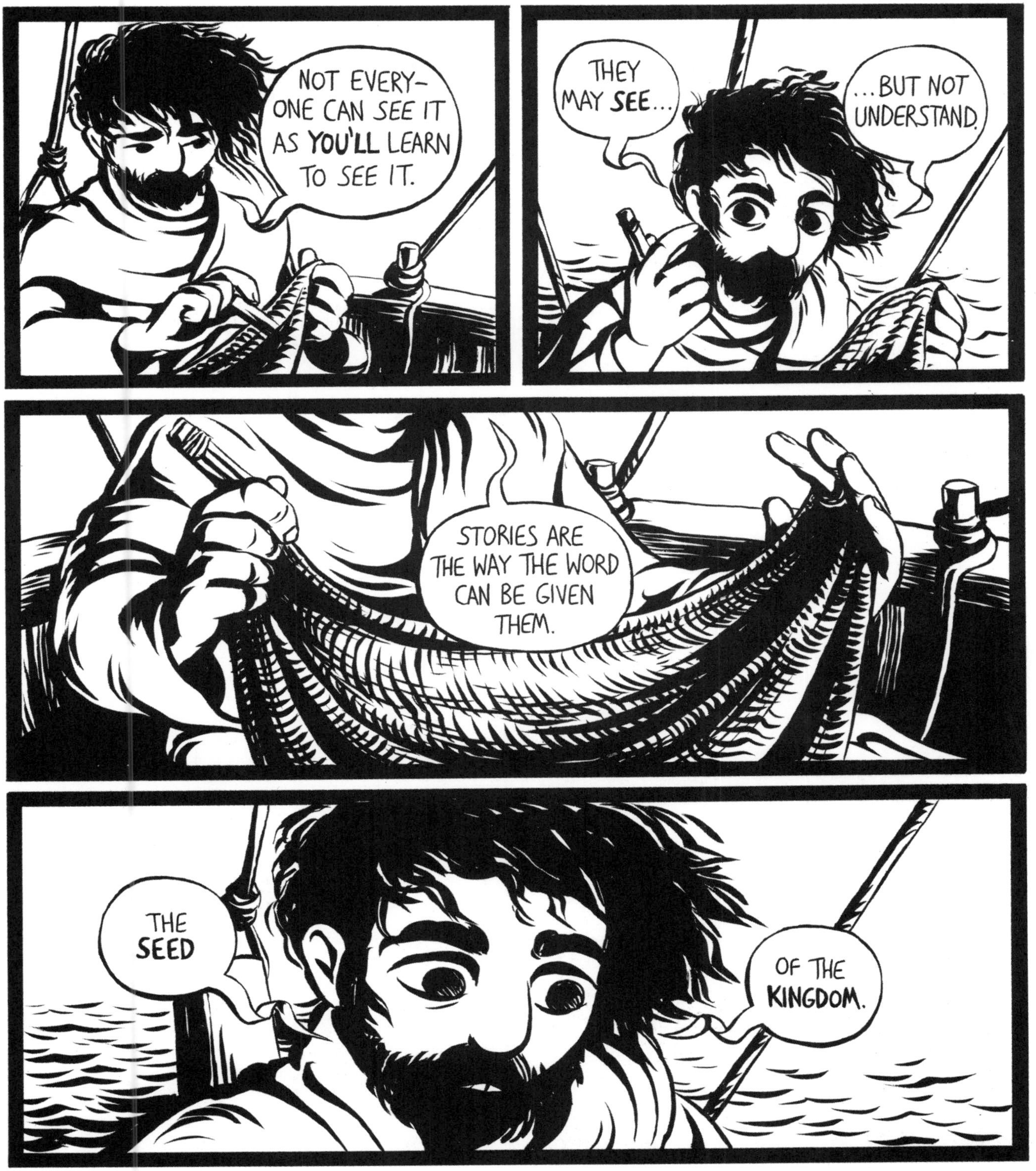
NOT EVERY-ONE CAN SEE IT AS **YOU'LL** LEARN TO SEE IT.
THEY MAY **SEE**...
...BUT NOT UNDERSTAND.
STORIES ARE THE WAY THE WORD CAN BE GIVEN THEM.
THE **SEED**
OF THE **KINGDOM**.

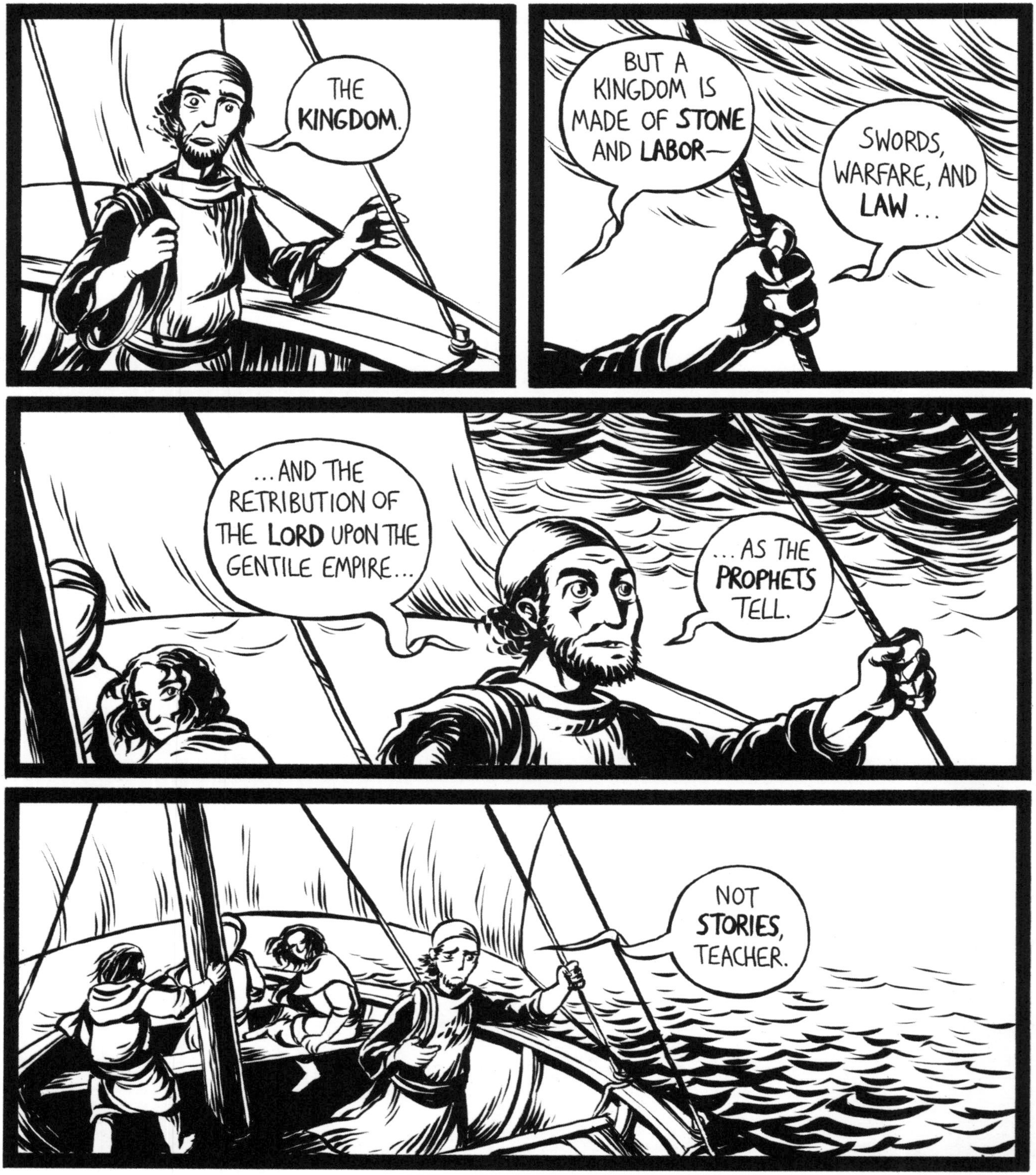
THE KINGDOM.
BUT A KINGDOM IS MADE OF STONE AND LABOR—
SWORDS, WARFARE, AND LAW...
...AND THE RETRIBUTION OF THE LORD UPON THE GENTILE EMPIRE...
...AS THE PROPHETS TELL.
NOT STORIES, TEACHER.

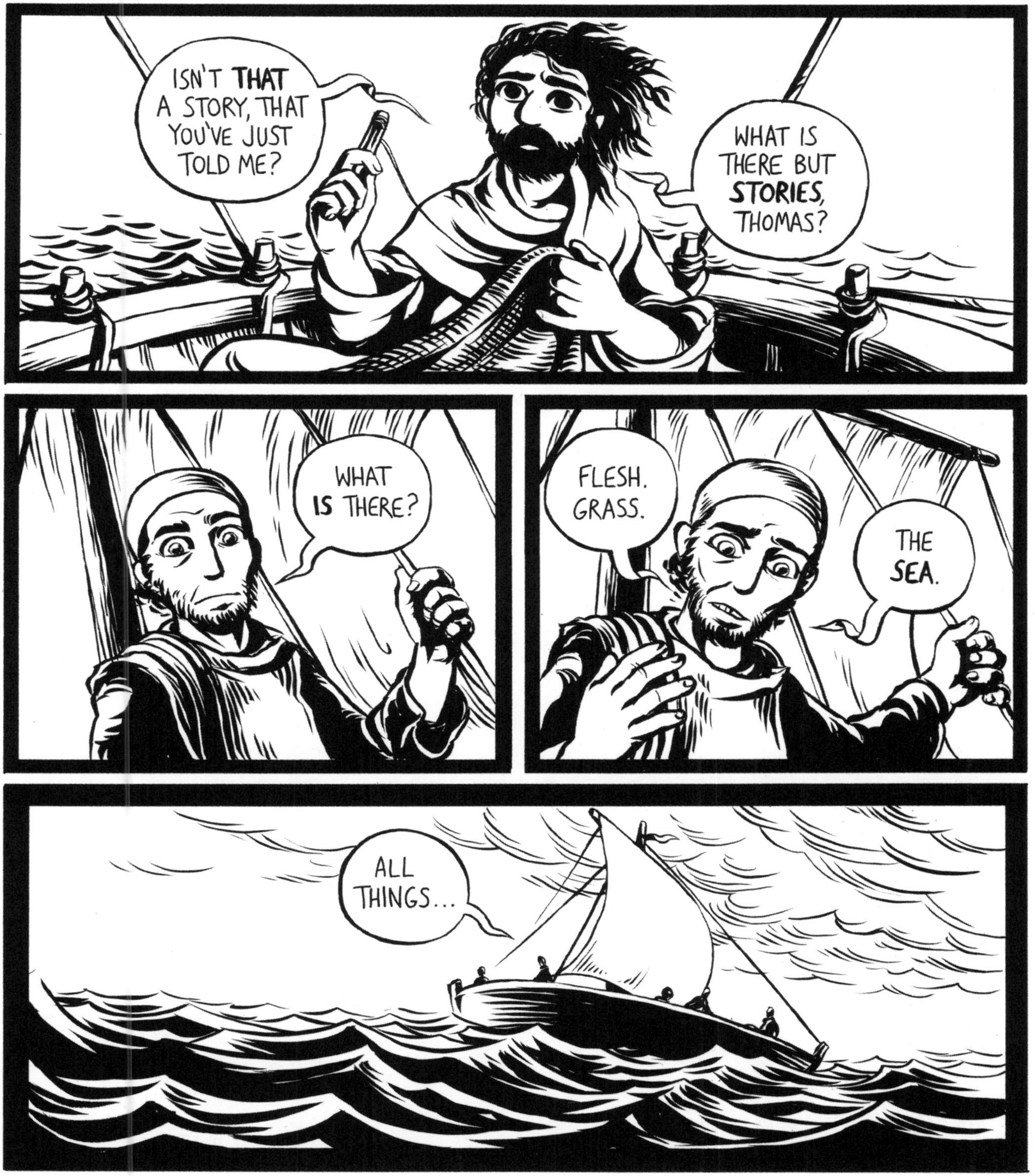
ISN'T **THAT** A STORY, THAT YOU'VE JUST TOLD ME?
WHAT IS THERE BUT **STORIES**, THOMAS?
WHAT **IS** THERE?
FLESH. GRASS.
THE **SEA**.
ALL THINGS...

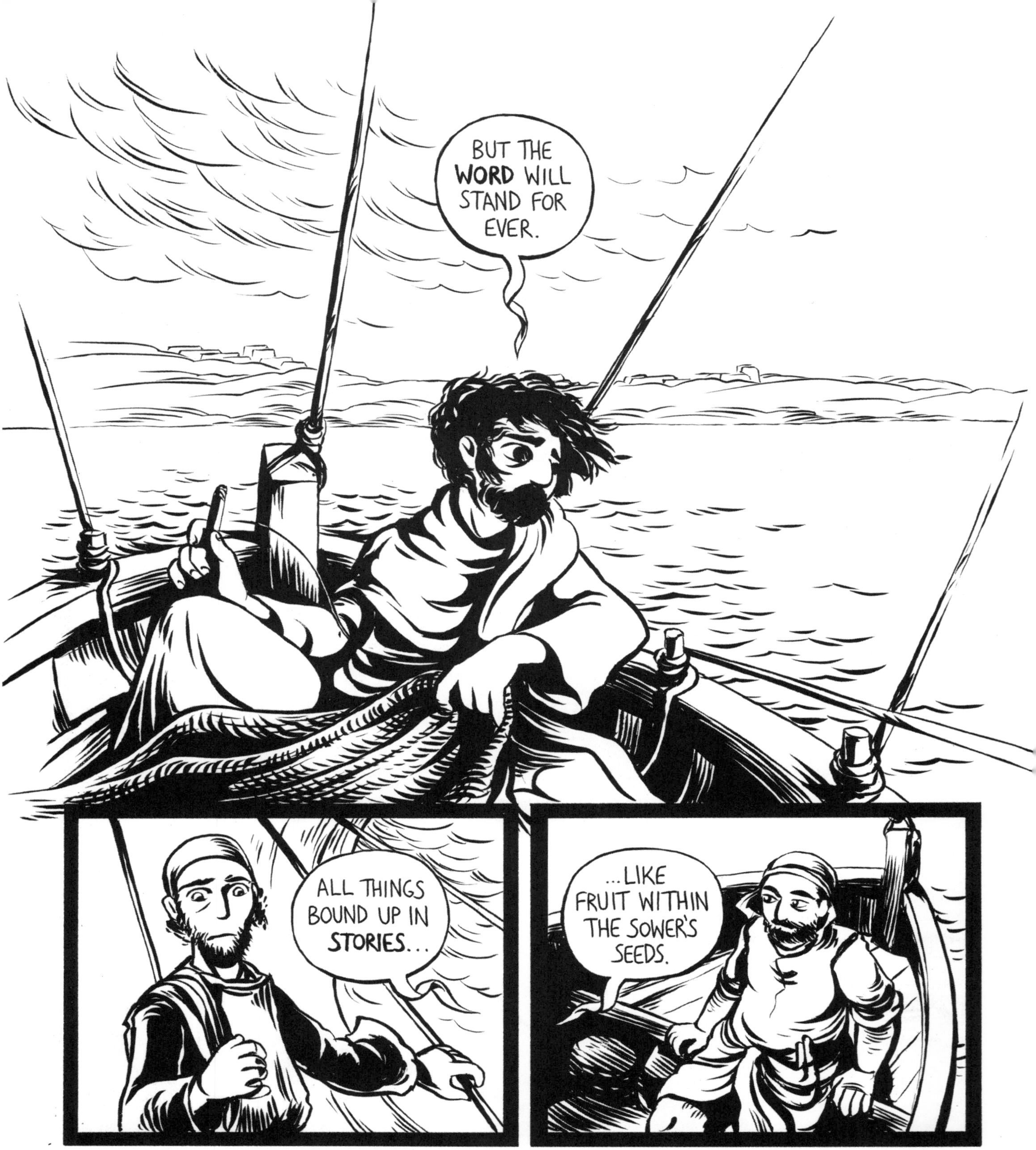
BUT THE WORD WILL STAND FOR EVER.
ALL THINGS BOUND UP IN STORIES...
...LIKE FRUIT WITHIN THE SOWER'S SEEDS.

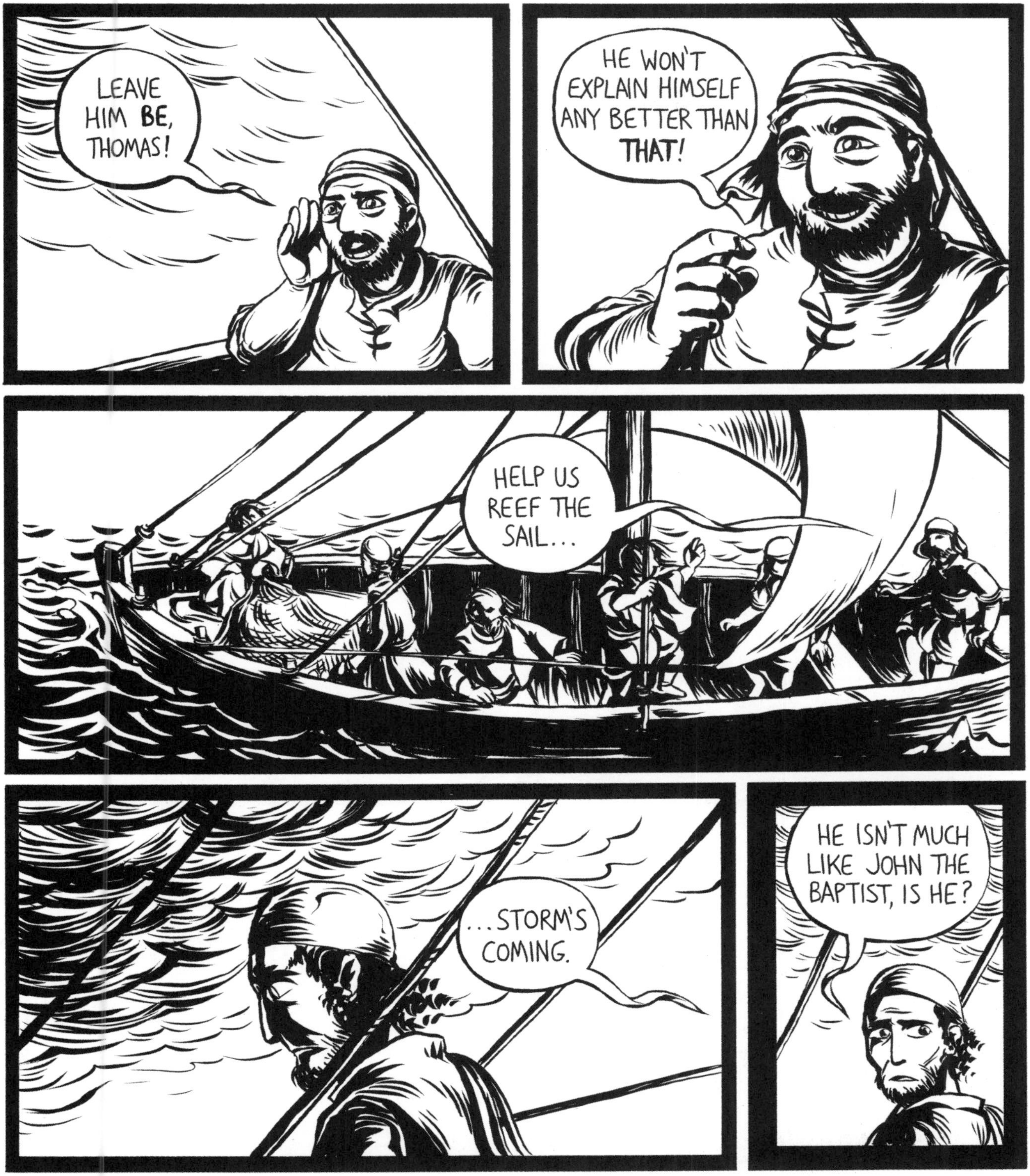
LEAVE HIM BE, THOMAS!
HE WON'T EXPLAIN HIMSELF ANY BETTER THAN THAT!
HELP US REEF THE SAIL...
...STORM'S COMING.
HE ISN'T MUCH LIKE JOHN THE BAPTIST, IS HE?

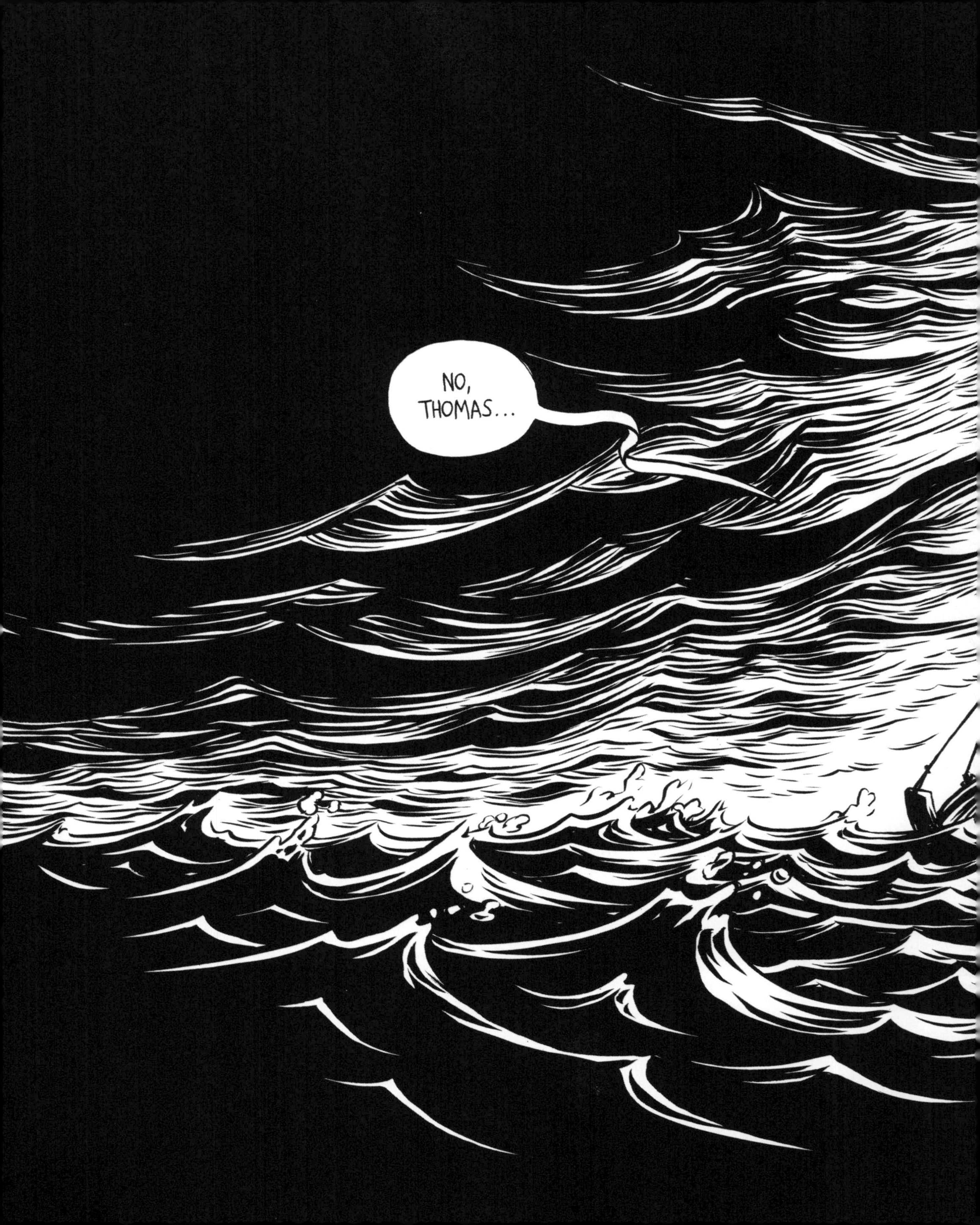
NO, THOMAS...

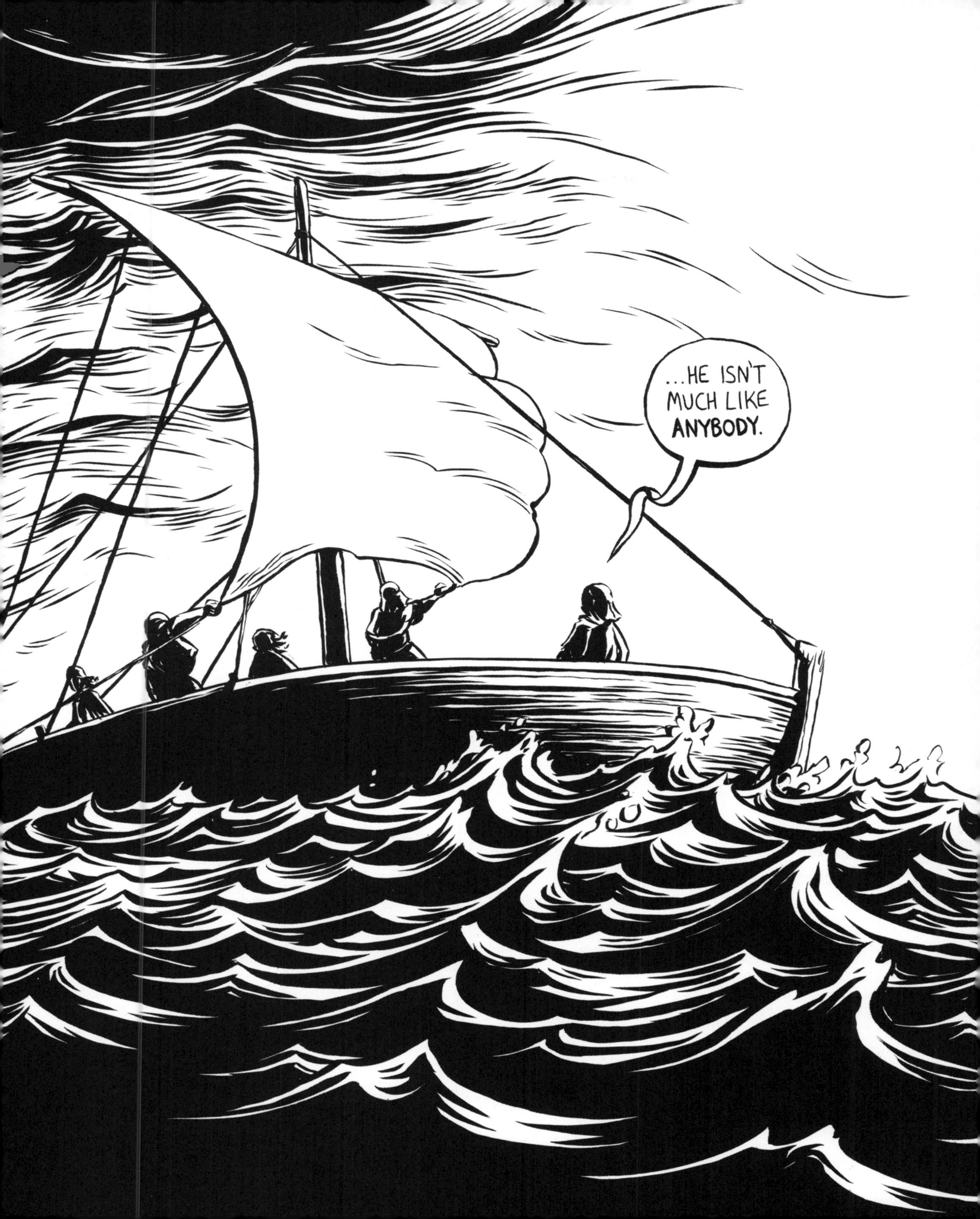
...HE ISN'T MUCH LIKE **ANYBODY**.

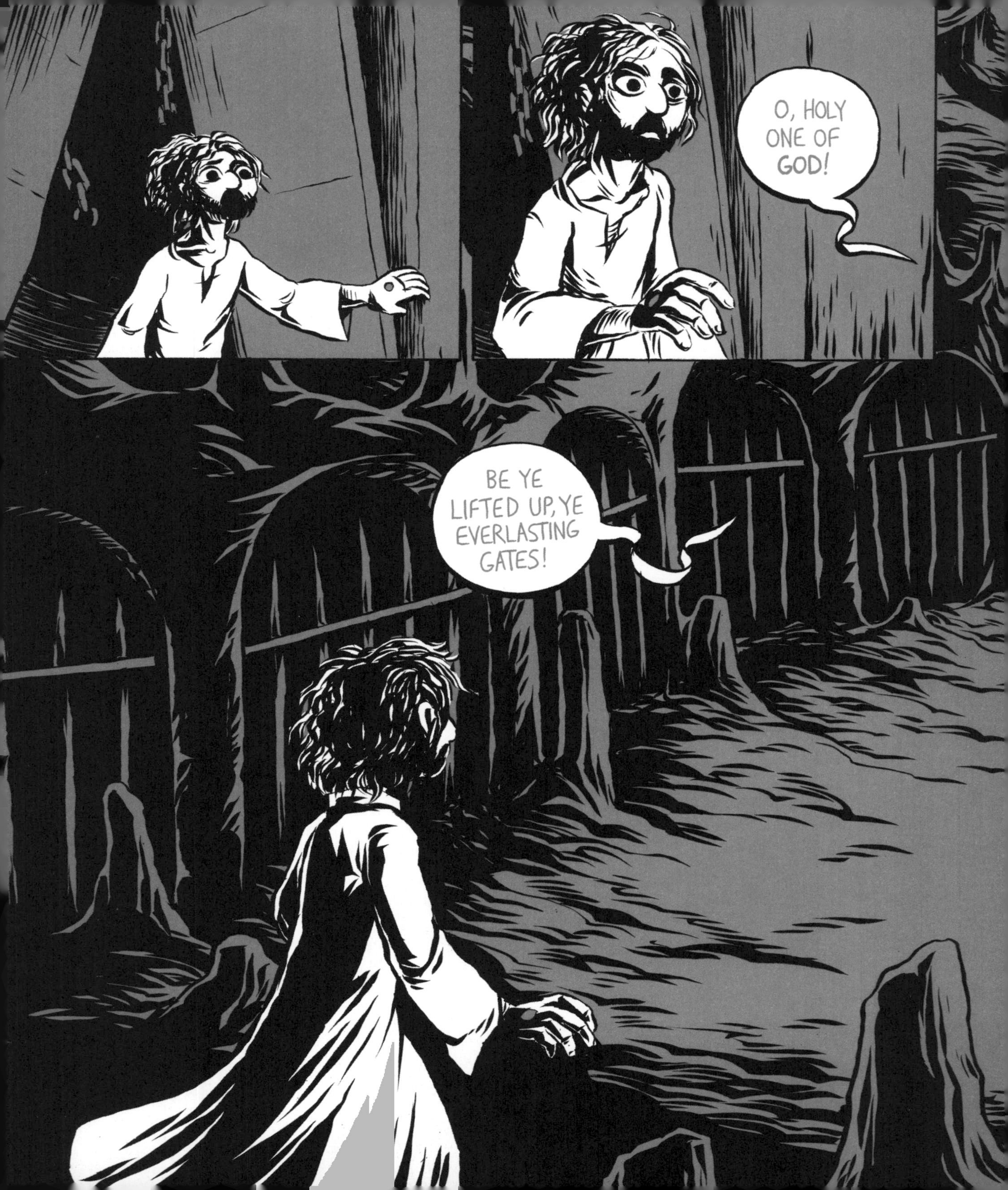
O, HOLY ONE OF GOD!
BE YE LIFTED UP, YE EVERLASTING GATES!

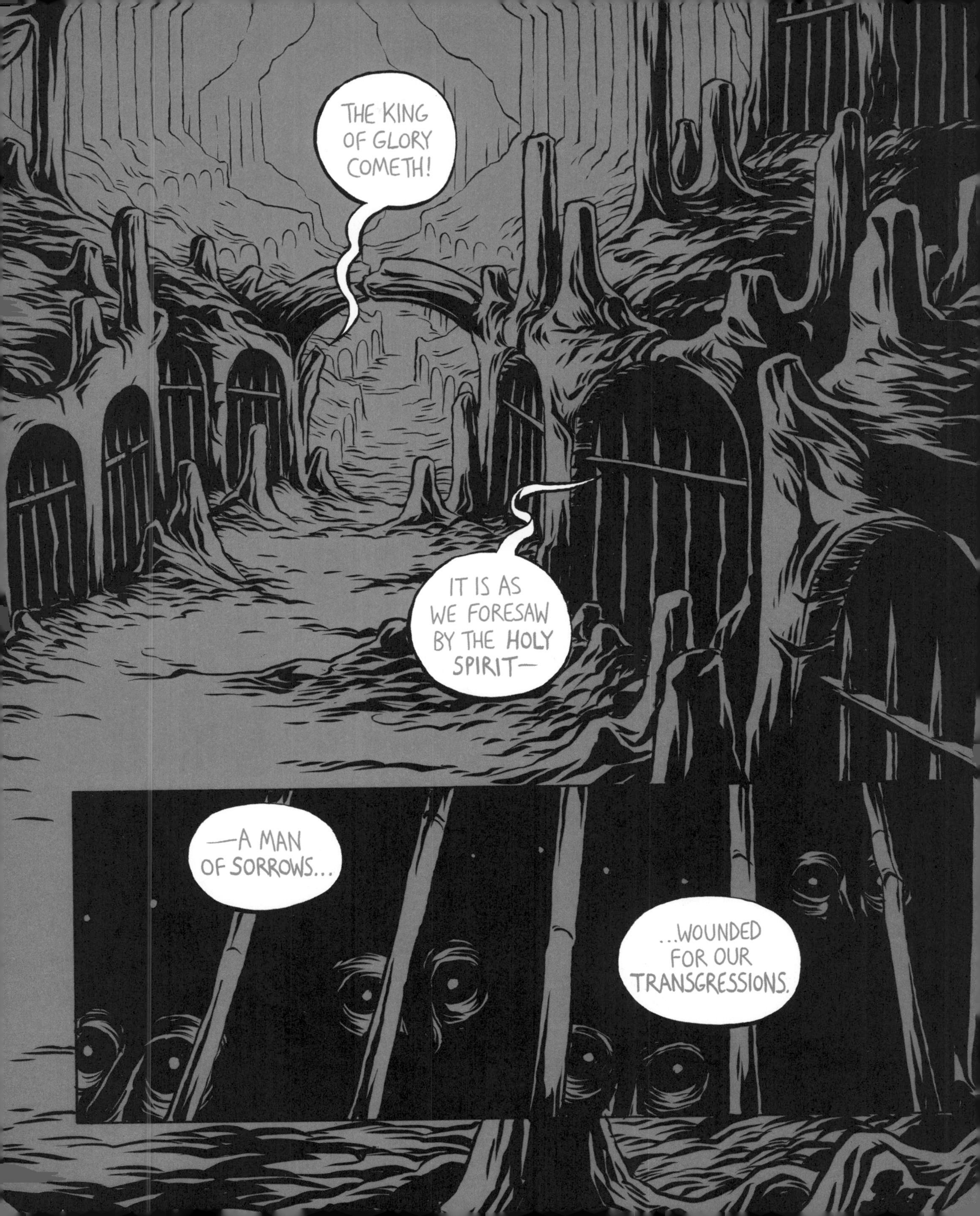
THE KING OF GLORY COMETH!
IT IS AS WE FORESAW BY THE HOLY SPIRIT—
—A MAN OF SORROWS...
...WOUNDED FOR OUR TRANSGRESSIONS.

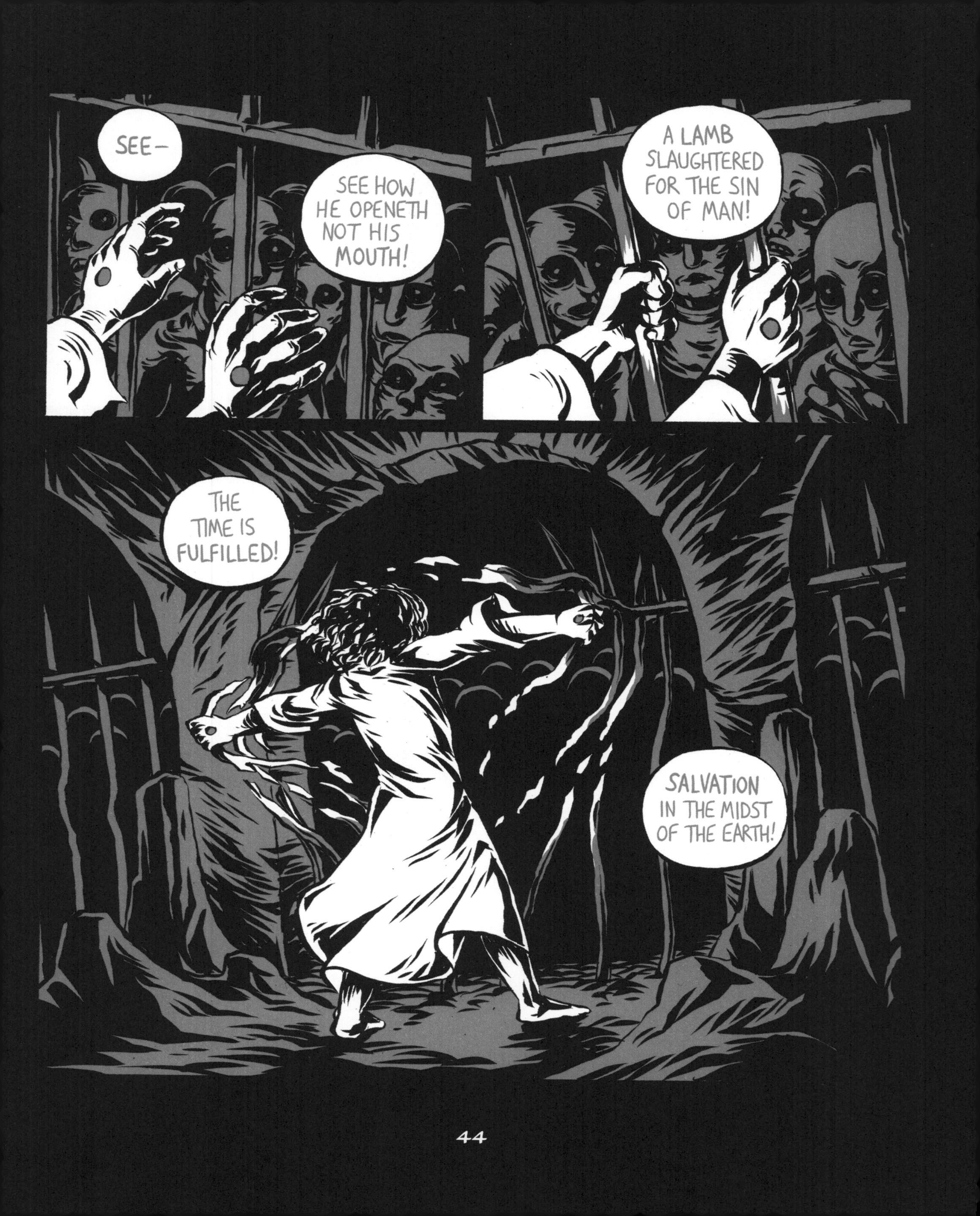
SEE—
SEE HOW HE OPENETH NOT HIS MOUTH!
A LAMB SLAUGHTERED FOR THE SIN OF MAN!
THE TIME IS FULFILLED!
SALVATION IN THE MIDST OF THE EARTH!

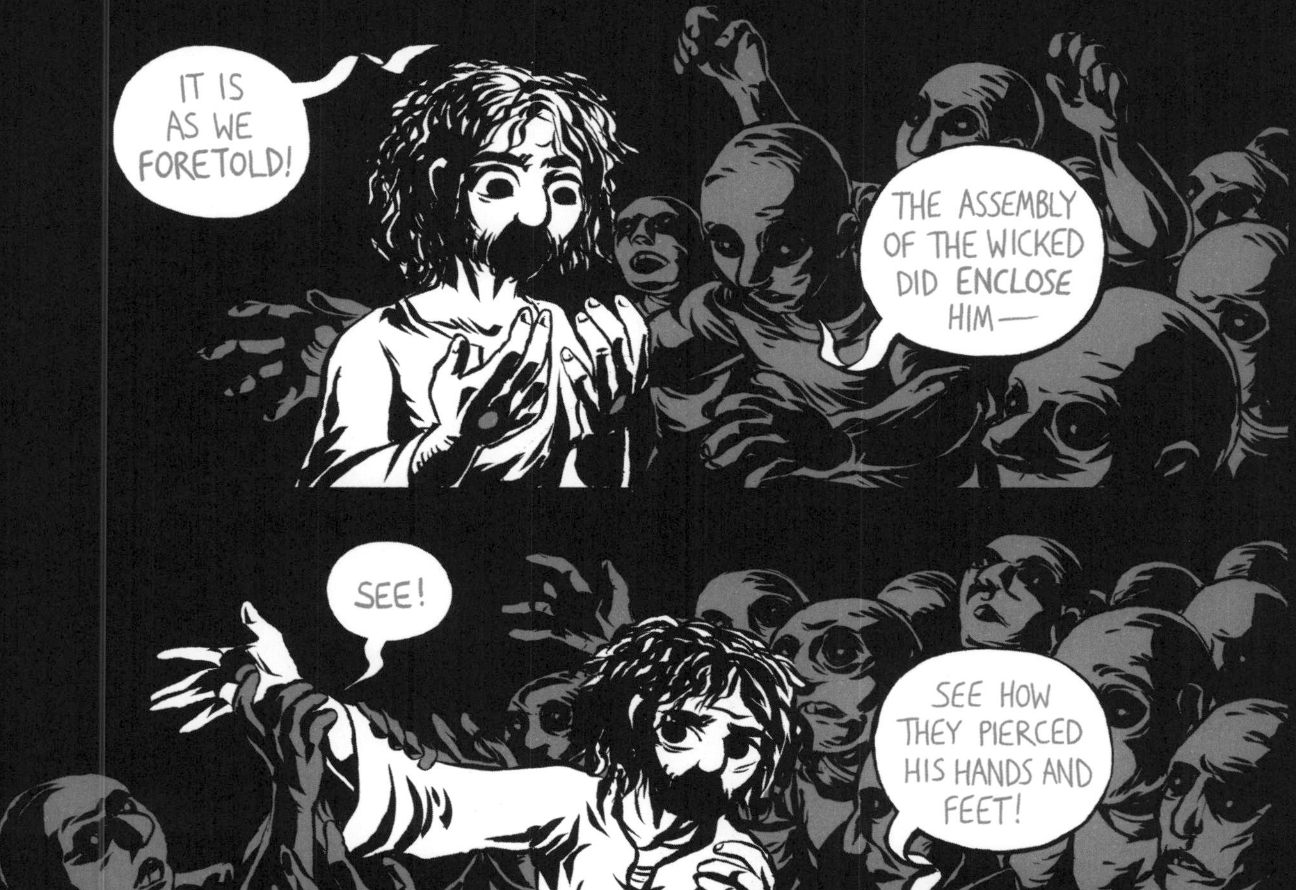
IT IS AS WE FORETOLD!
THE ASSEMBLY OF THE WICKED DID ENCLOSE HIM—
SEE!
SEE HOW THEY PIERCED HIS HANDS AND FEET!
WHO HATH BELIEVED OUR REPORT?

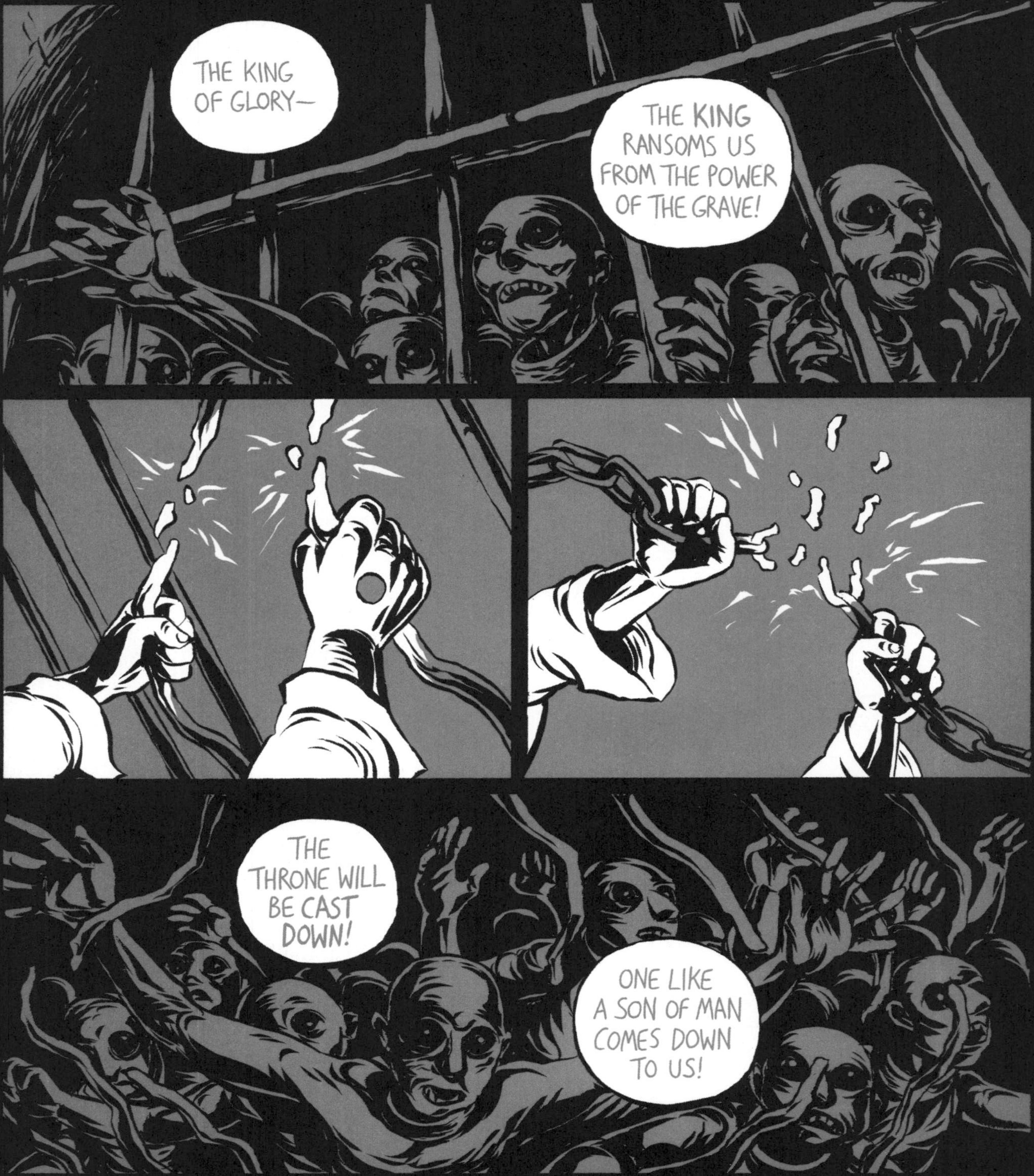
THE KING OF GLORY—
THE KING RANSOMS US FROM THE POWER OF THE GRAVE!
THE THRONE WILL BE CAST DOWN!
ONE LIKE A SON OF MAN COMES DOWN TO US!

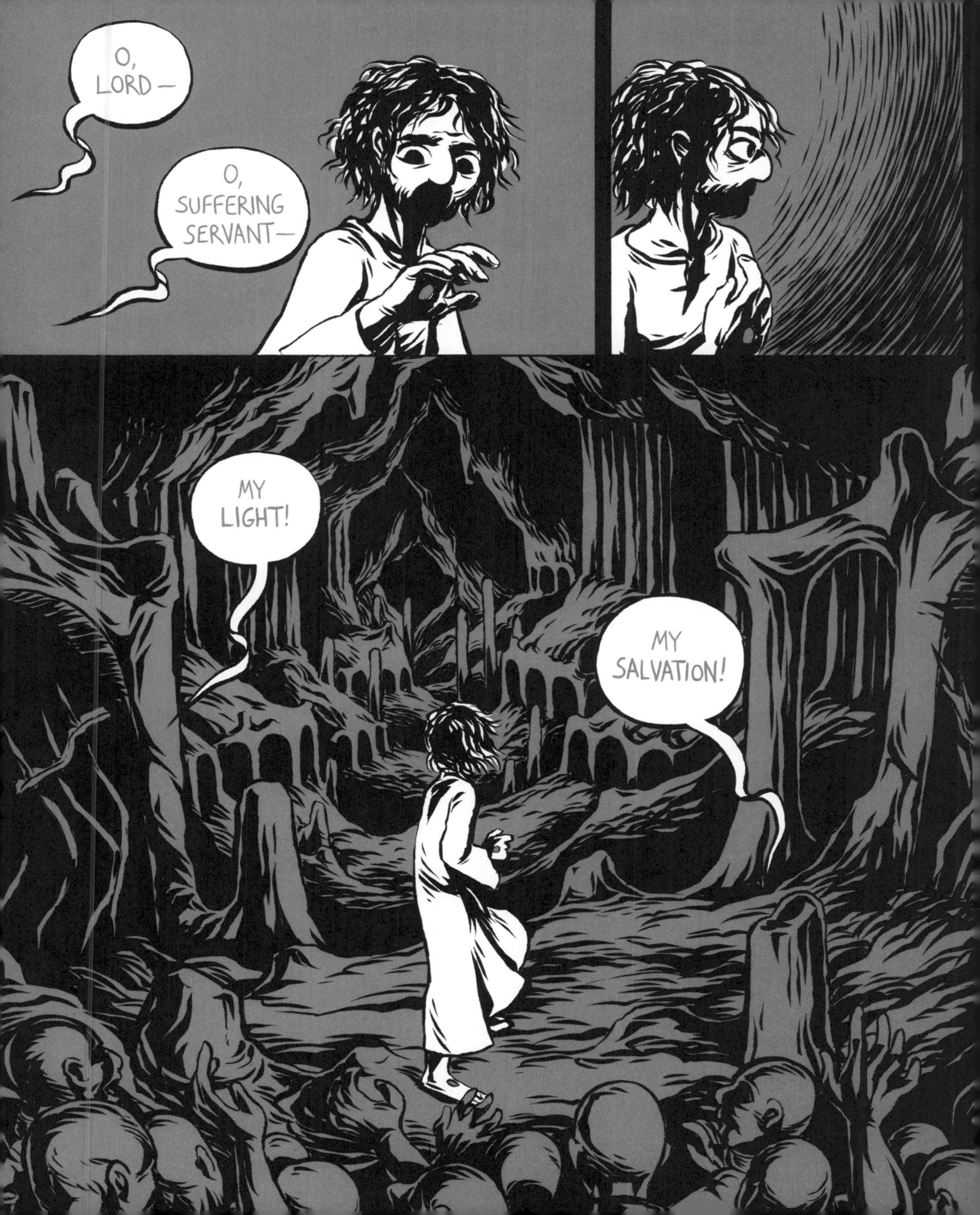
O, LORD—
O, SUFFERING SERVANT—
MY LIGHT!
MY SALVATION!

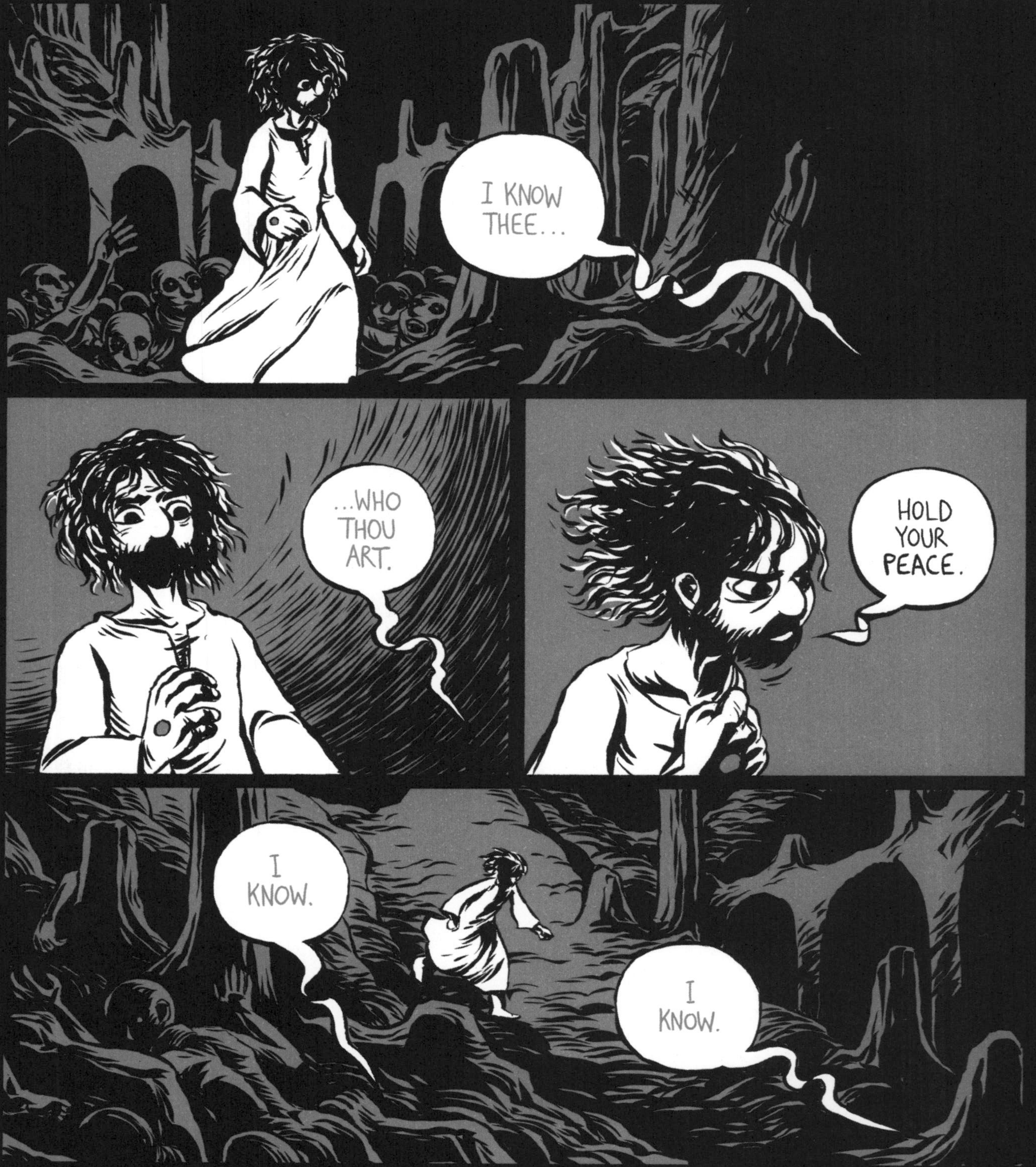
I KNOW THEE...
...WHO THOU ART.
HOLD YOUR PEACE.
I KNOW.
I KNOW.

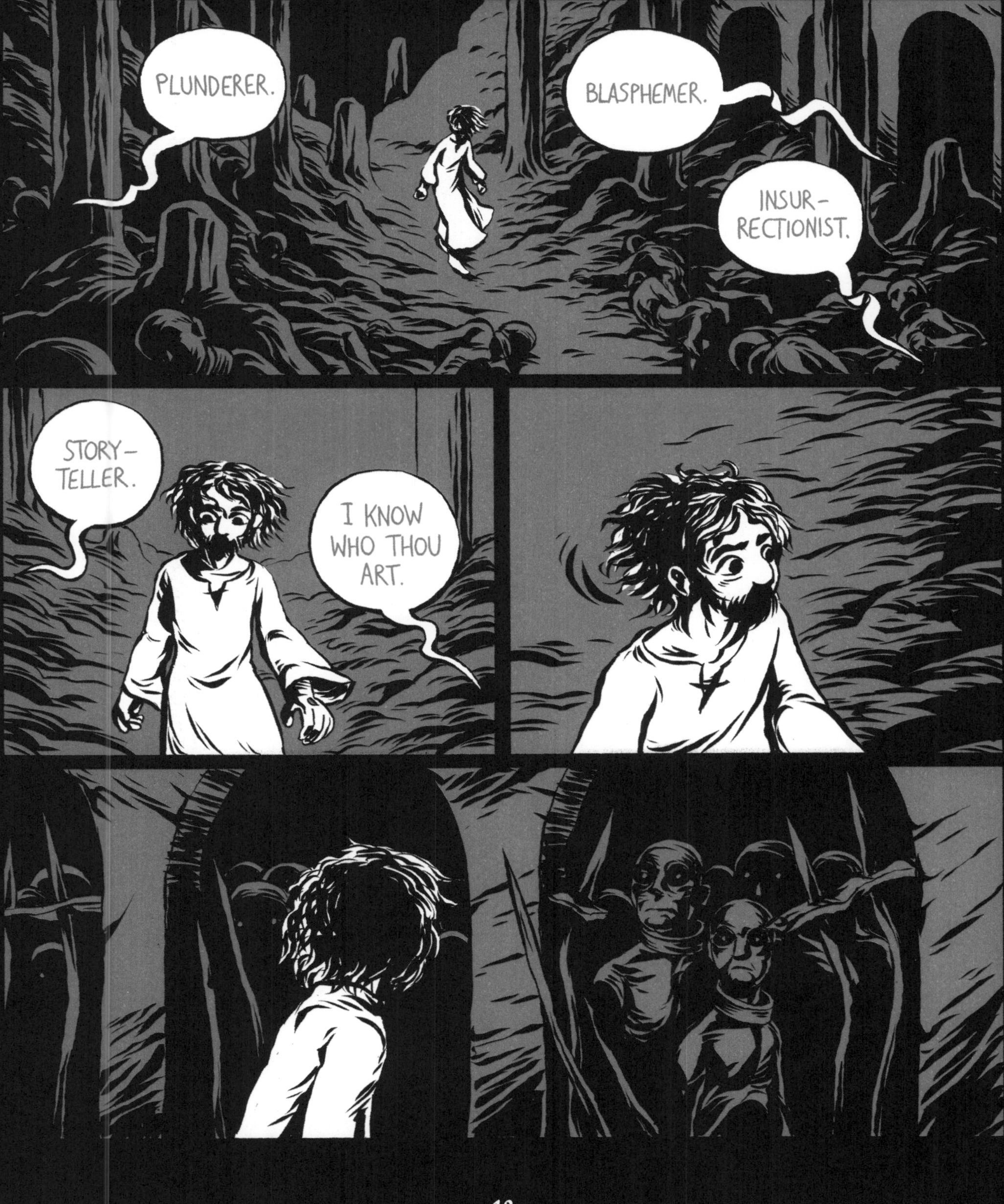
PLUNDERER.
BLASPHEMER.
INSUR-
RECTIONIST.
STORY-
TELLER.
I KNOW
WHO THOU
ART.

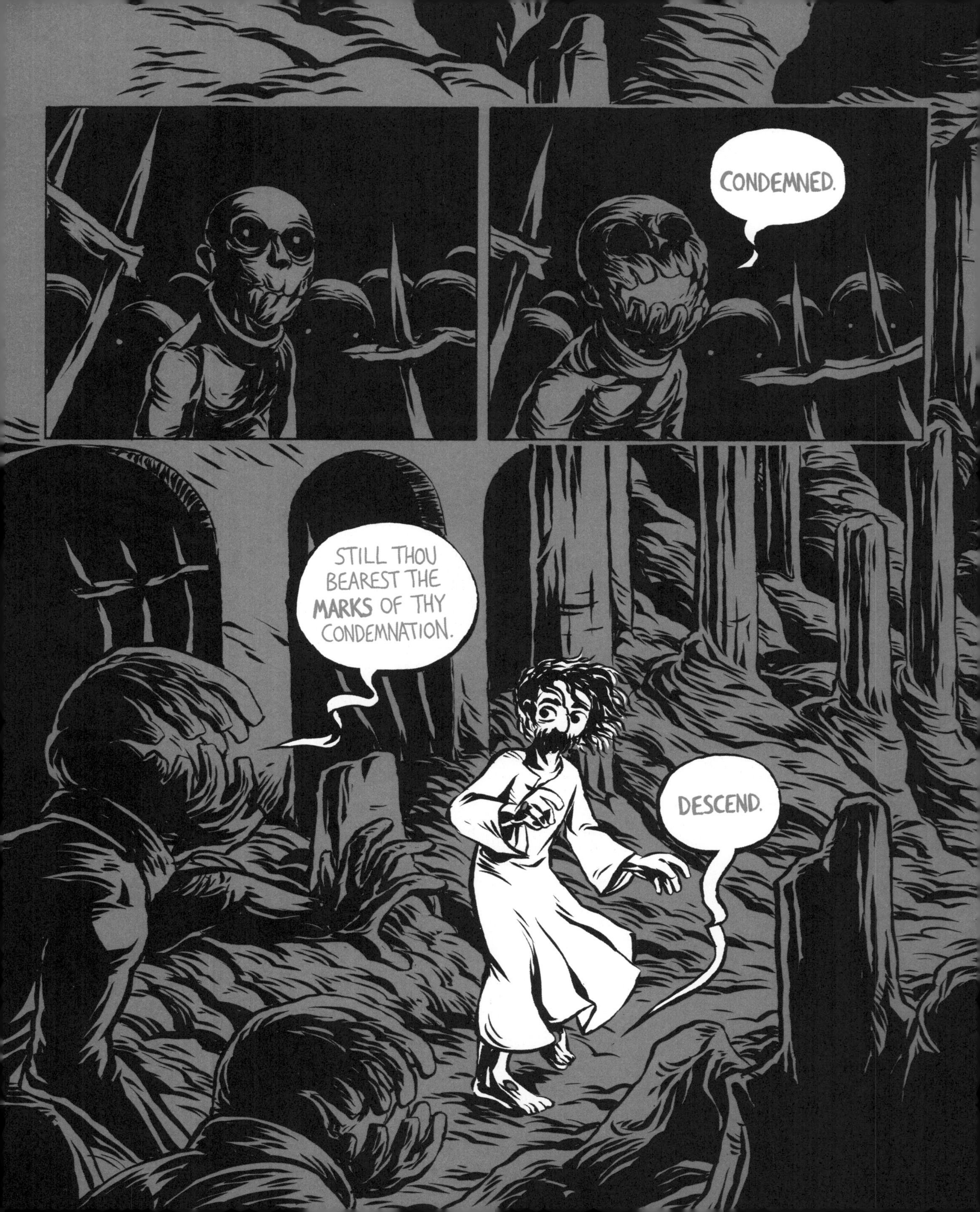
CONDEMNED.
STILL THOU BEAREST THE **MARKS** OF THY CONDEMNATION.
DESCEND.

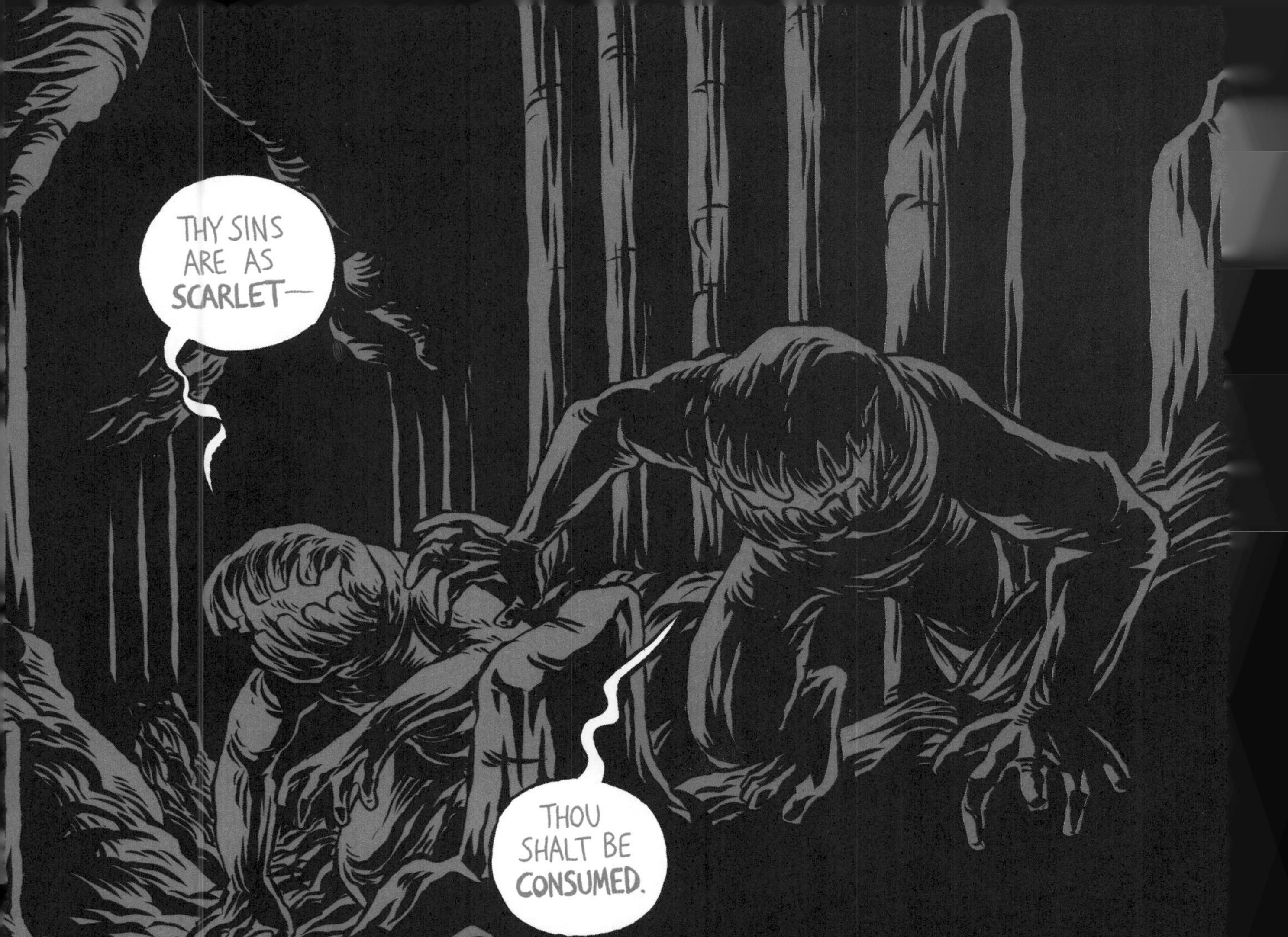
THY SINS ARE AS SCARLET—
THOU SHALT BE CONSUMED.
DESCEND.
SINNER.

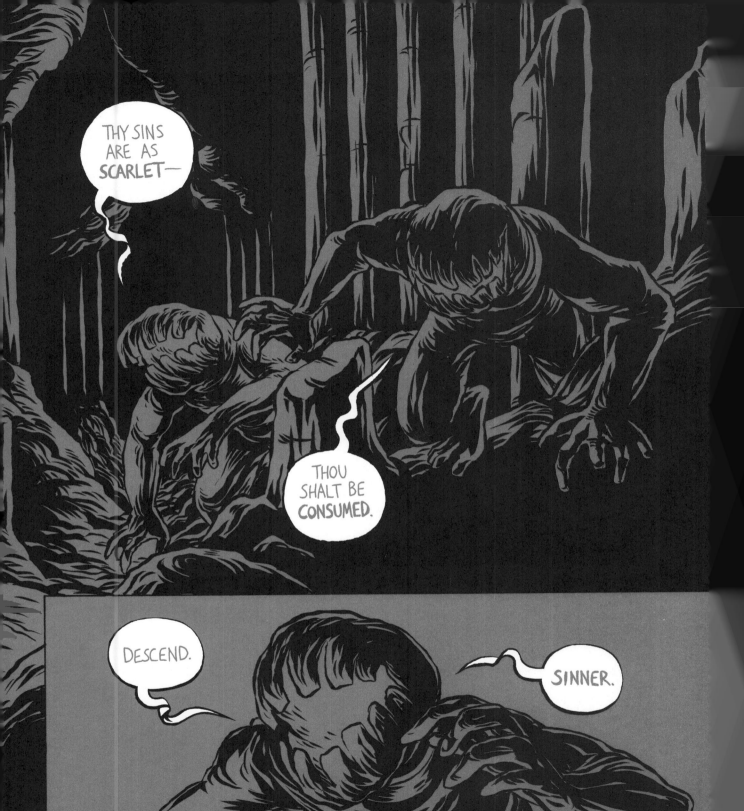

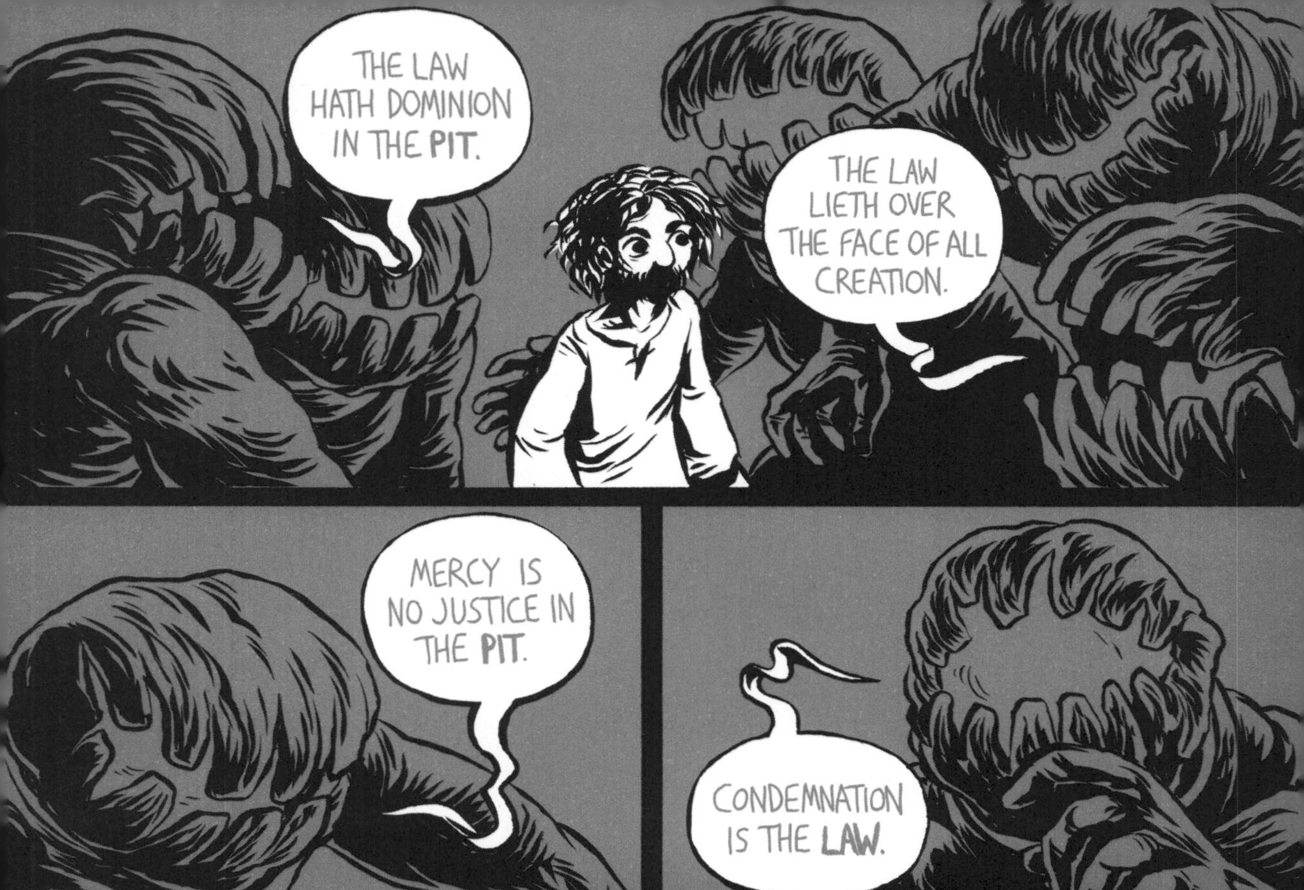
THE LAW HATH DOMINION IN THE **PIT**.
THE LAW LIETH OVER THE FACE OF ALL CREATION.
MERCY IS NO JUSTICE IN THE **PIT**.
CONDEMNATION IS THE **LAW**.
SINNER.
I KNOW WHO THOU ART.

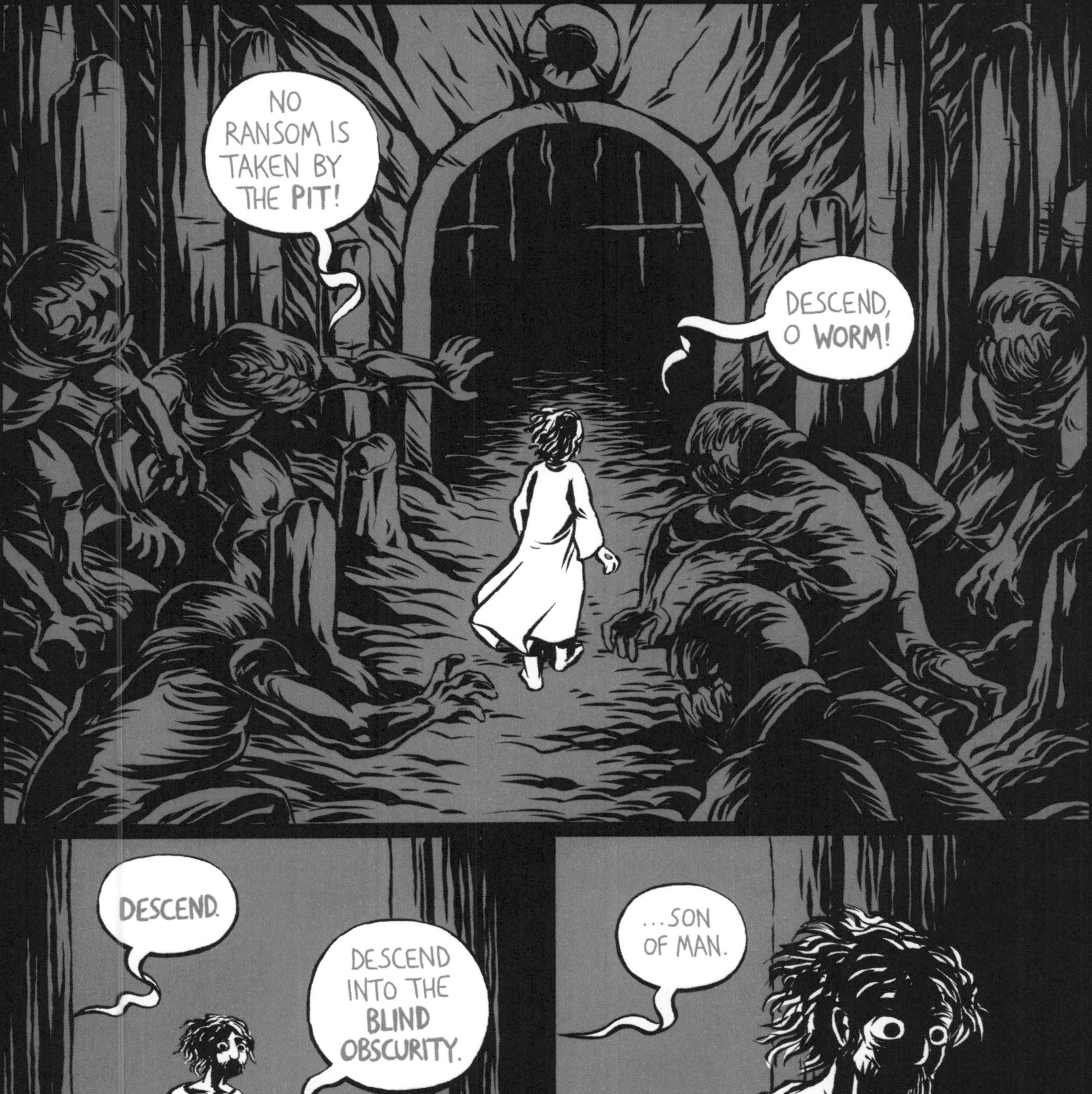
NO RANSOM IS TAKEN BY THE PIT!
DESCEND, O WORM!
DESCEND.
DESCEND INTO THE BLIND OBSCURITY.
...SON OF MAN.

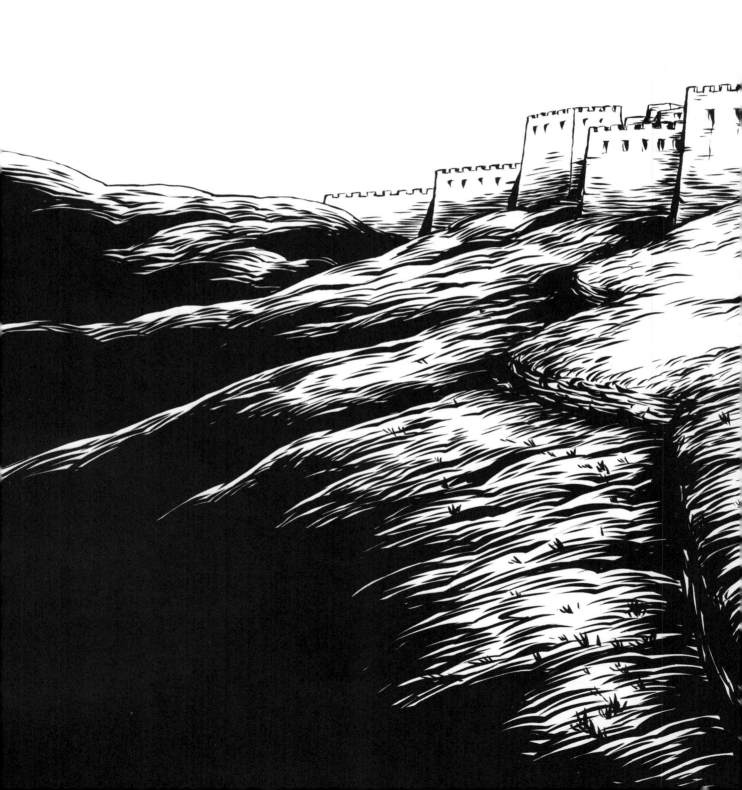

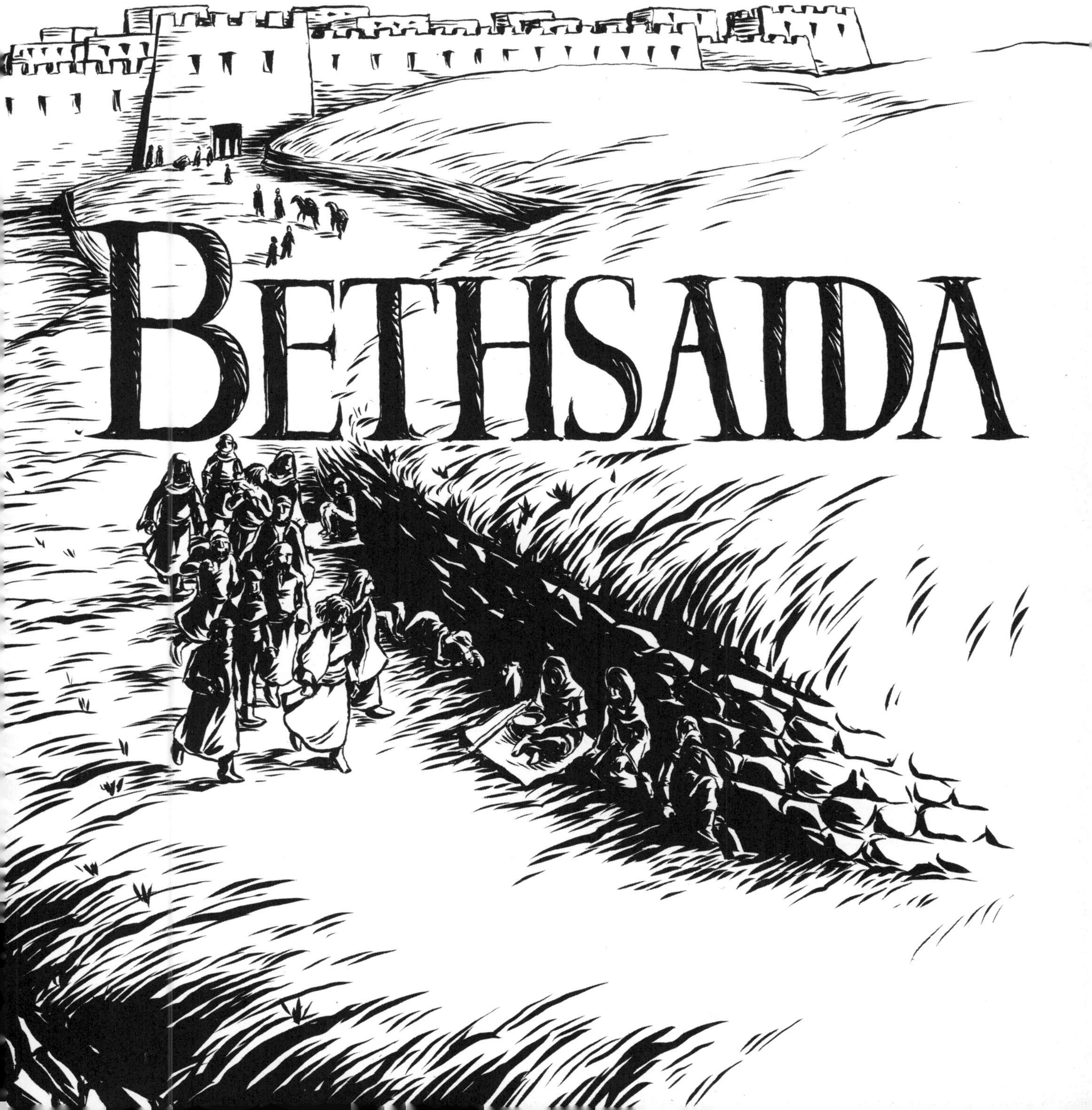
BETHSAIDA

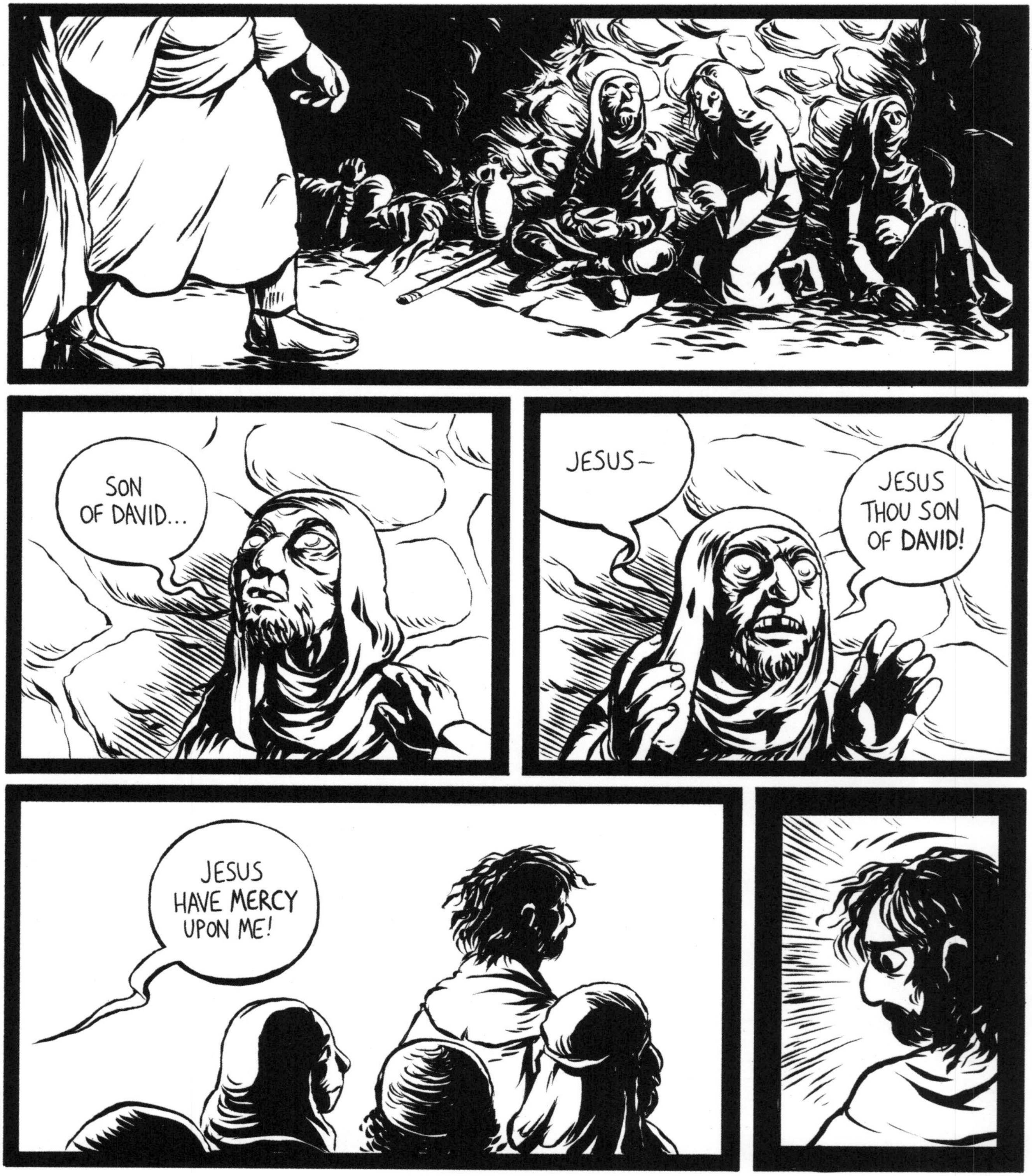
SON OF DAVID...
JESUS-
JESUS THOU SON OF DAVID!
JESUS HAVE MERCY UPON ME!

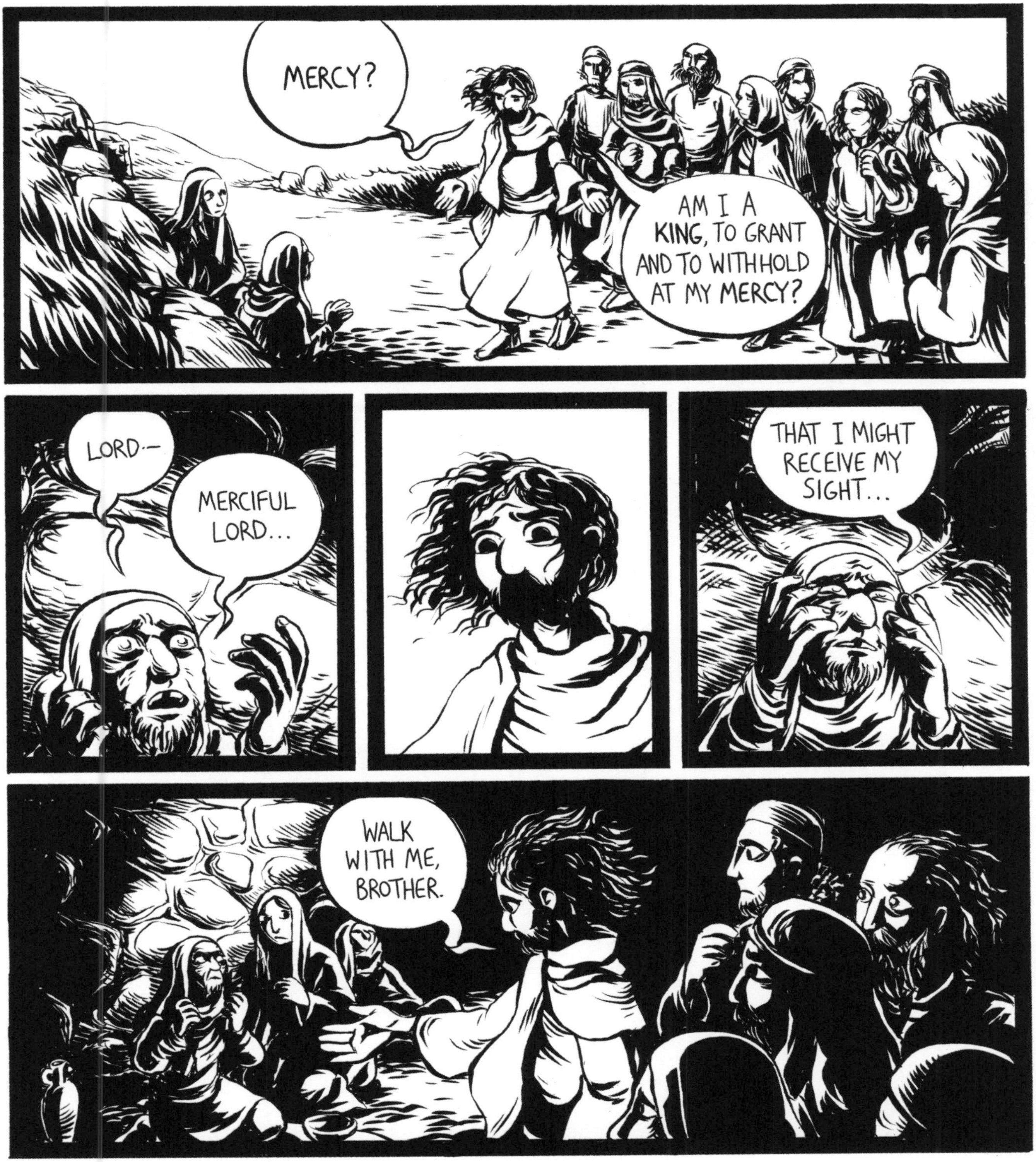
MERCY?
AM I A KING, TO GRANT AND TO WITHHOLD AT MY MERCY?
LORD.—
MERCIFUL LORD...
THAT I MIGHT RECEIVE MY SIGHT...
WALK WITH ME, BROTHER.

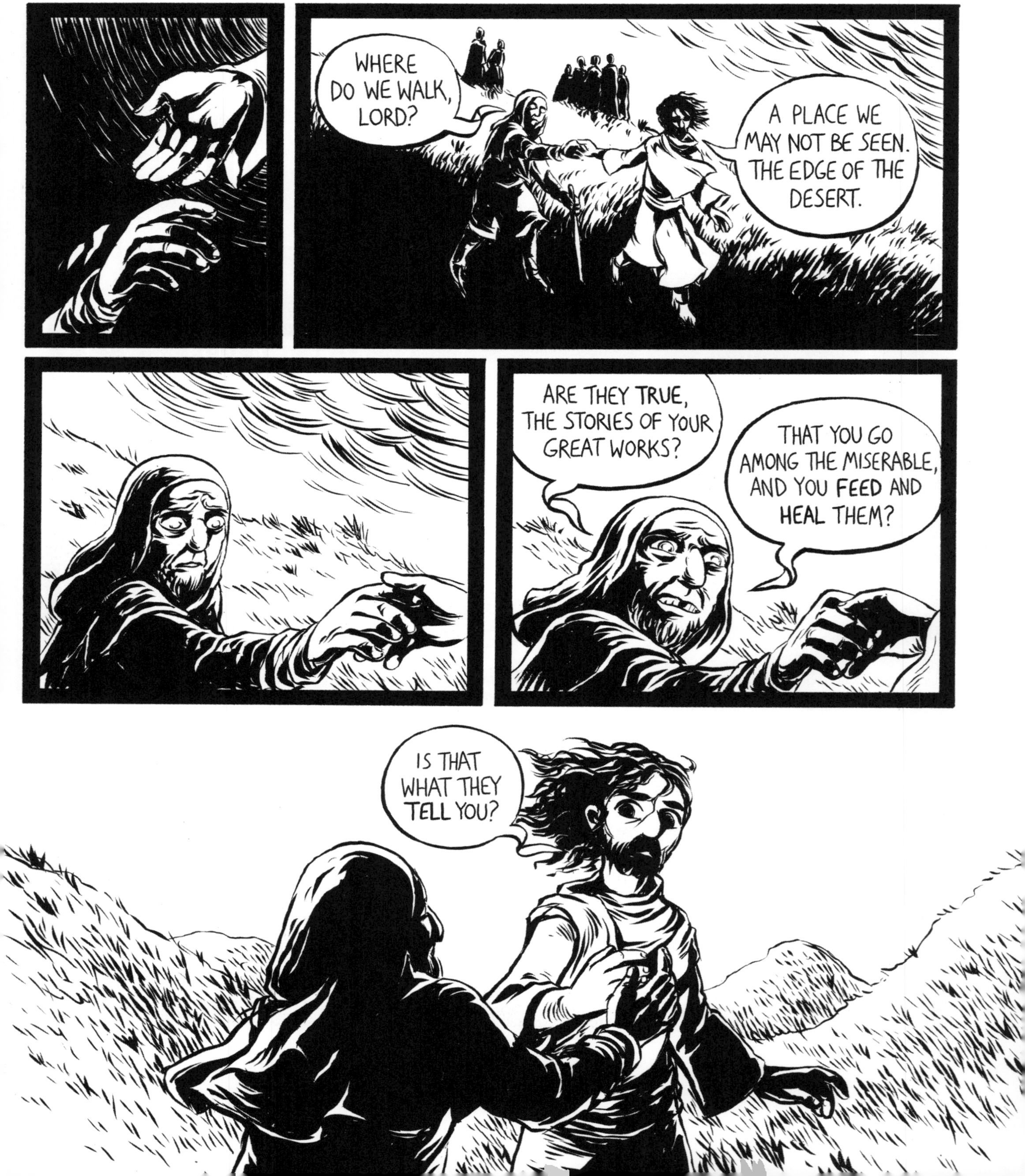
WHERE DO WE WALK, LORD?
A PLACE WE MAY NOT BE SEEN. THE EDGE OF THE DESERT.
ARE THEY TRUE, THE STORIES OF YOUR GREAT WORKS?
THAT YOU GO AMONG THE MISERABLE, AND YOU FEED AND HEAL THEM?
IS THAT WHAT THEY TELL YOU?

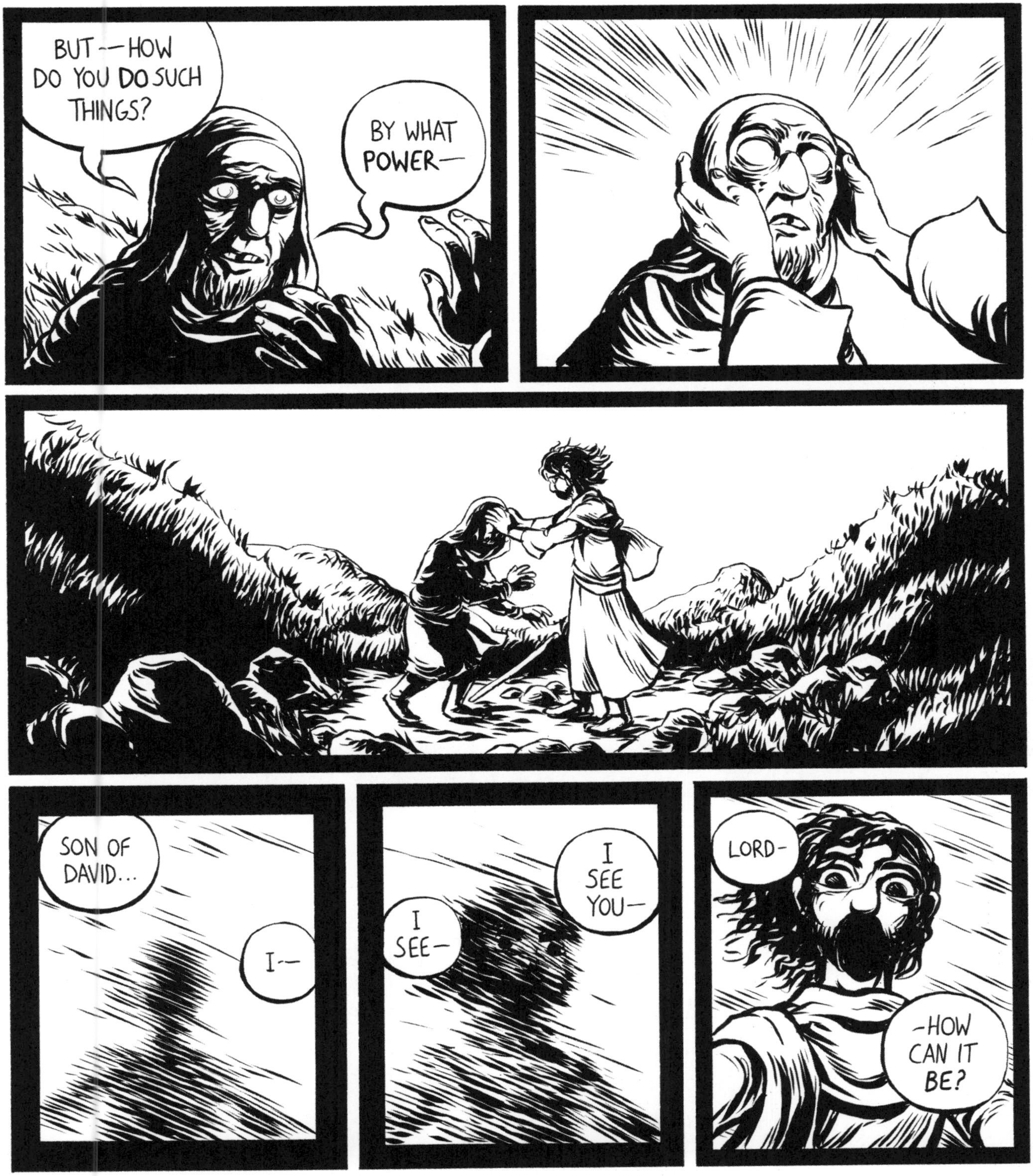
BUT--HOW DO YOU DO SUCH THINGS?
BY WHAT POWER—
SON OF DAVID...
I-—
I SEE YOU—
I SEE—
LORD-
-HOW CAN IT BE?

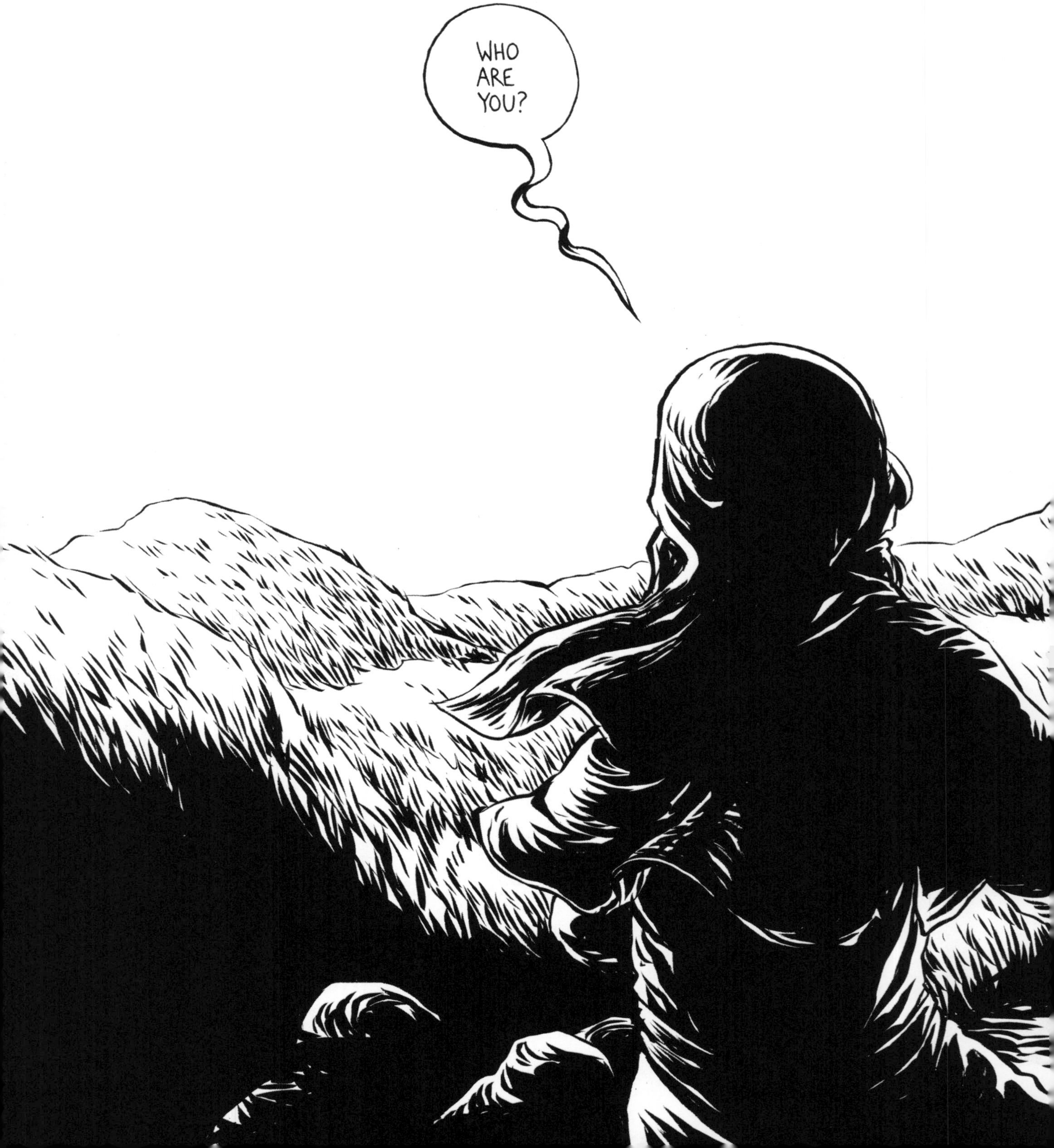
WHO ARE YOU?

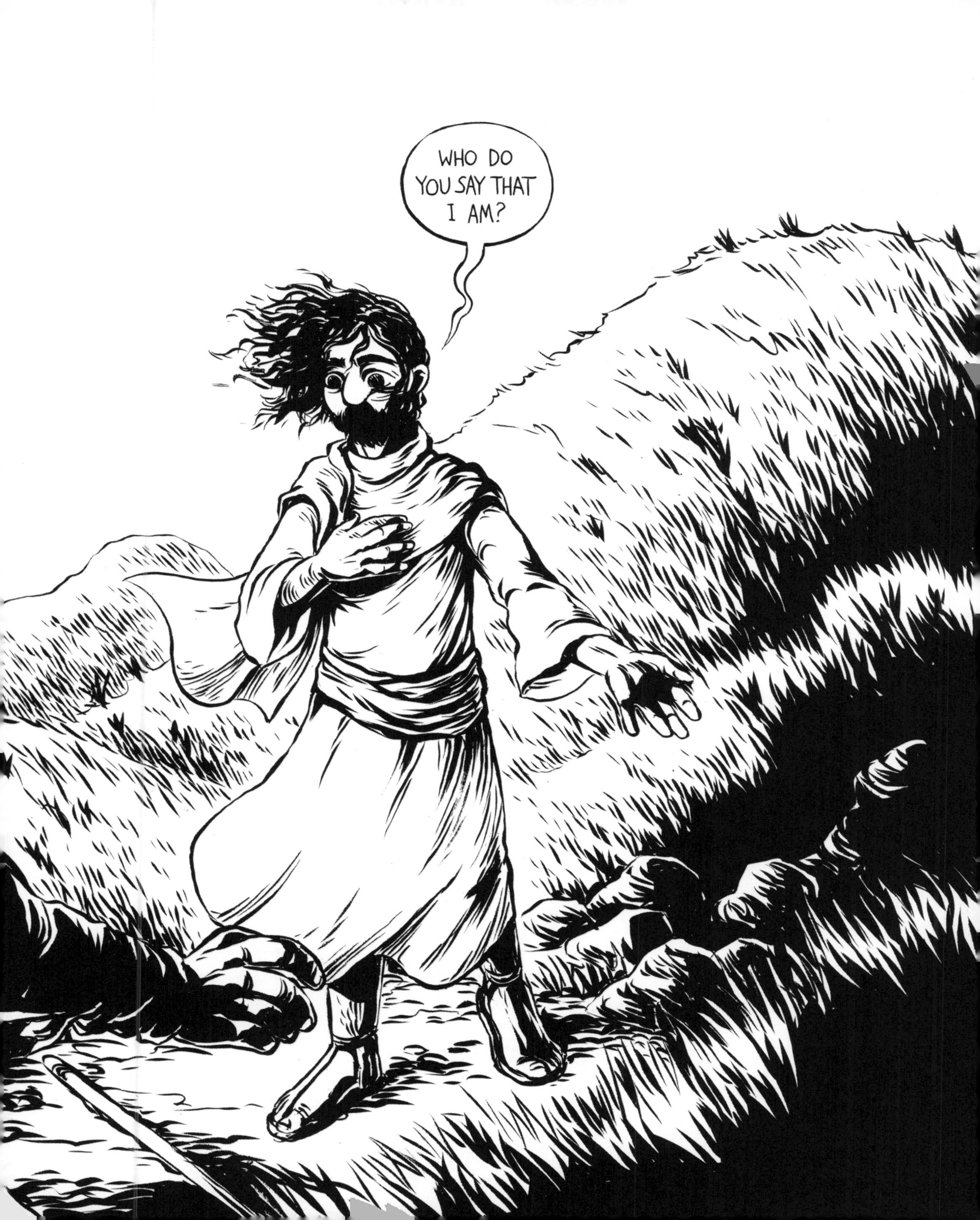
WHO DO YOU SAY THAT I AM?

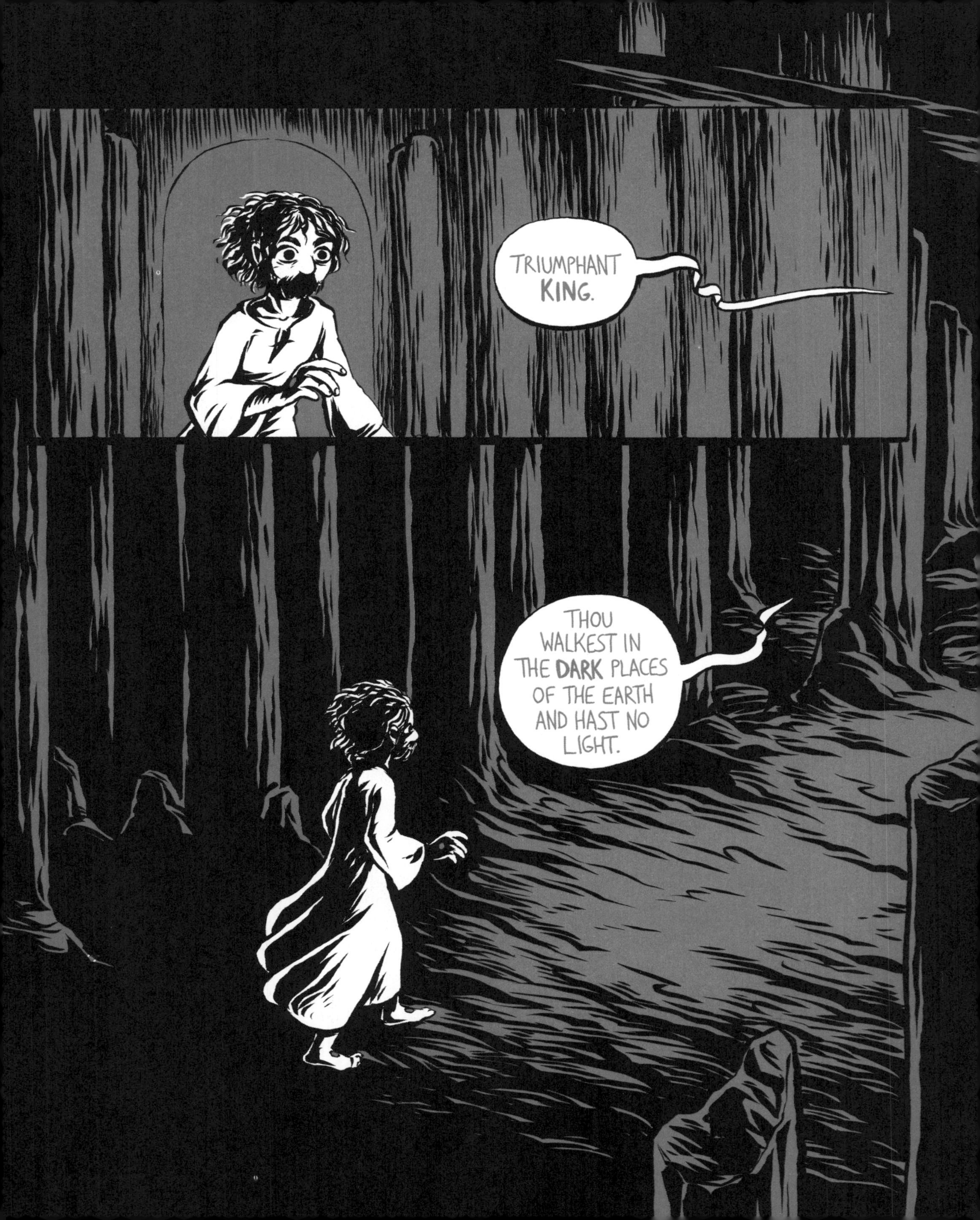
TRIUMPHANT KING.
THOU WALKEST IN THE DARK PLACES OF THE EARTH AND HAST NO LIGHT.

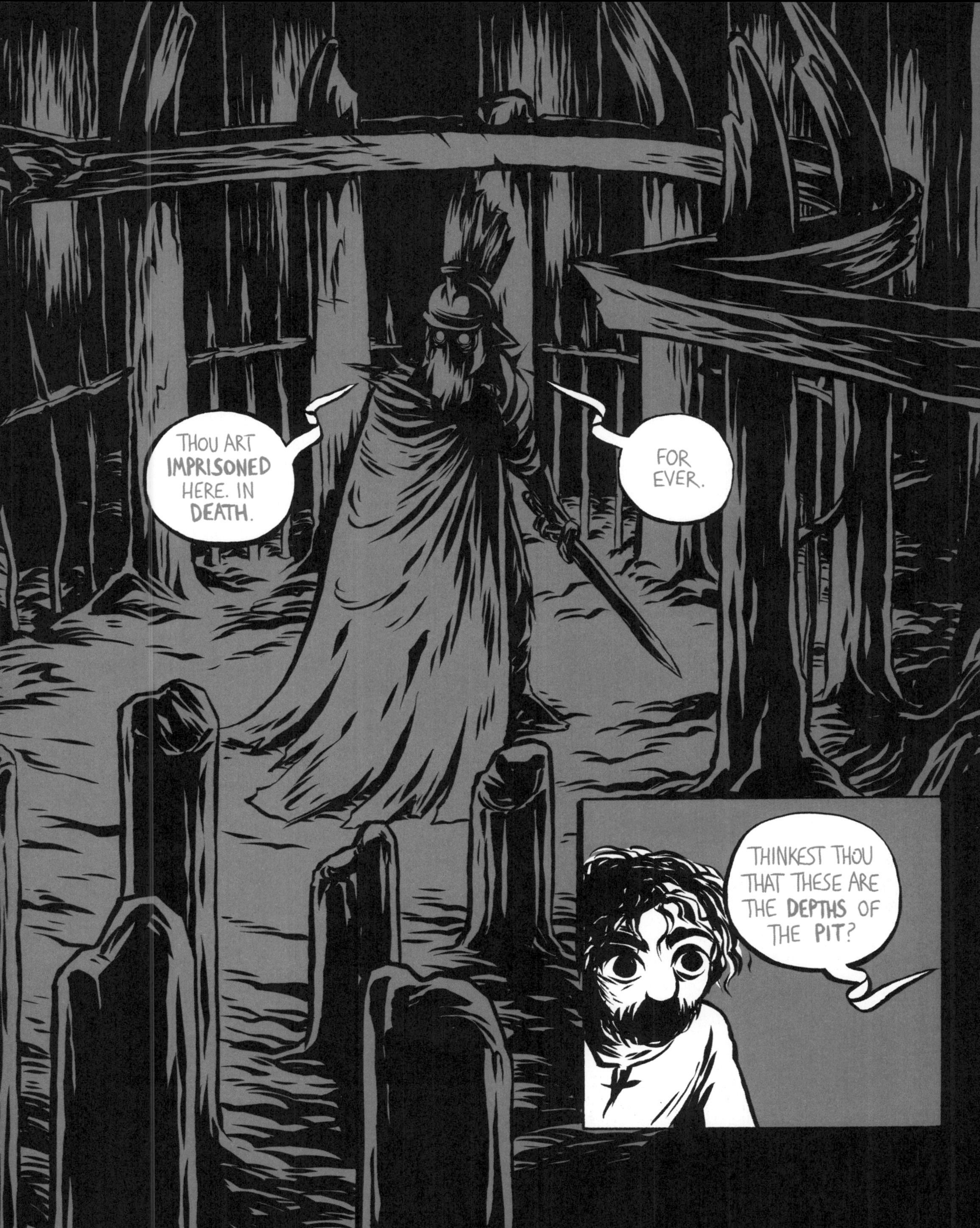
THOU ART IMPRISONED HERE. IN DEATH.
FOR EVER.
THINKEST THOU THAT THESE ARE THE DEPTHS OF THE PIT?

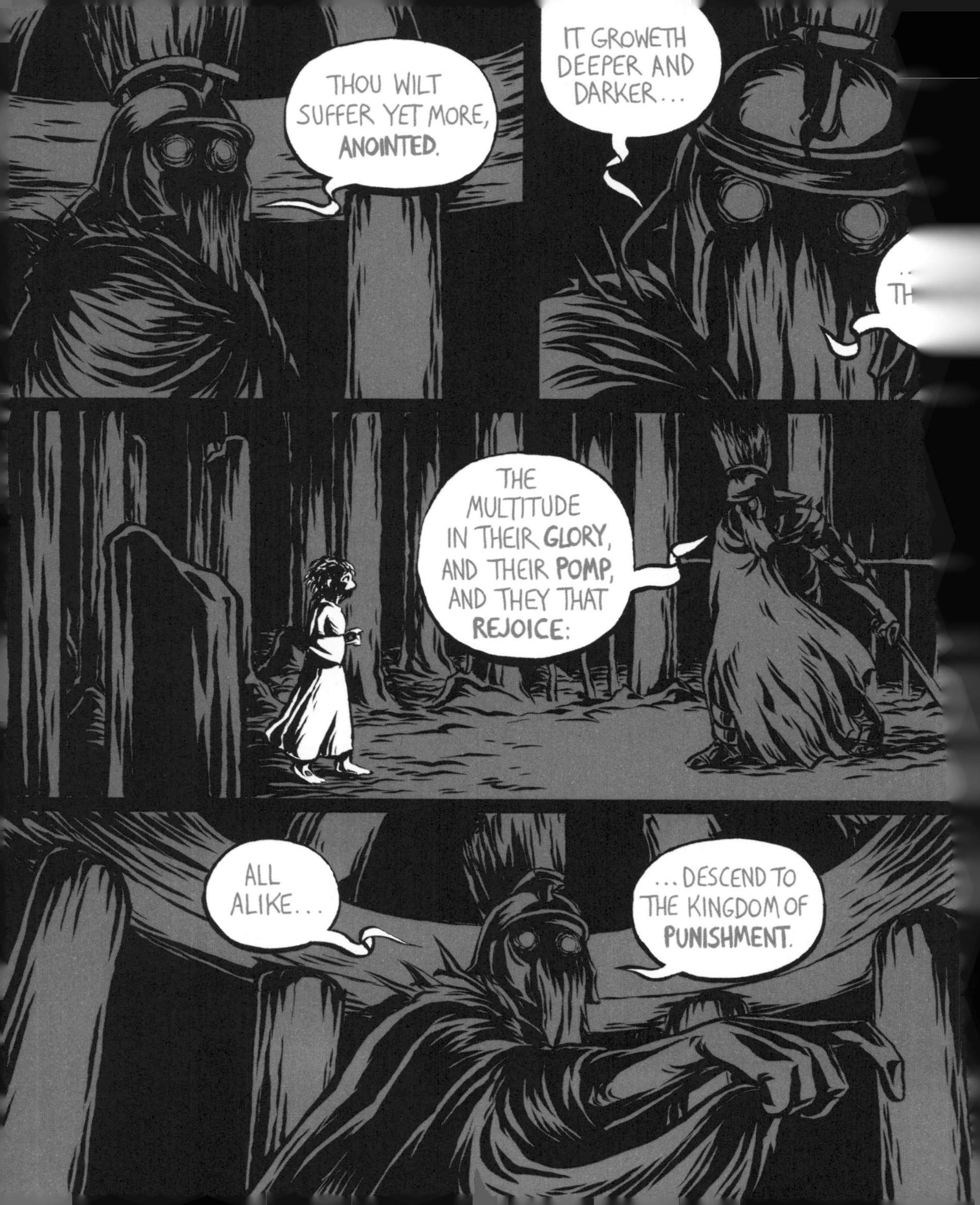
THOU WILT SUFFER YET MORE, ANOINTED.
IT GROWETH DEEPER AND DARKER...
THE MULTITUDE IN THEIR GLORY, AND THEIR POMP, AND THEY THAT REJOICE:
ALL ALIKE...
...DESCEND TO THE KINGDOM OF PUNISHMENT.

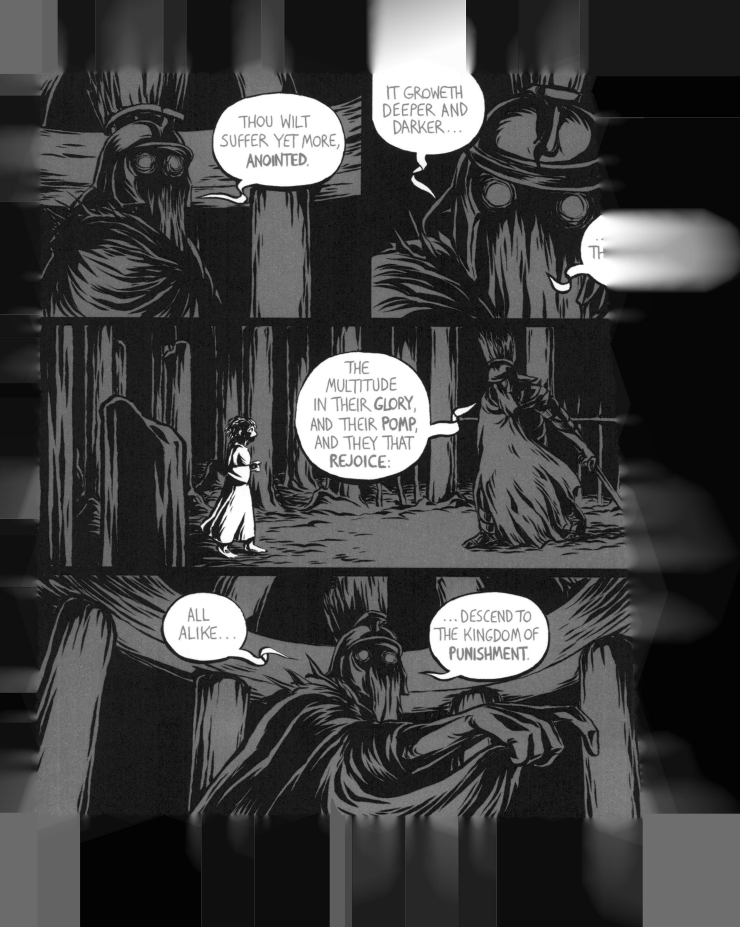

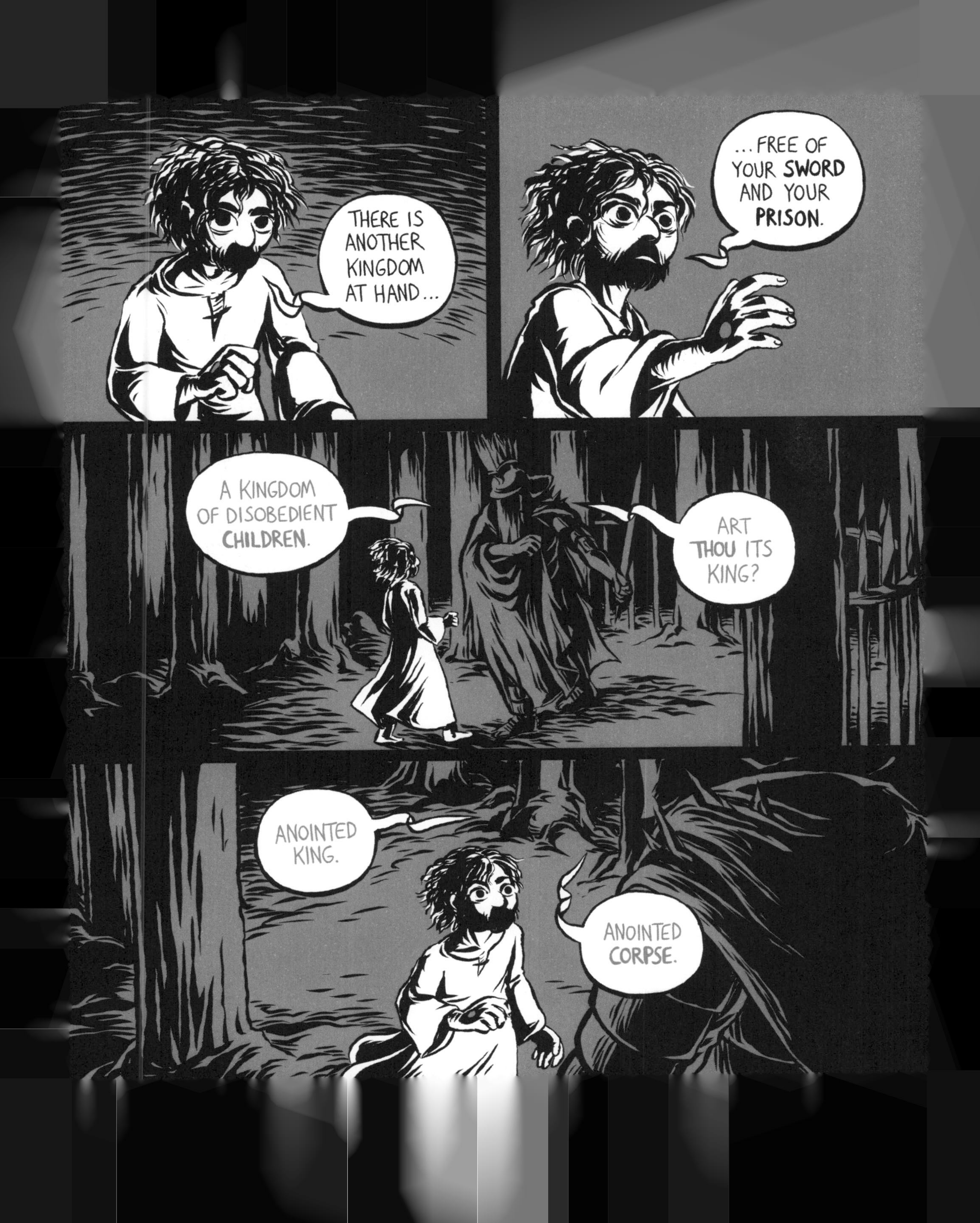
THERE IS ANOTHER KINGDOM AT HAND...
...FREE OF YOUR SWORD AND YOUR PRISON.
A KINGDOM OF DISOBEDIENT CHILDREN.
ART THOU ITS KING?
ANOINTED KING.
ANOINTED CORPSE.

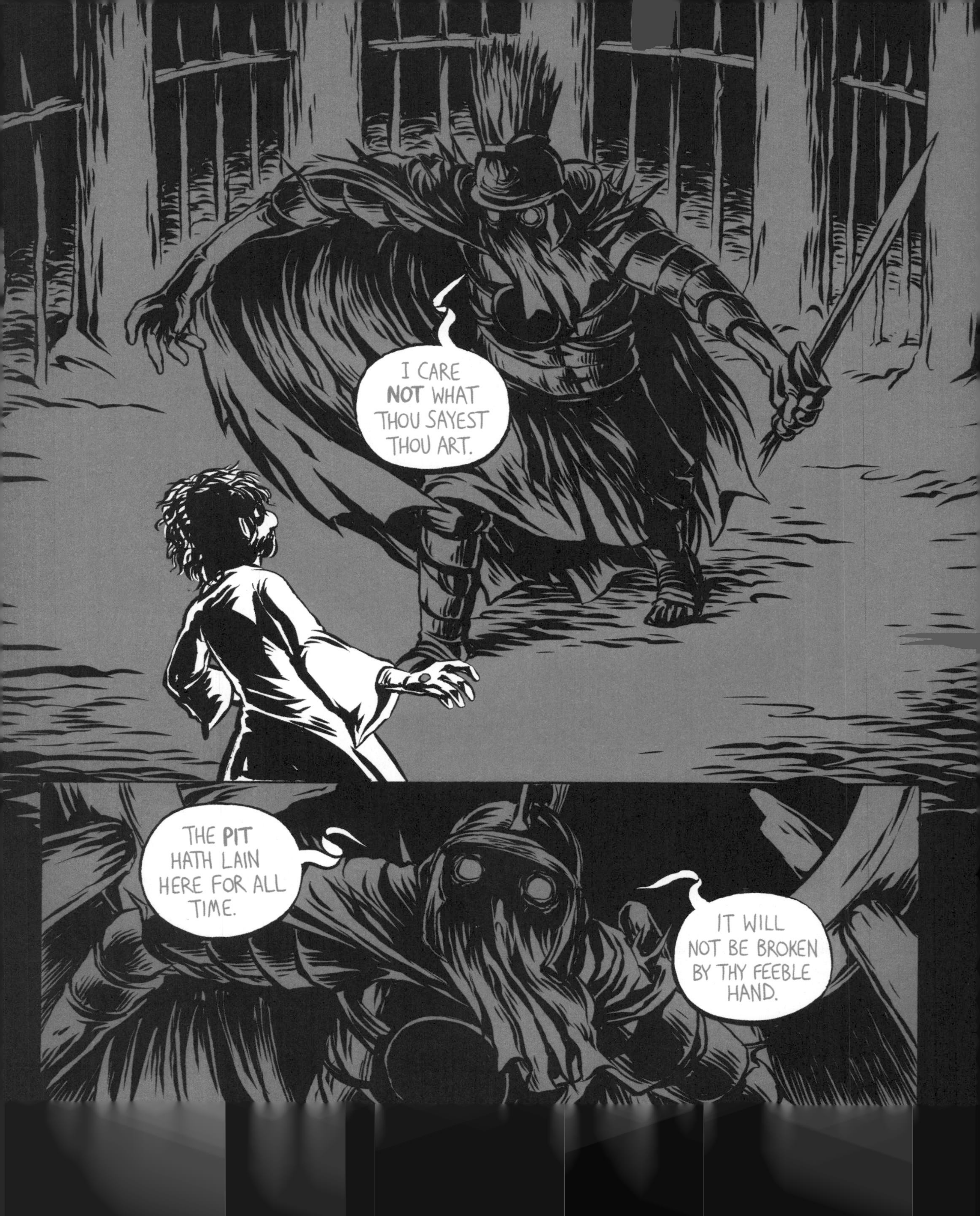
I CARE **NOT** WHAT THOU SAYEST THOU ART.
THE **PIT** HATH LAIN HERE FOR ALL TIME.
IT WILL NOT BE BROKEN BY THY FEEBLE HAND.

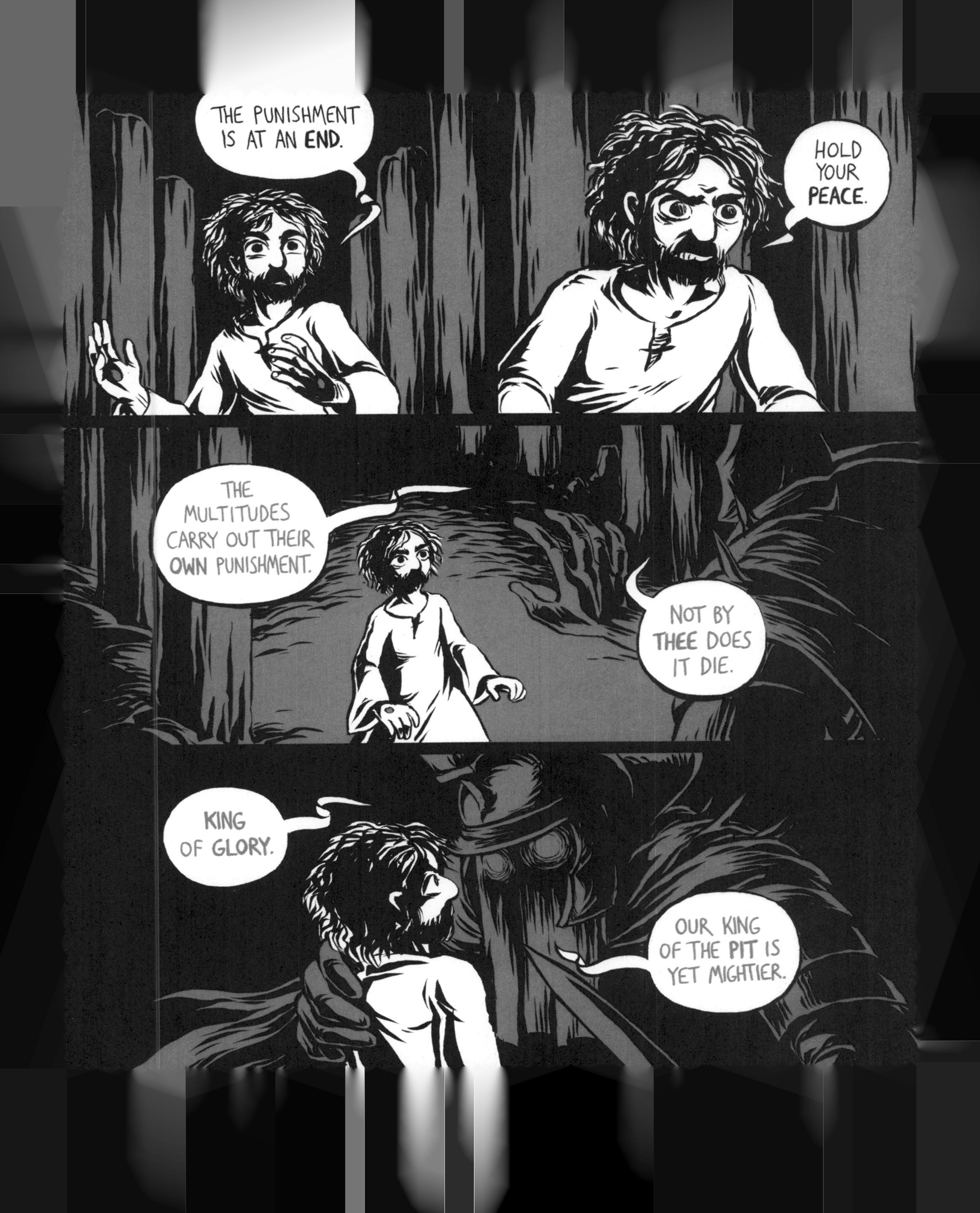
THE PUNISHMENT IS AT AN END.
HOLD YOUR PEACE.
THE MULTITUDES CARRY OUT THEIR OWN PUNISHMENT.
NOT BY THEE DOES IT DIE.
KING OF GLORY.
OUR KING OF THE PIT IS YET MIGHTIER.

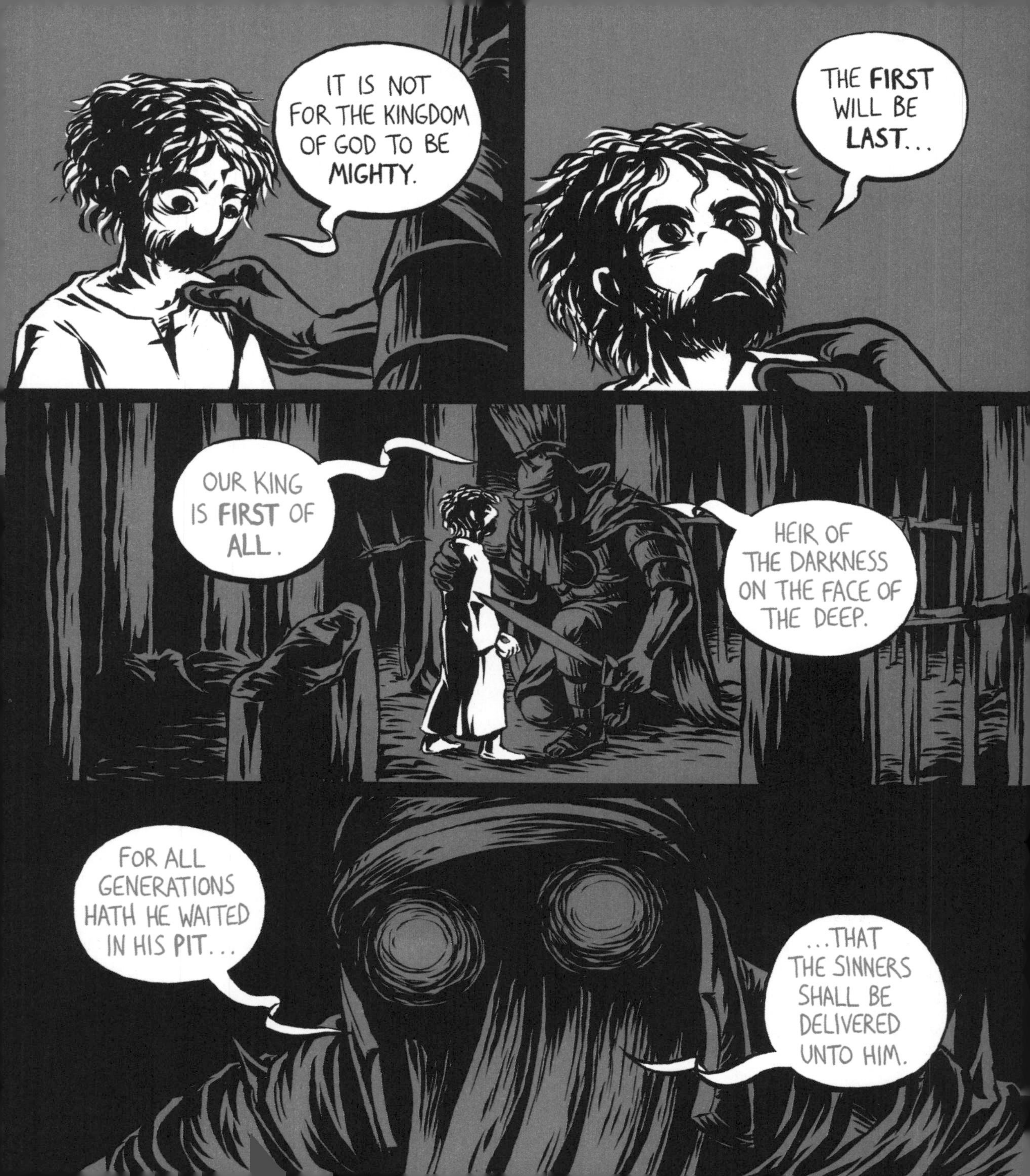
IT IS NOT FOR THE KINGDOM OF GOD TO BE MIGHTY.
THE FIRST WILL BE LAST...
OUR KING IS FIRST OF ALL.
HEIR OF THE DARKNESS ON THE FACE OF THE DEEP.
FOR ALL GENERATIONS HATH HE WAITED IN HIS PIT...
...THAT THE SINNERS SHALL BE DELIVERED UNTO HIM.

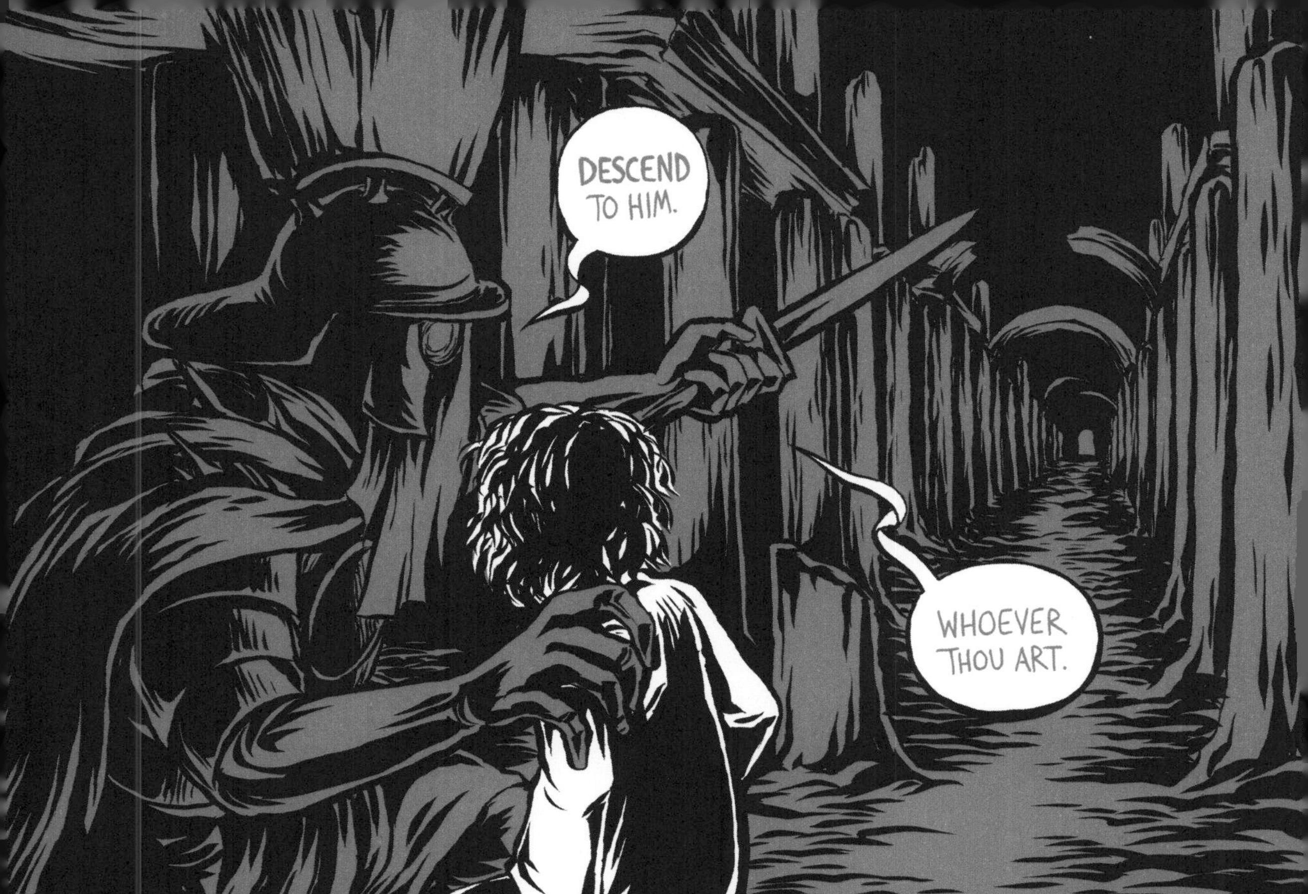
DESCEND TO HIM.
WHOEVER THOU ART.
PREPARE YE THE WAY OF THE **LORD**...

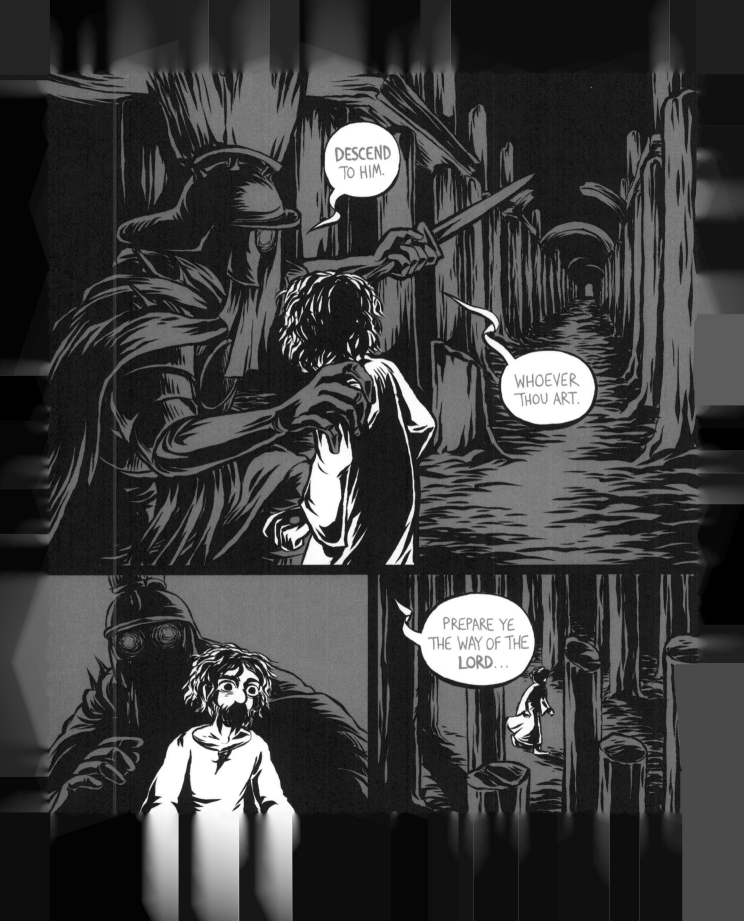

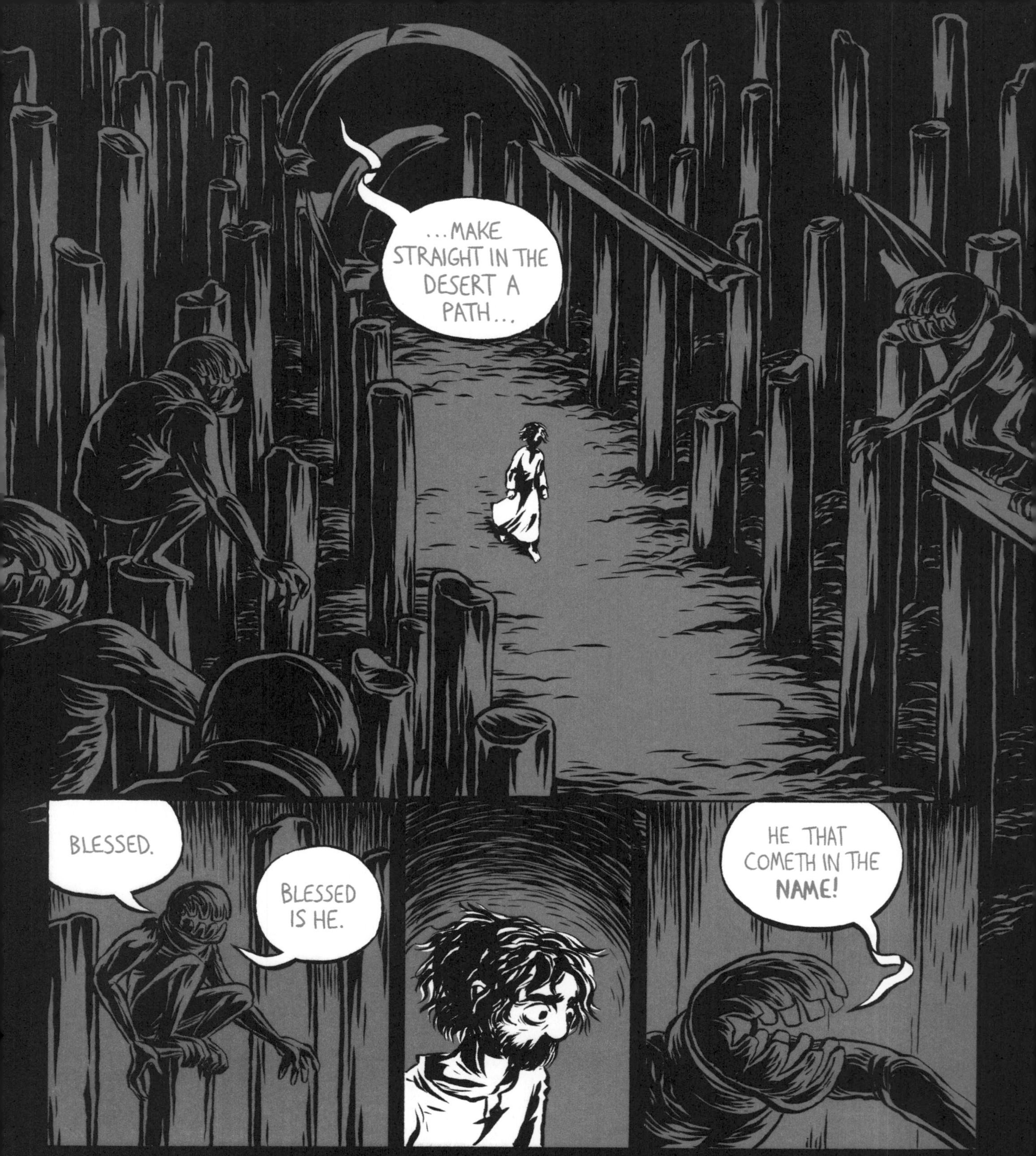
...MAKE STRAIGHT IN THE DESERT A PATH...
BLESSED.
BLESSED IS HE.
HE THAT COMETH IN THE **NAME!**

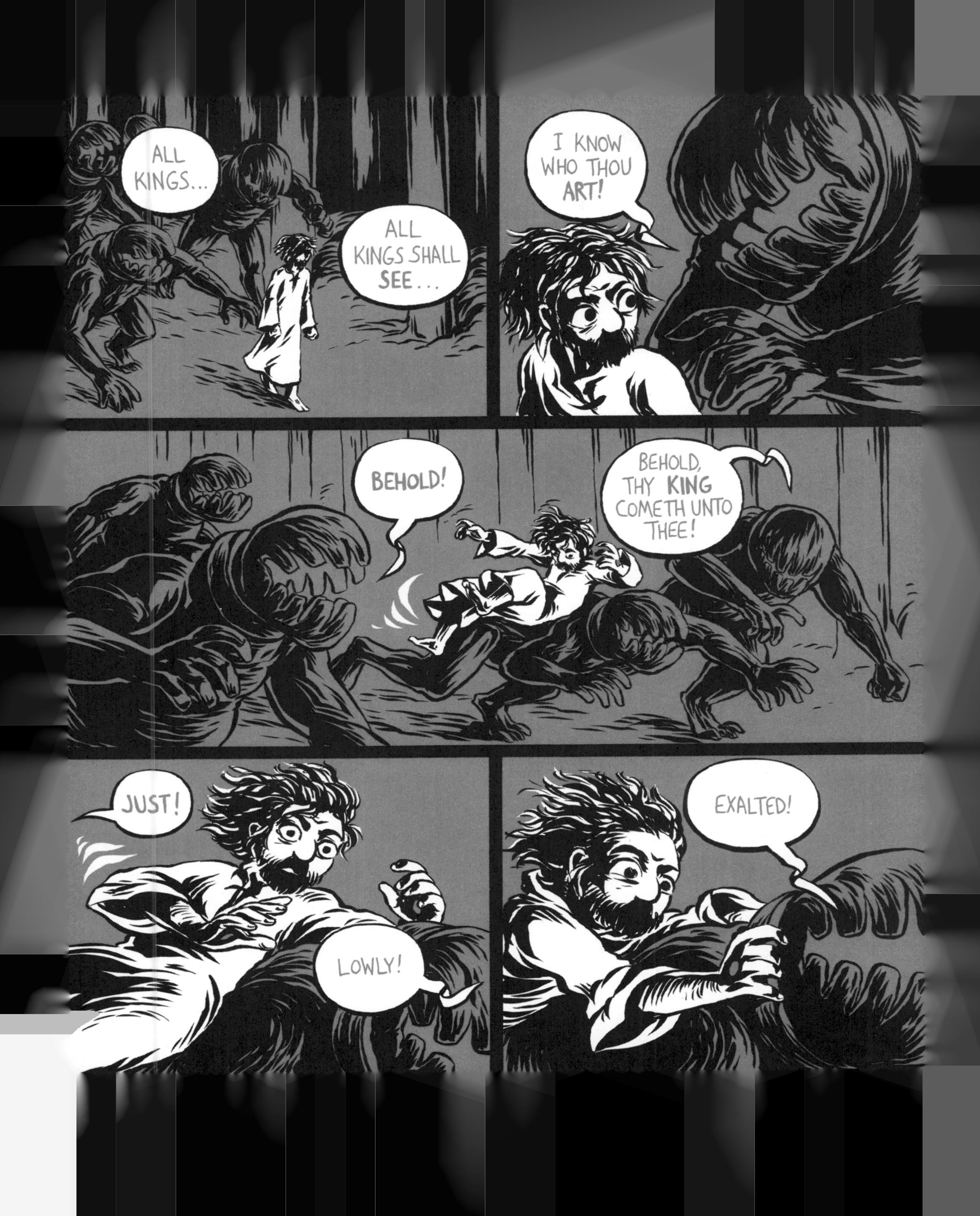
ALL KINGS...
ALL KINGS SHALL SEE...
I KNOW WHO THOU ART!
BEHOLD!
BEHOLD, THY KING COMETH UNTO THEE!
JUST!
LOWLY!
EXALTED!

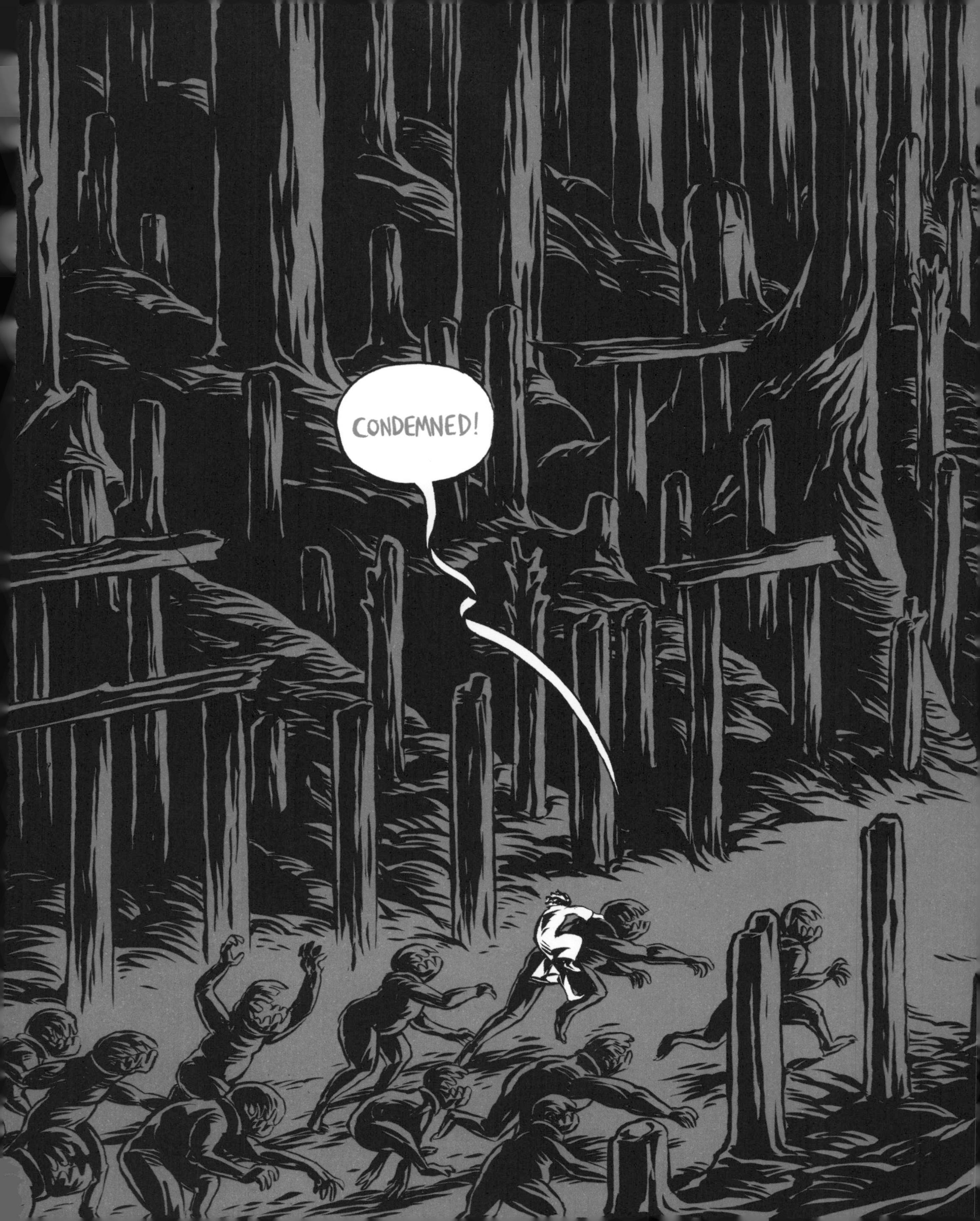
CONDEMNED!

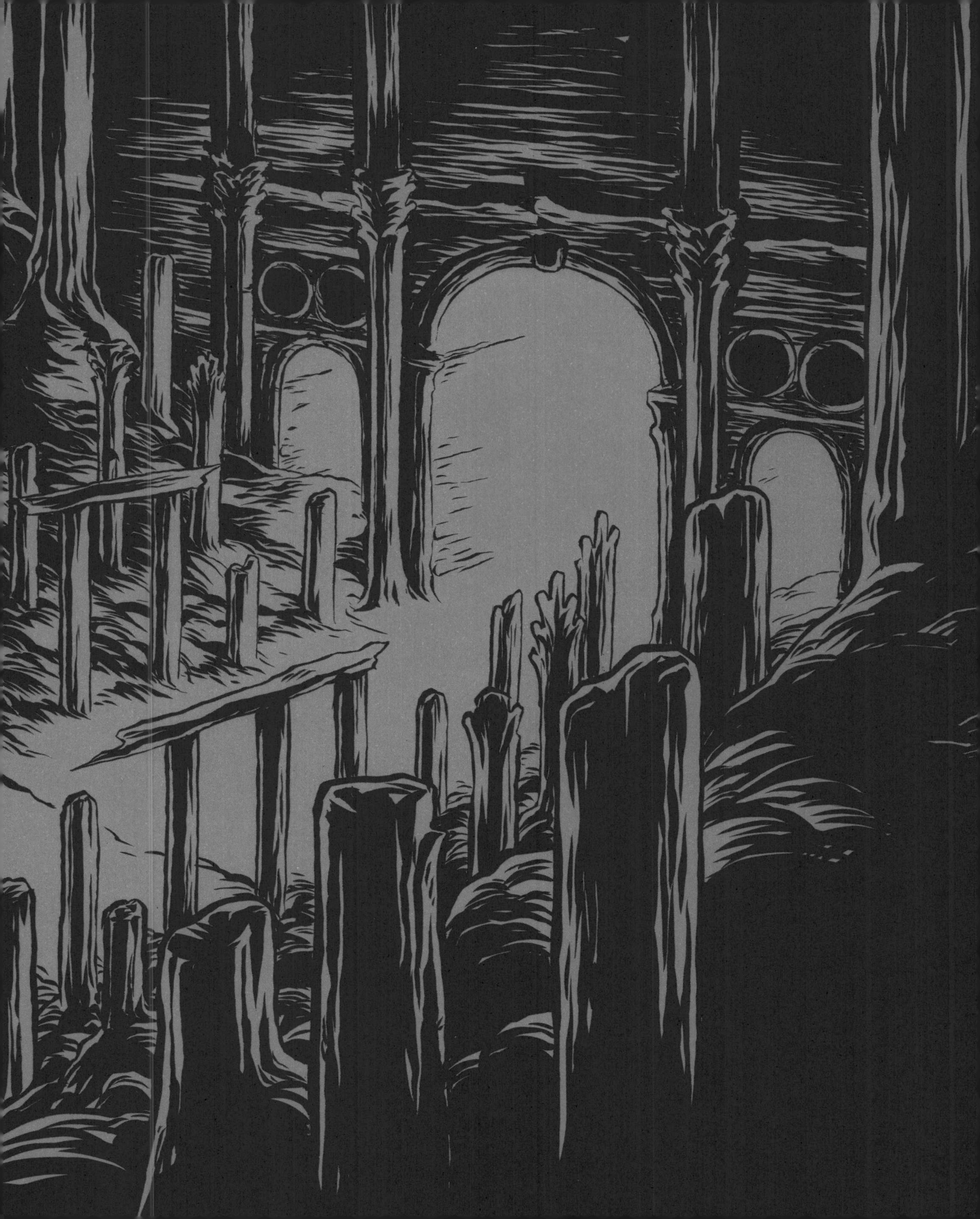

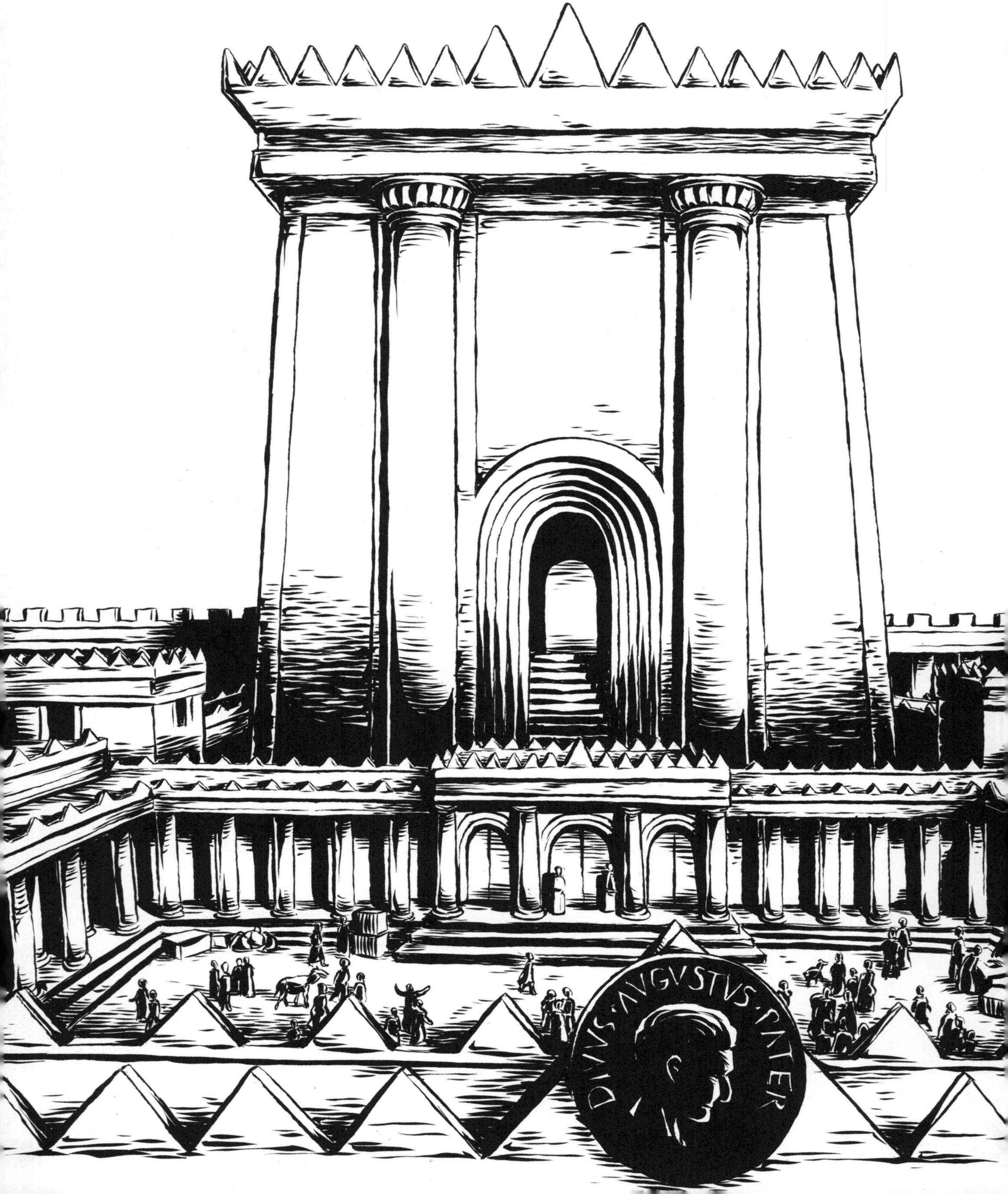
DIVVS·AVGVSTVS·PATER

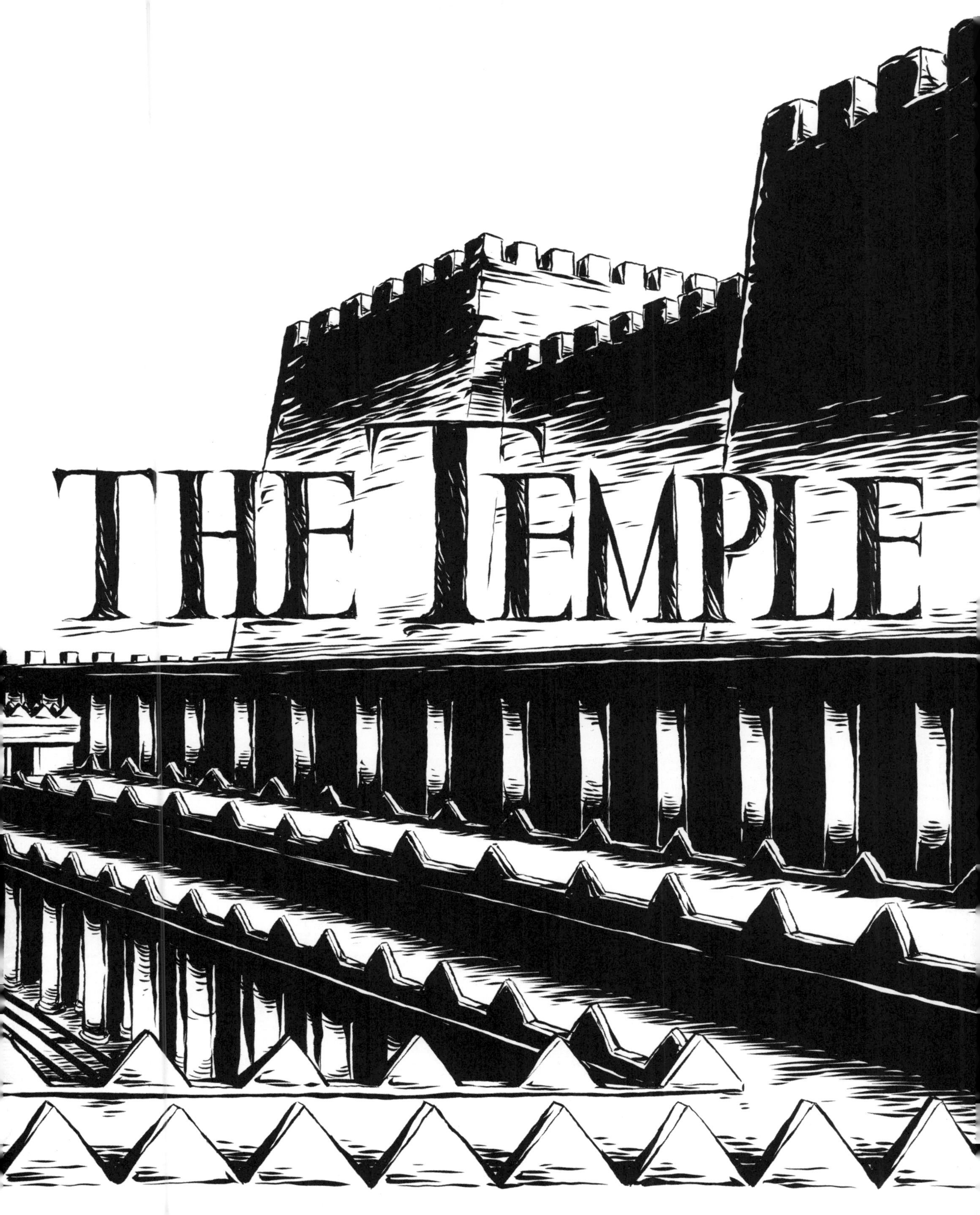
THE TEMPLE

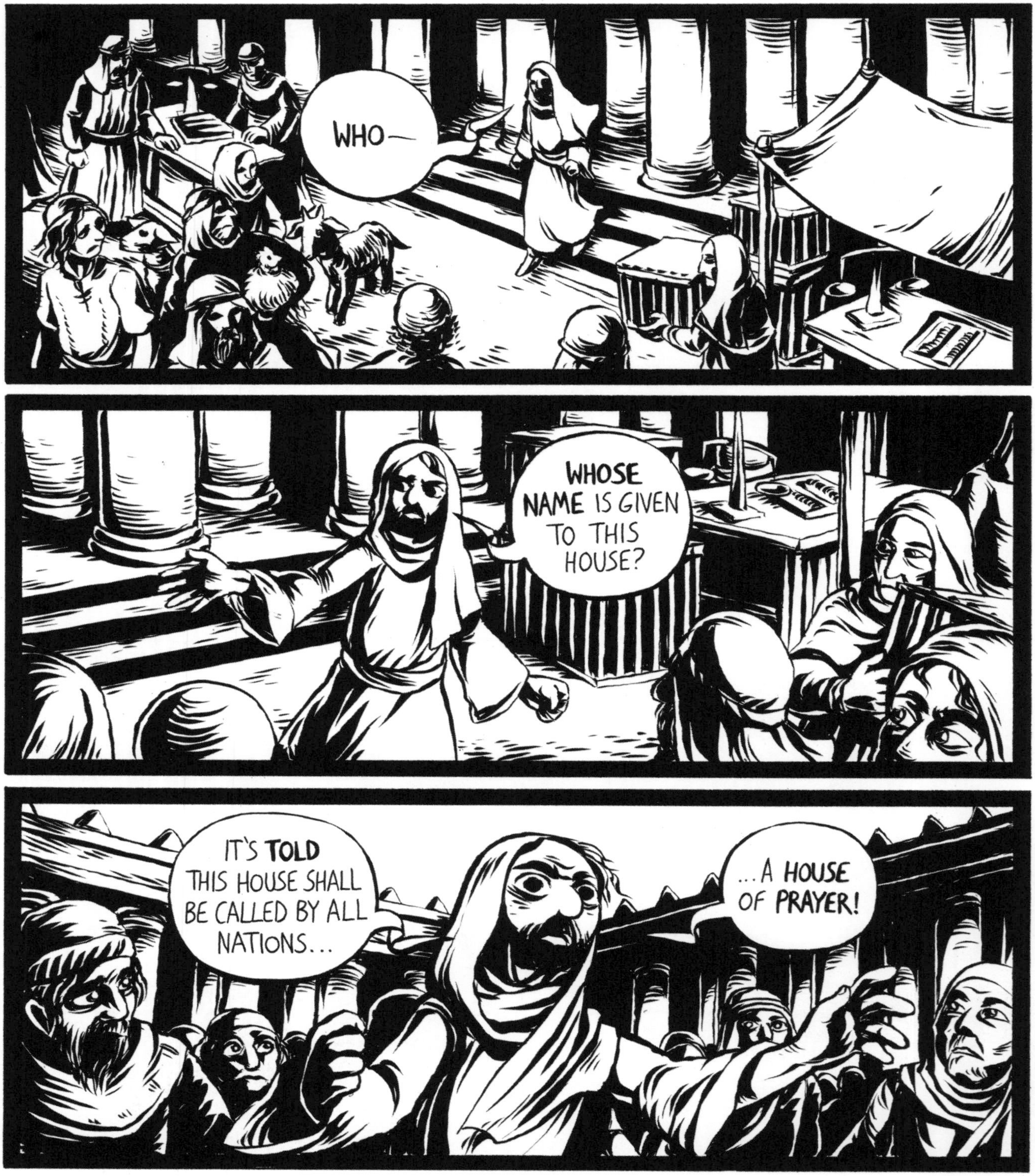
WHO—
WHOSE NAME IS GIVEN TO THIS HOUSE?
IT'S TOLD THIS HOUSE SHALL BE CALLED BY ALL NATIONS...
...A HOUSE OF PRAYER!

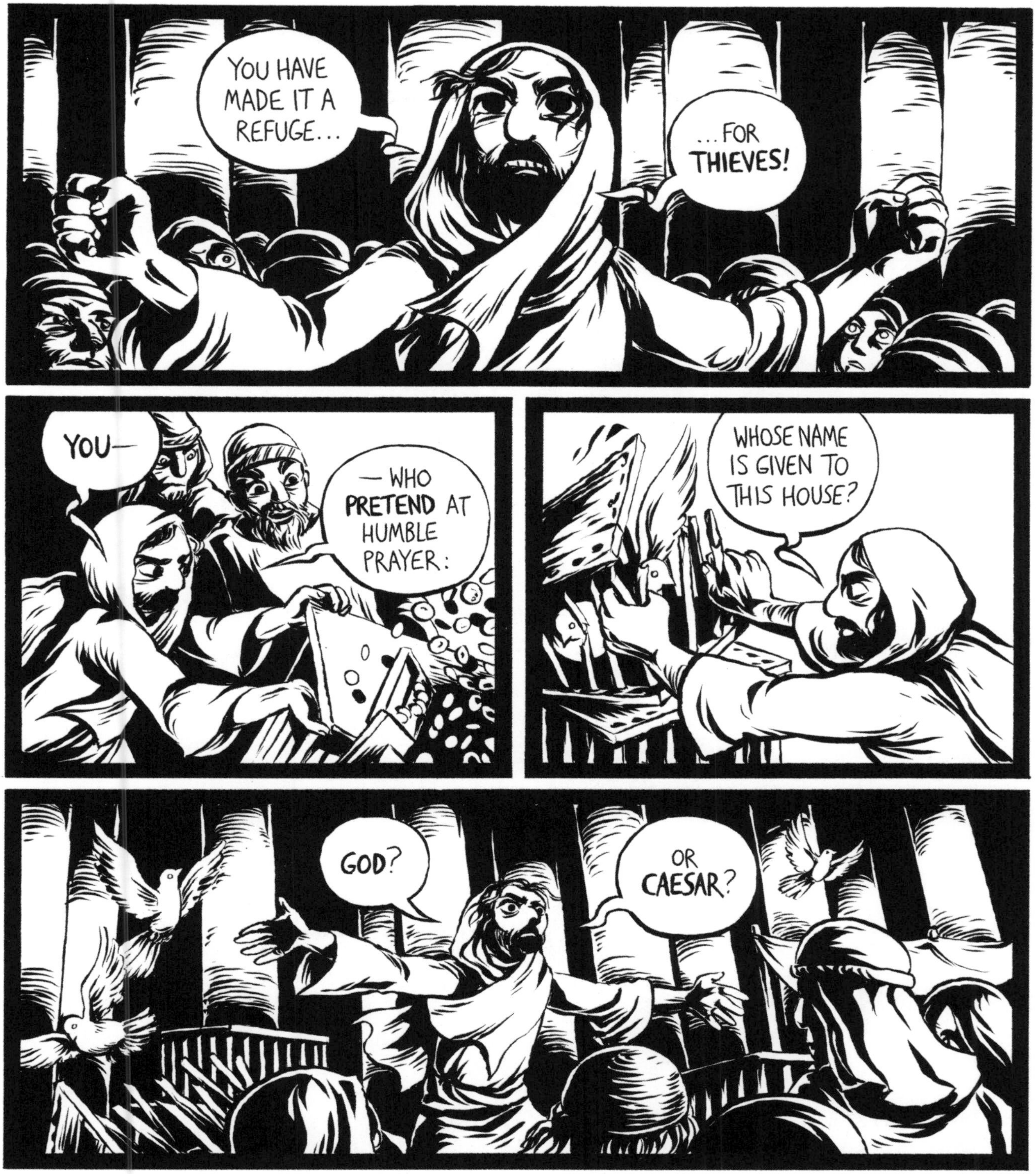
YOU HAVE MADE IT A REFUGE...
...FOR THIEVES!
YOU—
—WHO PRETEND AT HUMBLE PRAYER:
WHOSE NAME IS GIVEN TO THIS HOUSE?
GOD?
OR CAESAR?

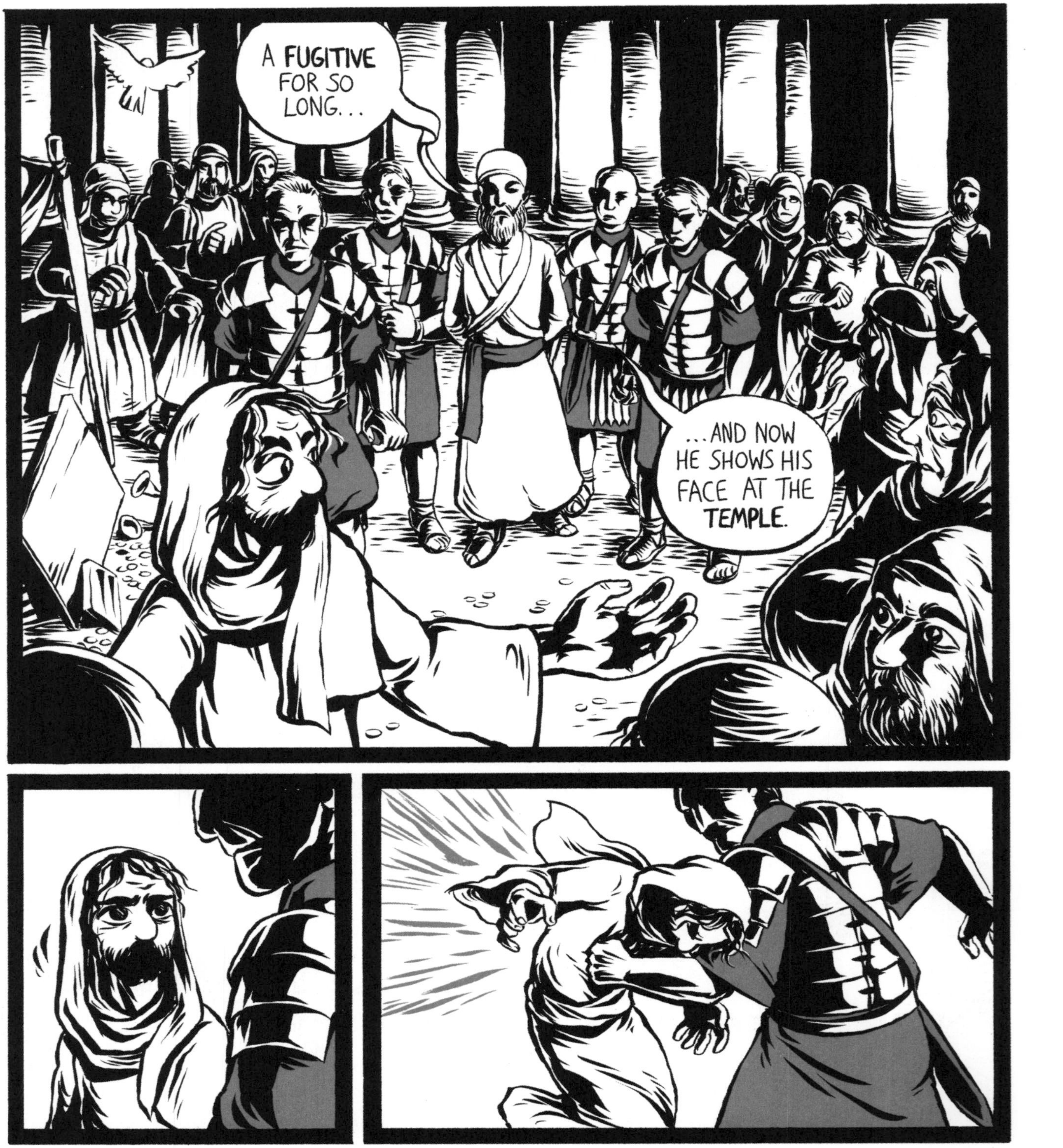
A **FUGITIVE** FOR SO LONG...
...AND NOW HE SHOWS HIS FACE AT THE **TEMPLE**.

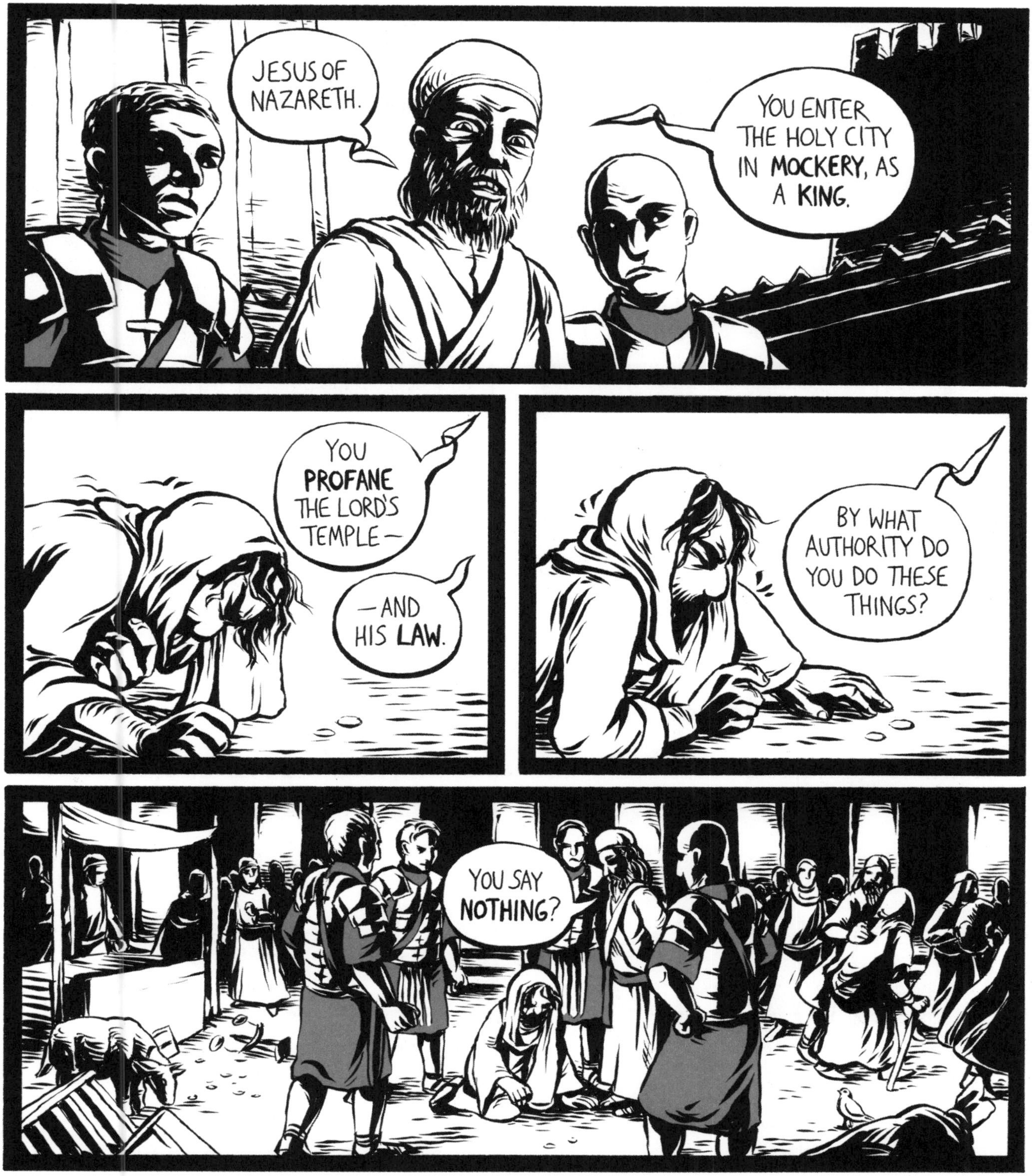
JESUS OF NAZARETH.
YOU ENTER THE HOLY CITY IN MOCKERY, AS A KING.
YOU PROFANE THE LORD'S TEMPLE—
—AND HIS LAW.
BY WHAT AUTHORITY DO YOU DO THESE THINGS?
YOU SAY NOTHING?

YOU **PREACH** AND YOU **BLASPHEME**...
...BUT NOW YOU HAVE NOTHING MORE TO TELL?
YOU WILL BE **PUNISHED** FOR THIS.
STORIES.
YOU TALK IN **STORIES**.
YOU, AND THE GENTILE EMPIRE.

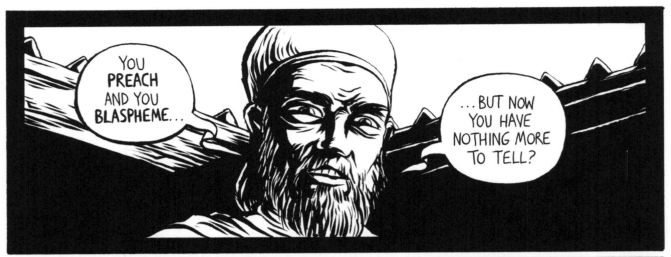

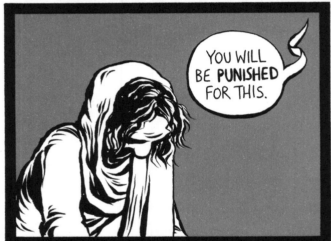

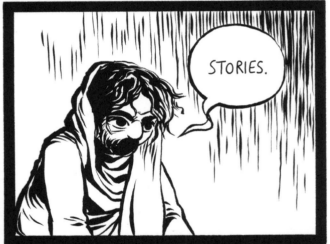

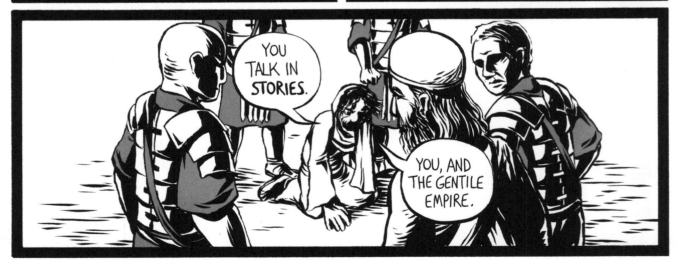

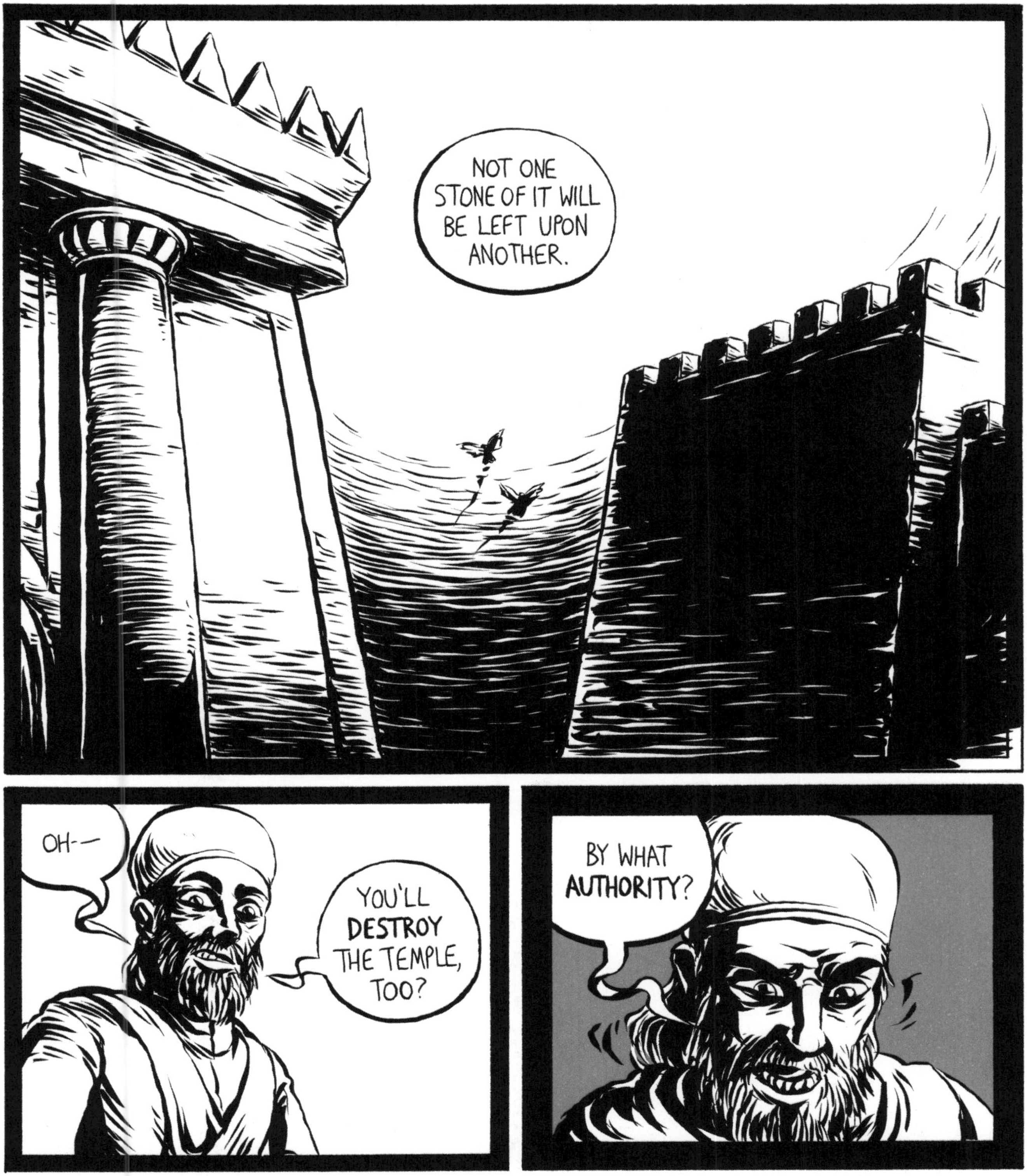
NOT ONE STONE OF IT WILL BE LEFT UPON ANOTHER.
OH-—
YOU'LL **DESTROY** THE TEMPLE, TOO?
BY WHAT **AUTHORITY**?

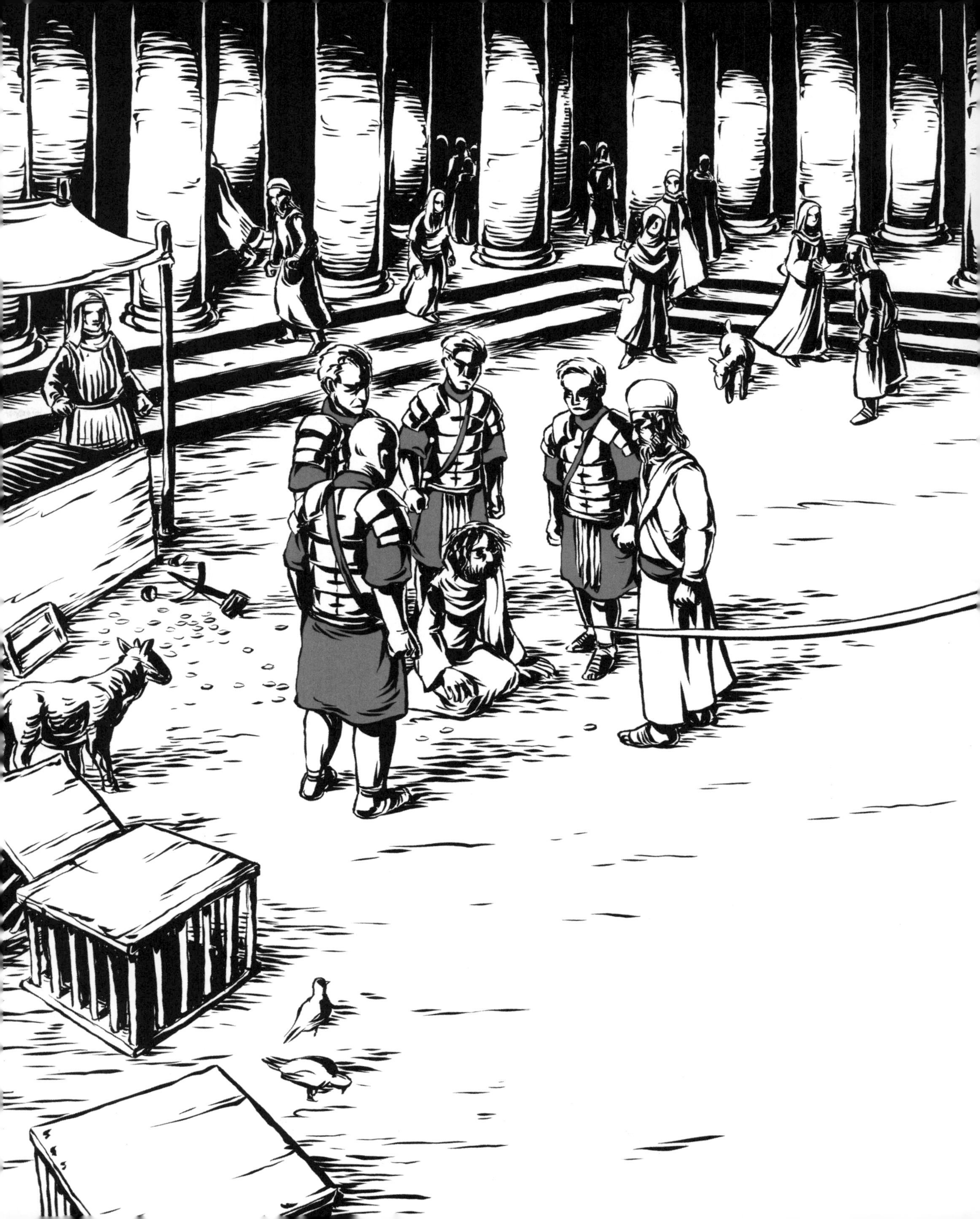

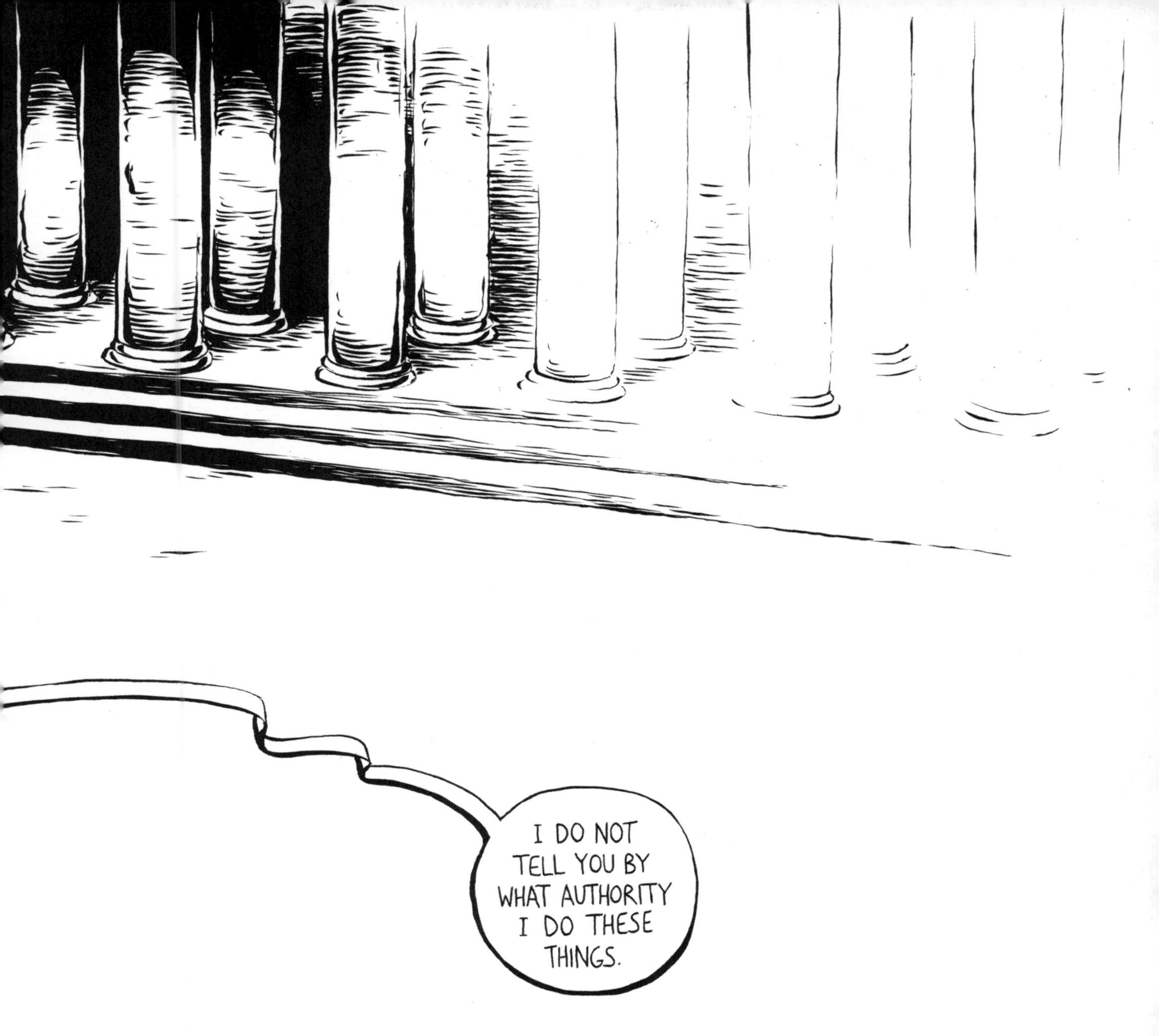
I DO NOT TELL YOU BY WHAT AUTHORITY I DO THESE THINGS.

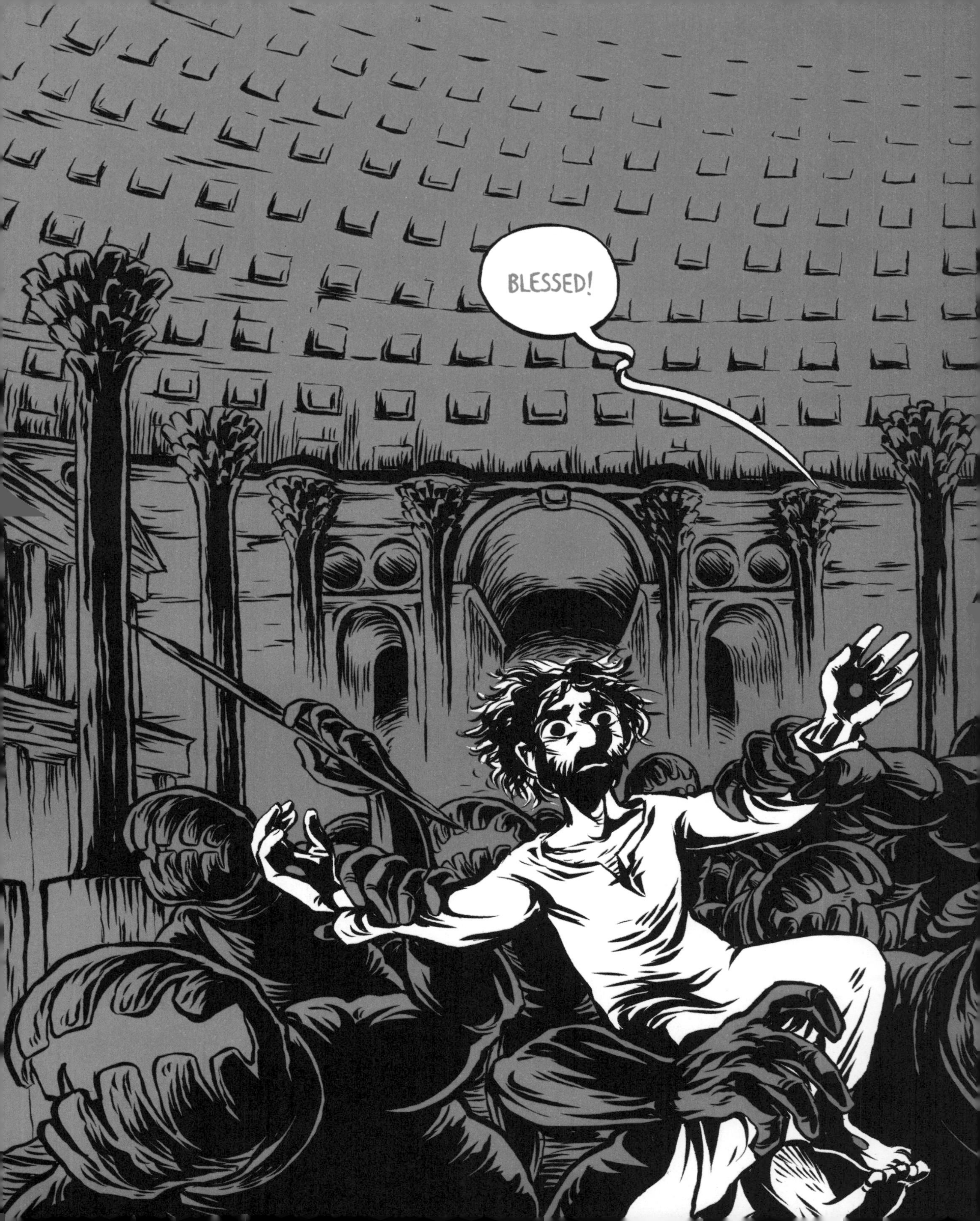
BLESSED!

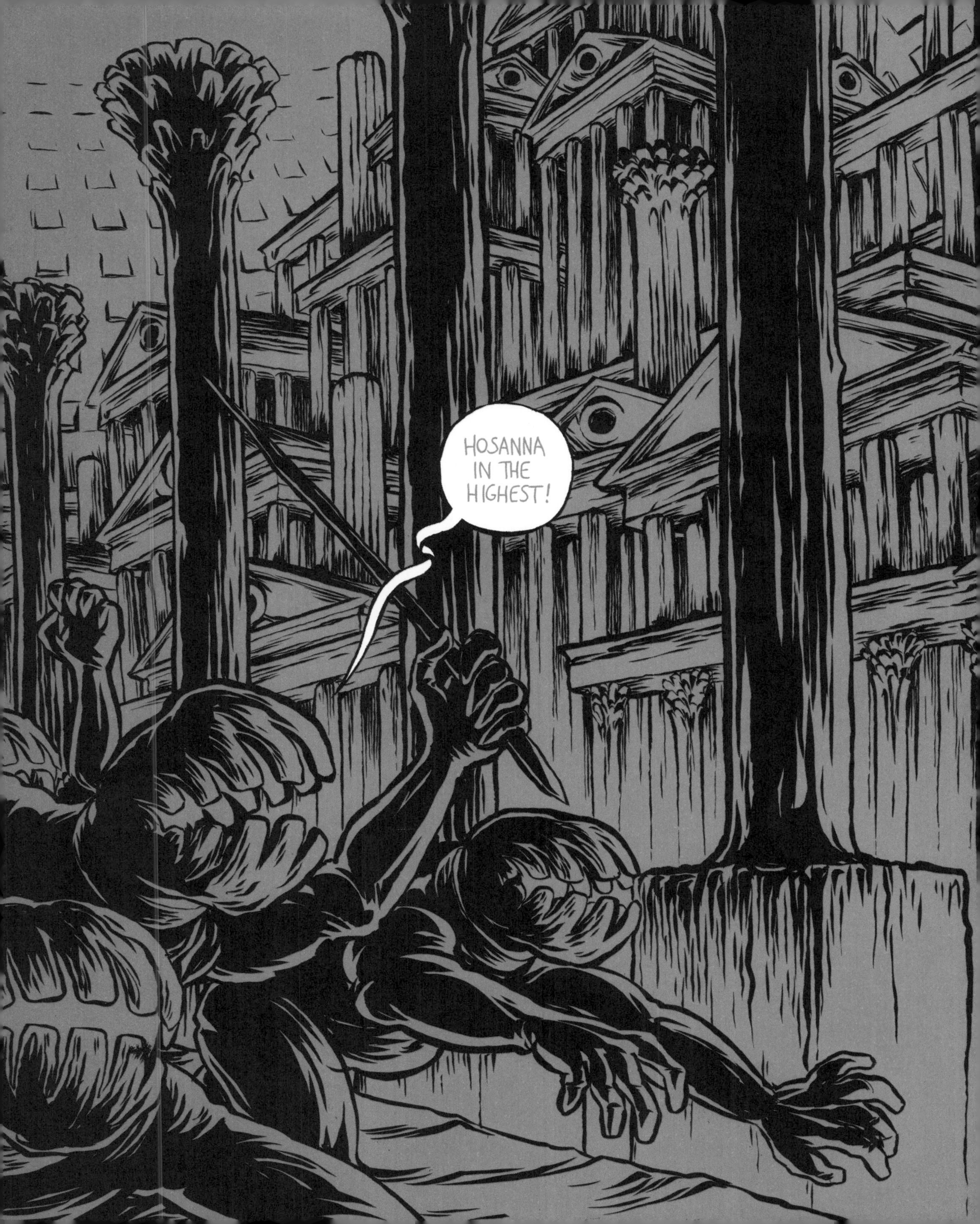
HOSANNA IN THE HIGHEST!

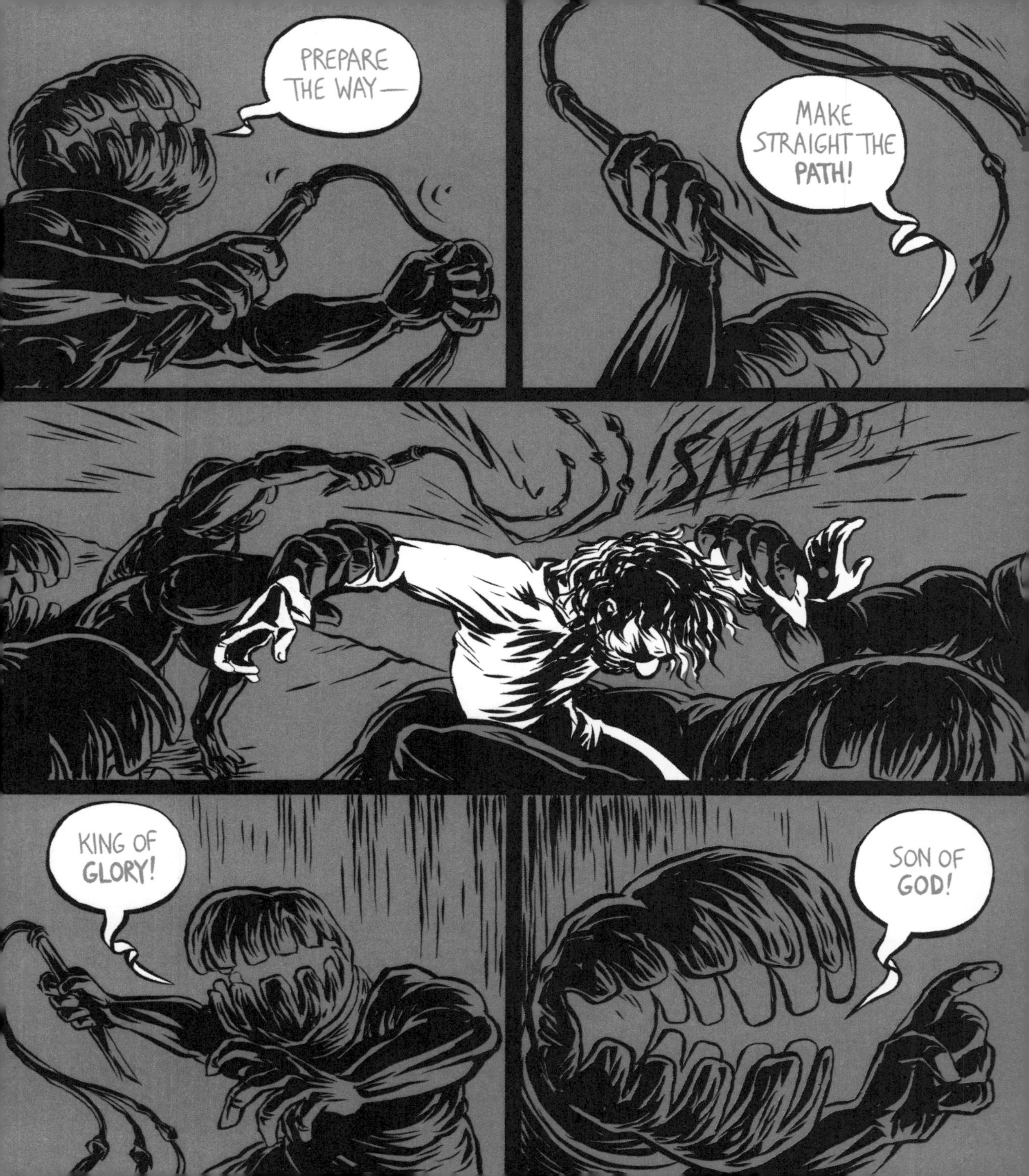
PREPARE THE WAY—
MAKE STRAIGHT THE PATH!
SNAP
KING OF GLORY!
SON OF GOD!

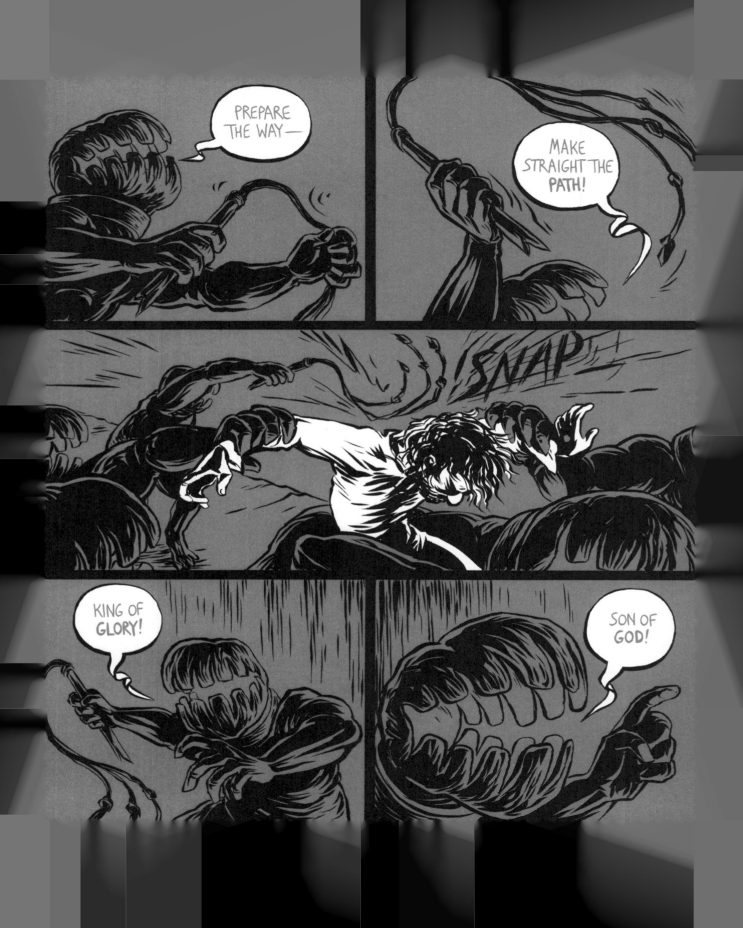

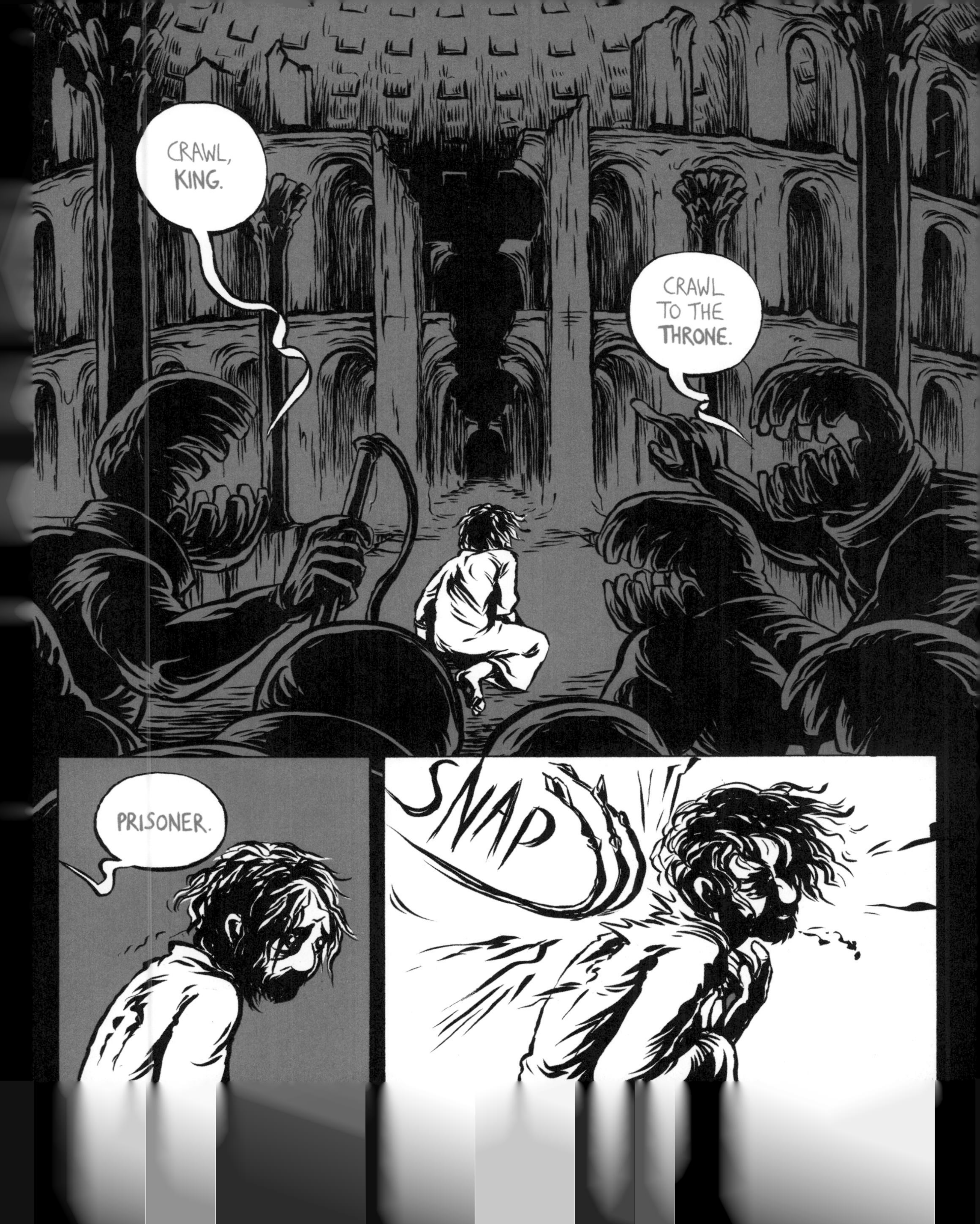
CRAWL, KING.
CRAWL TO THE THRONE.
PRISONER.
SNAP

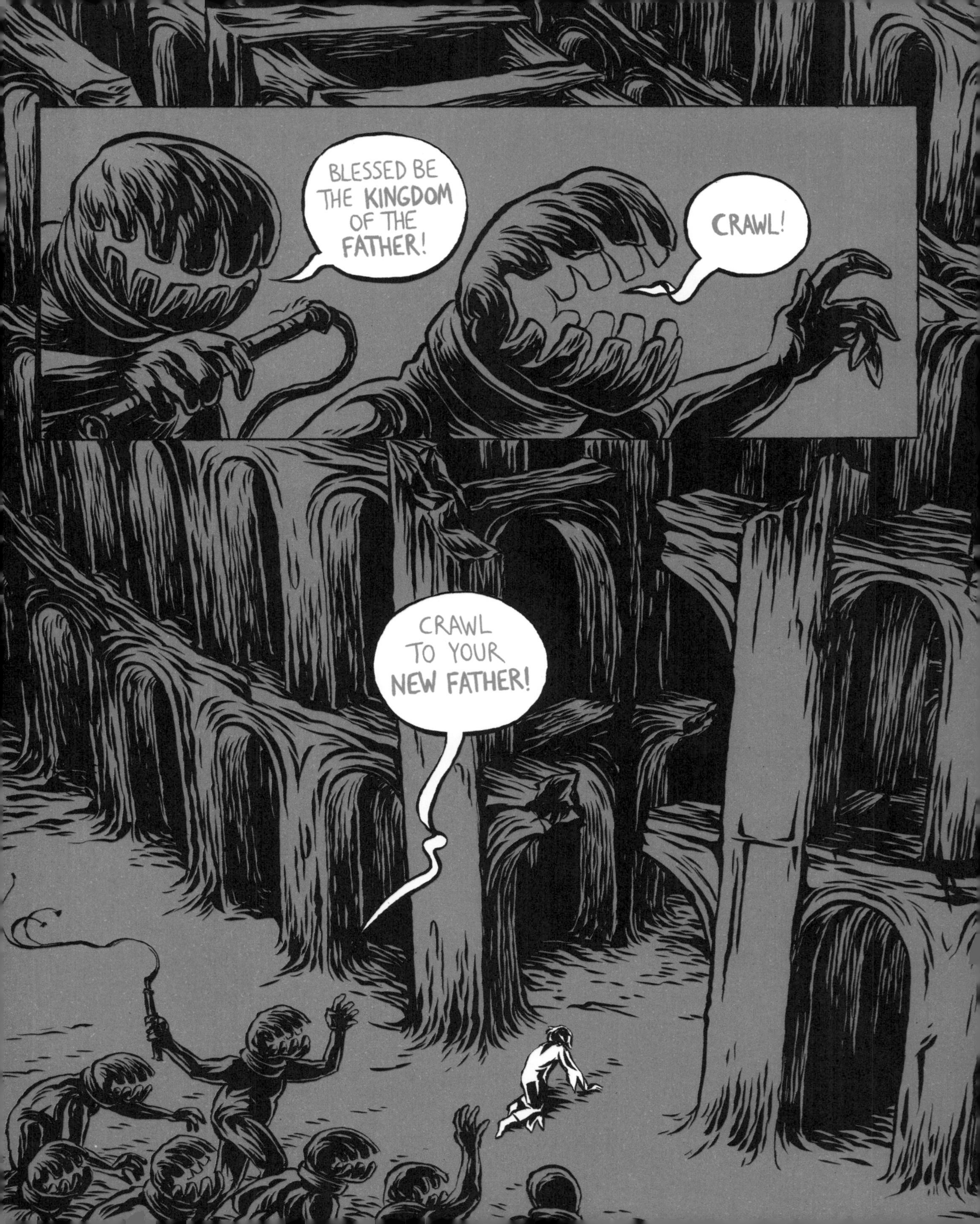
BLESSED BE THE KINGDOM OF THE FATHER!
CRAWL!
CRAWL TO YOUR NEW FATHER!

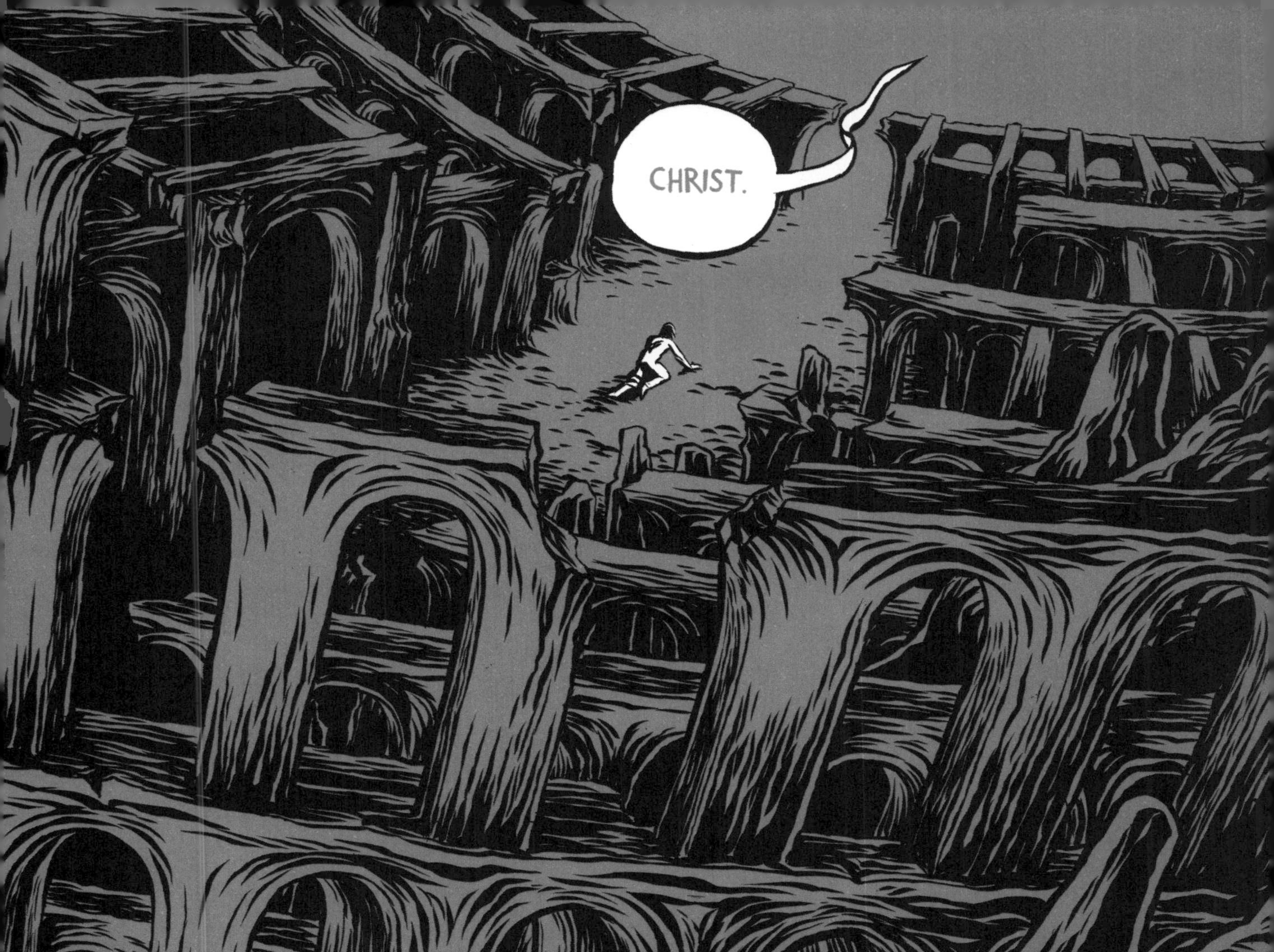
CHRIST.
ART THOU THE CHRIST?
I SAY THAT THOU ART.

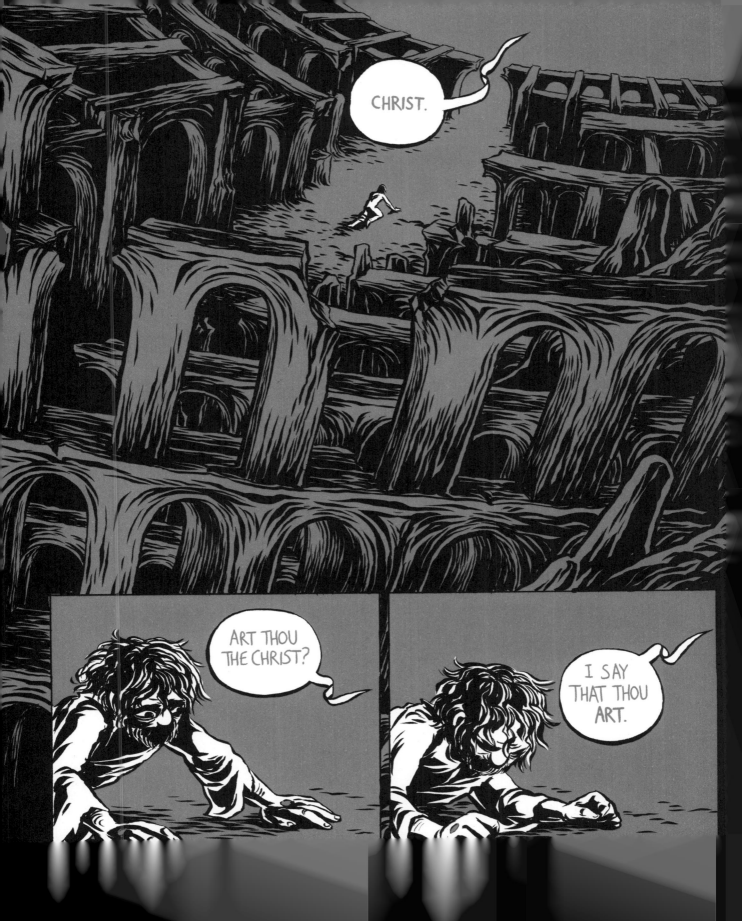

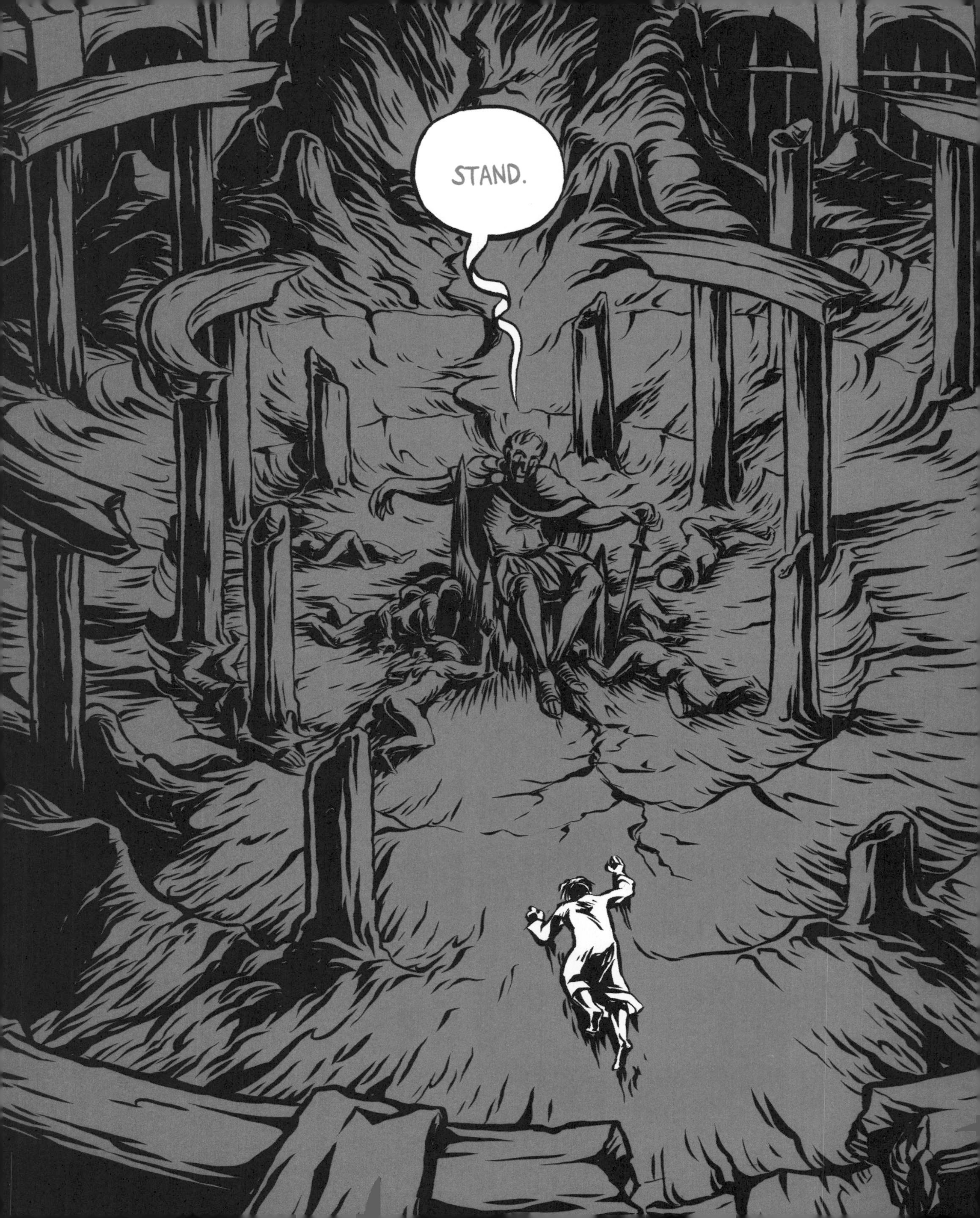
STAND.

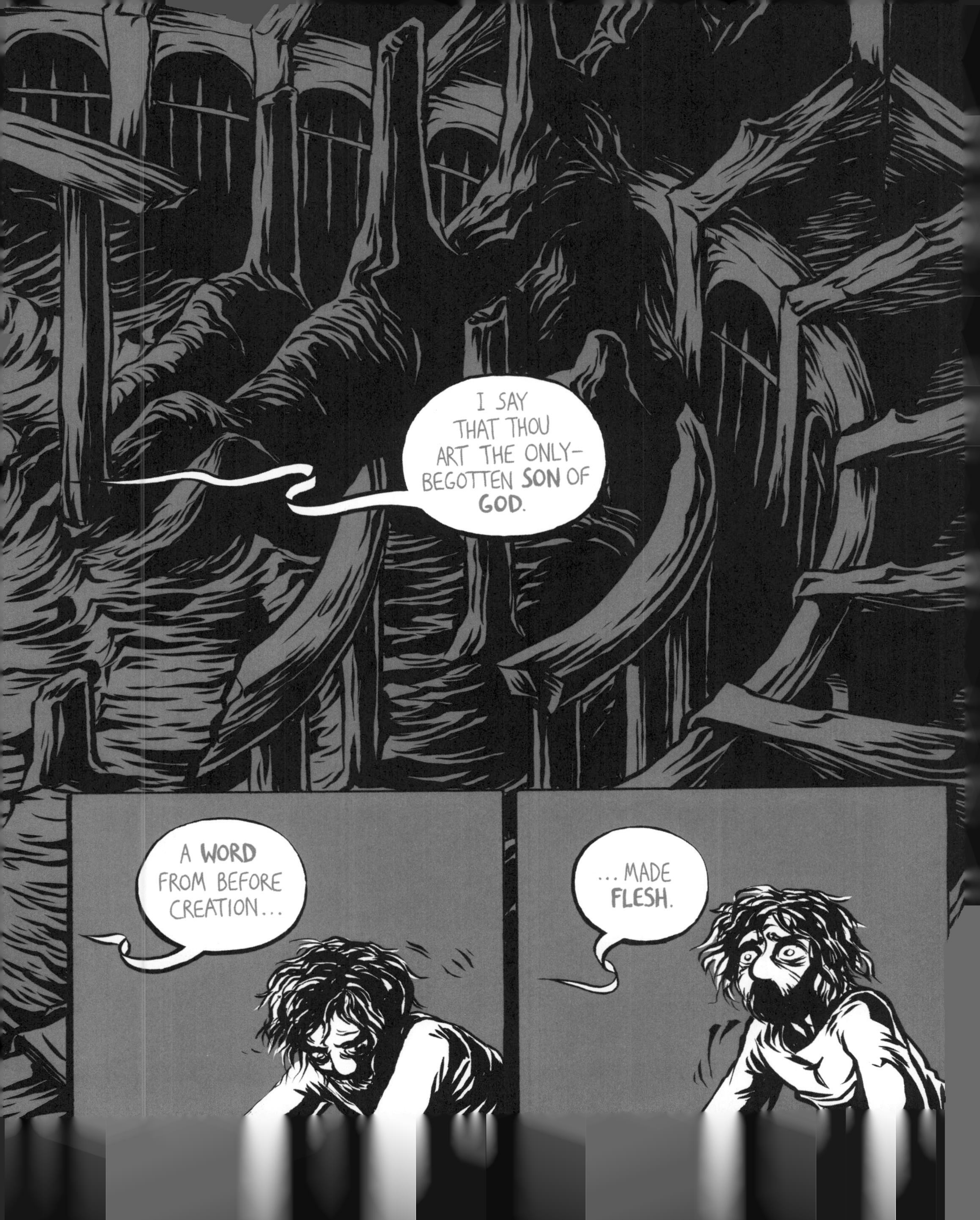
I SAY THAT THOU ART THE ONLY-BEGOTTEN SON OF GOD.
A WORD FROM BEFORE CREATION...
...MADE FLESH.

I SAY THAT THOU SHALT BE CALLED BY A **NEW** NAME—
—WHICH MINE OWN MOUTH SHALL NAME.
HOLD YOUR **PEACE**, ADVERSARY!

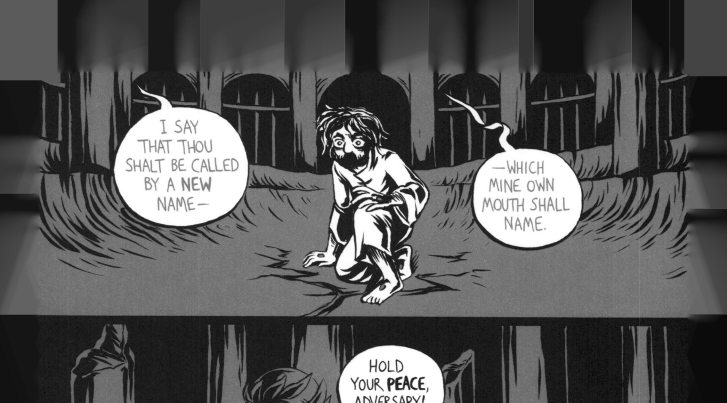

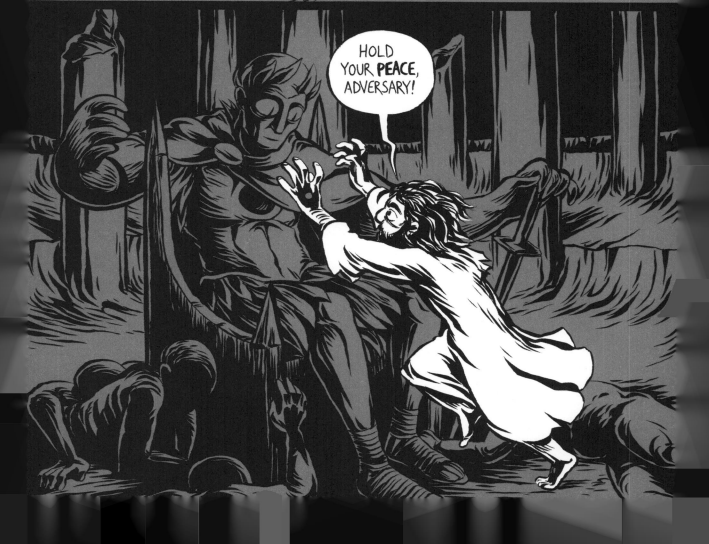

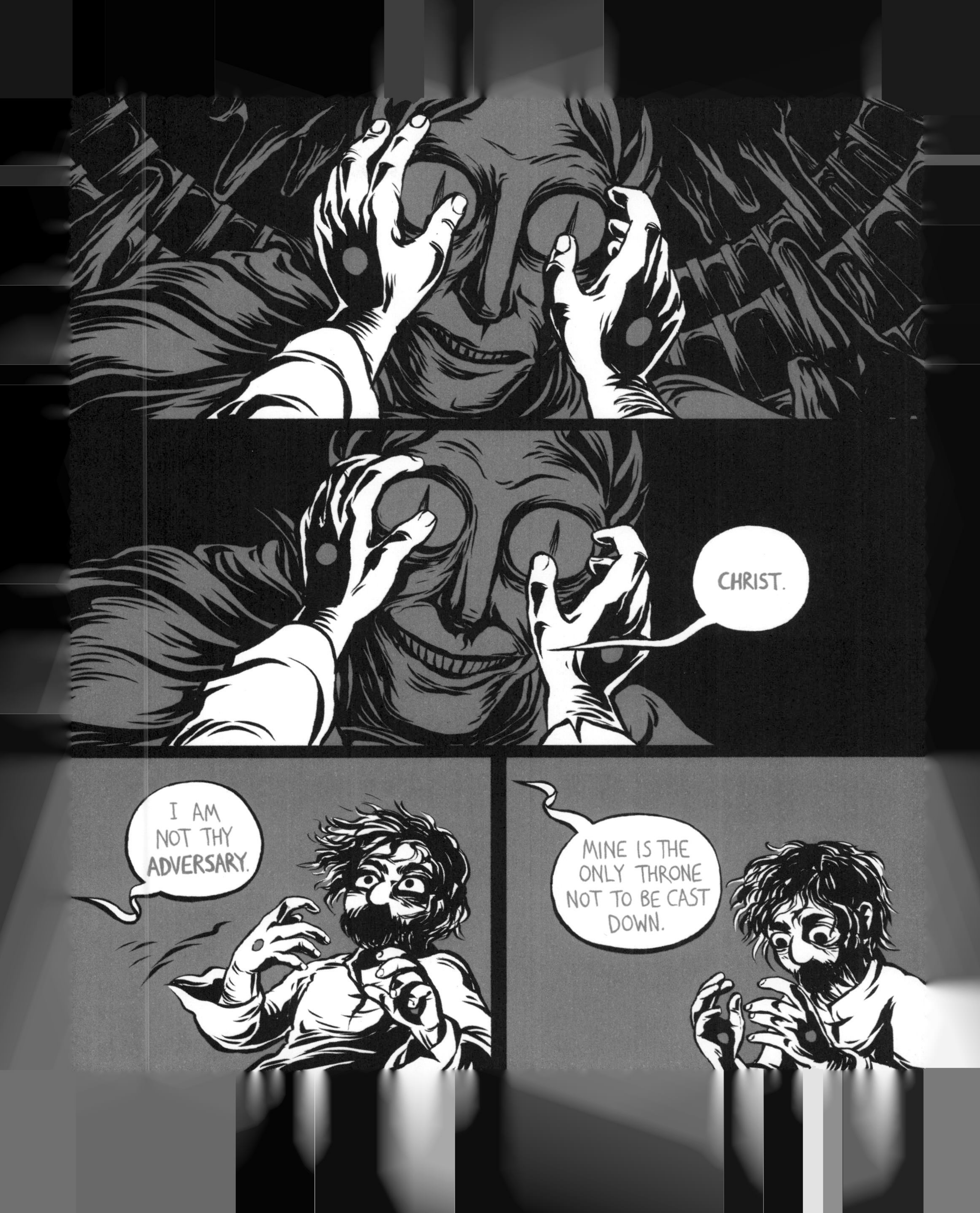
CHRIST.
I AM NOT THY ADVERSARY.
MINE IS THE ONLY THRONE NOT TO BE CAST DOWN.

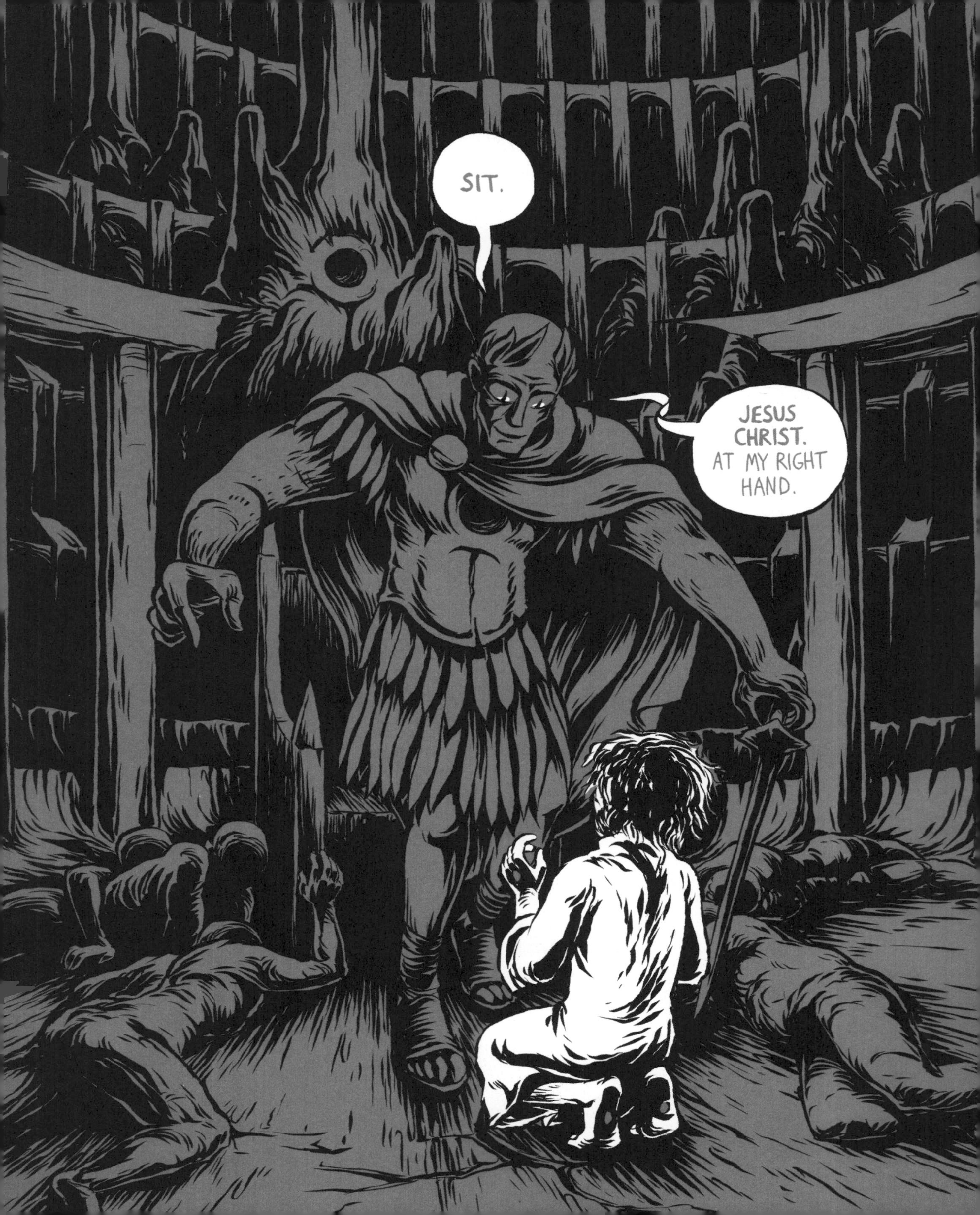
SIT.
JESUS CHRIST. AT MY RIGHT HAND.

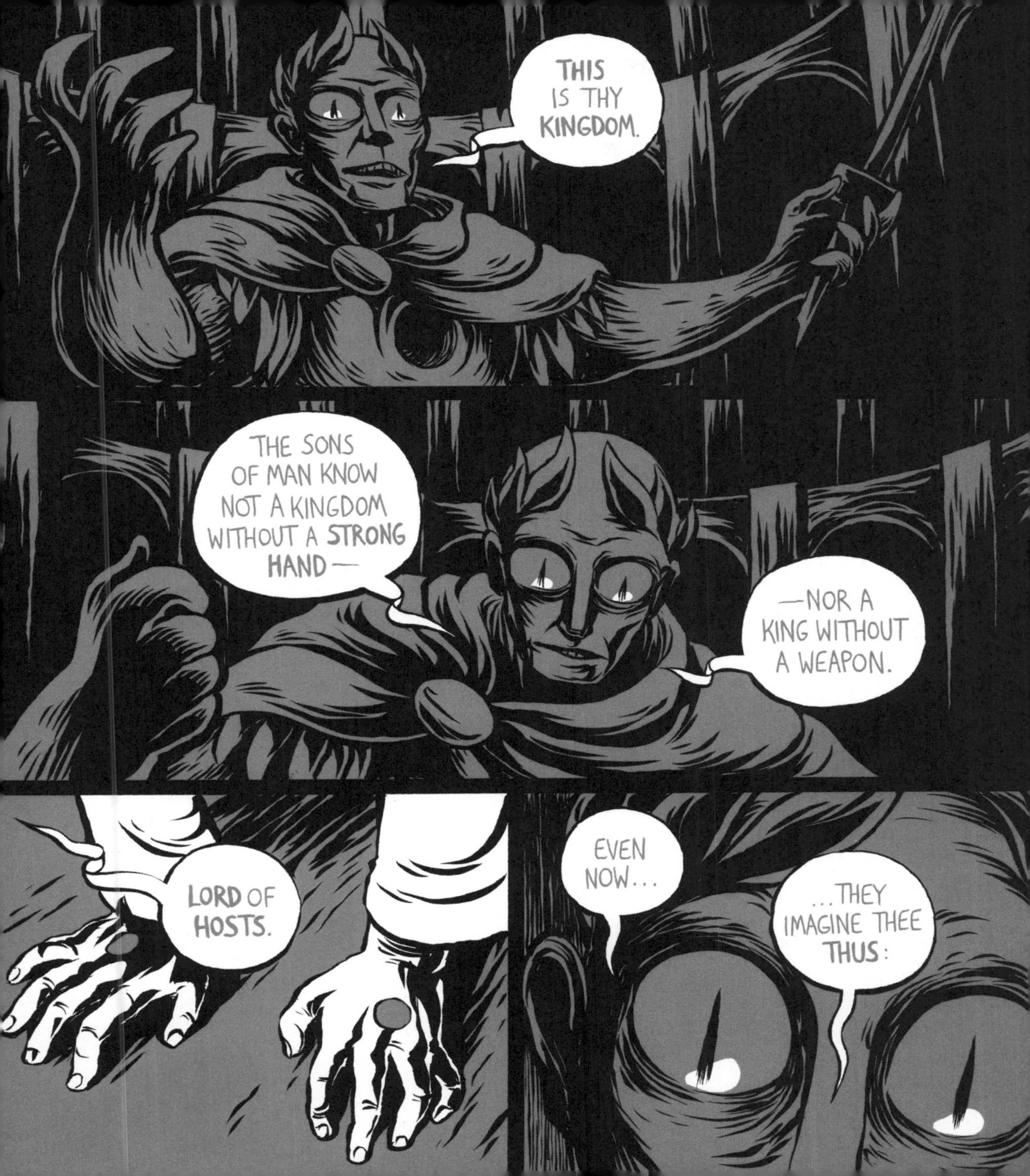
THIS IS THY KINGDOM.
THE SONS OF MAN KNOW NOT A KINGDOM WITHOUT A STRONG HAND—
—NOR A KING WITHOUT A WEAPON.
LORD OF HOSTS.
EVEN NOW...
...THEY IMAGINE THEE THUS:

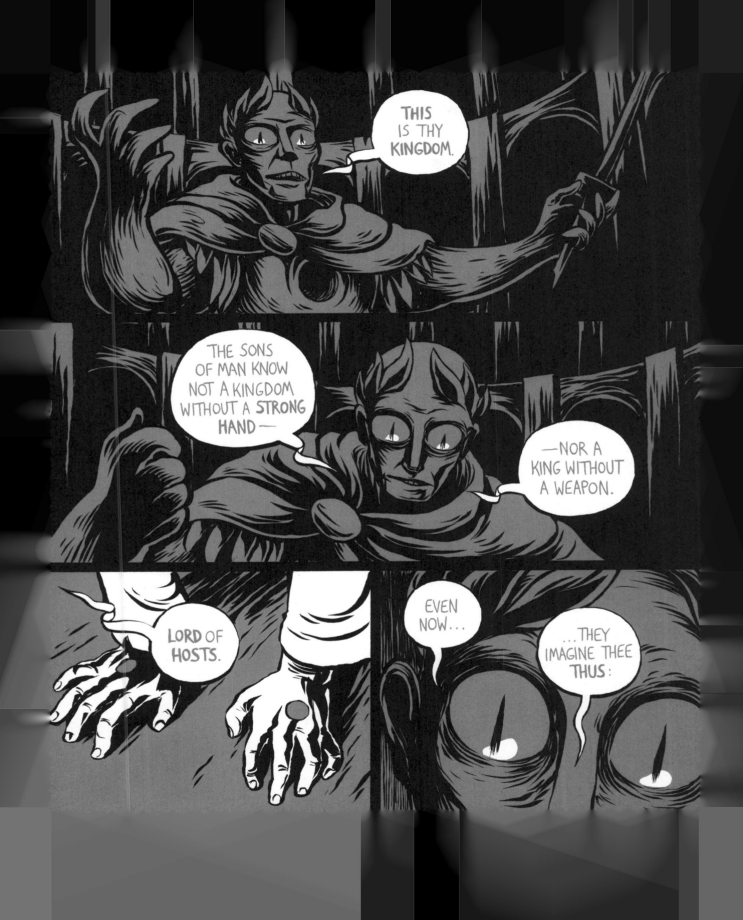

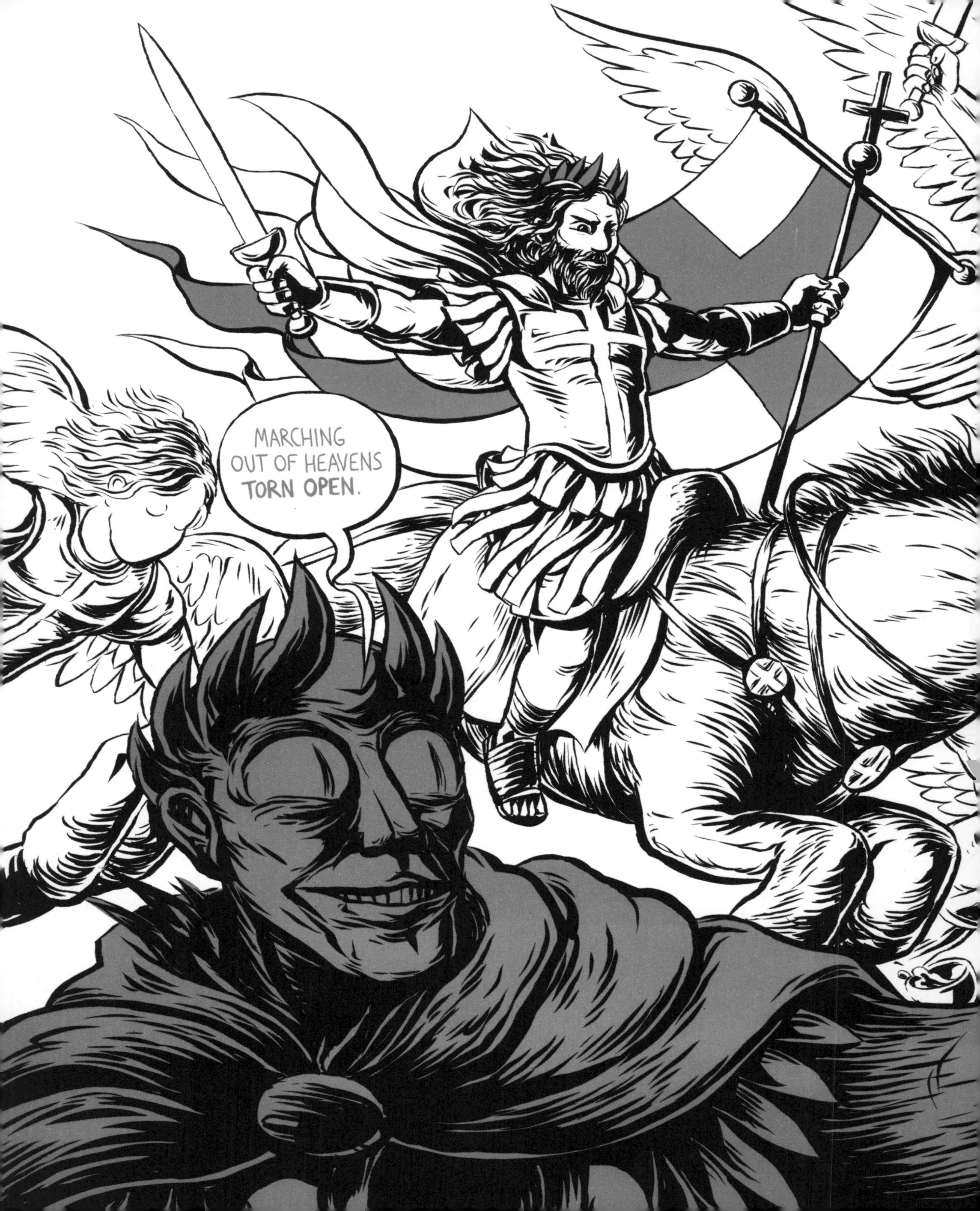
MARCHING OUT OF HEAVENS TORN OPEN.

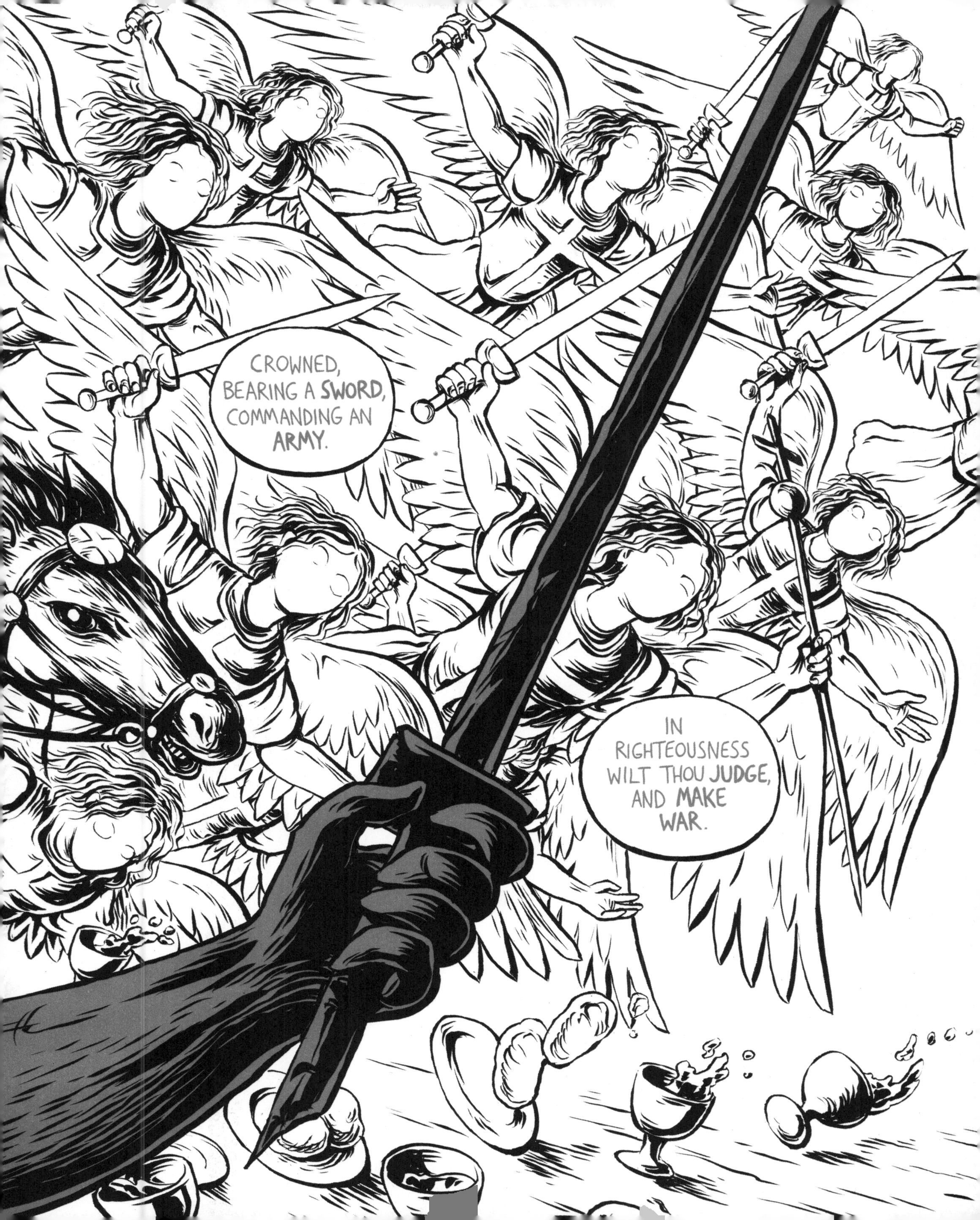
CROWNED, BEARING A SWORD, COMMANDING AN ARMY.
IN RIGHTEOUSNESS WILT THOU JUDGE, AND MAKE WAR.

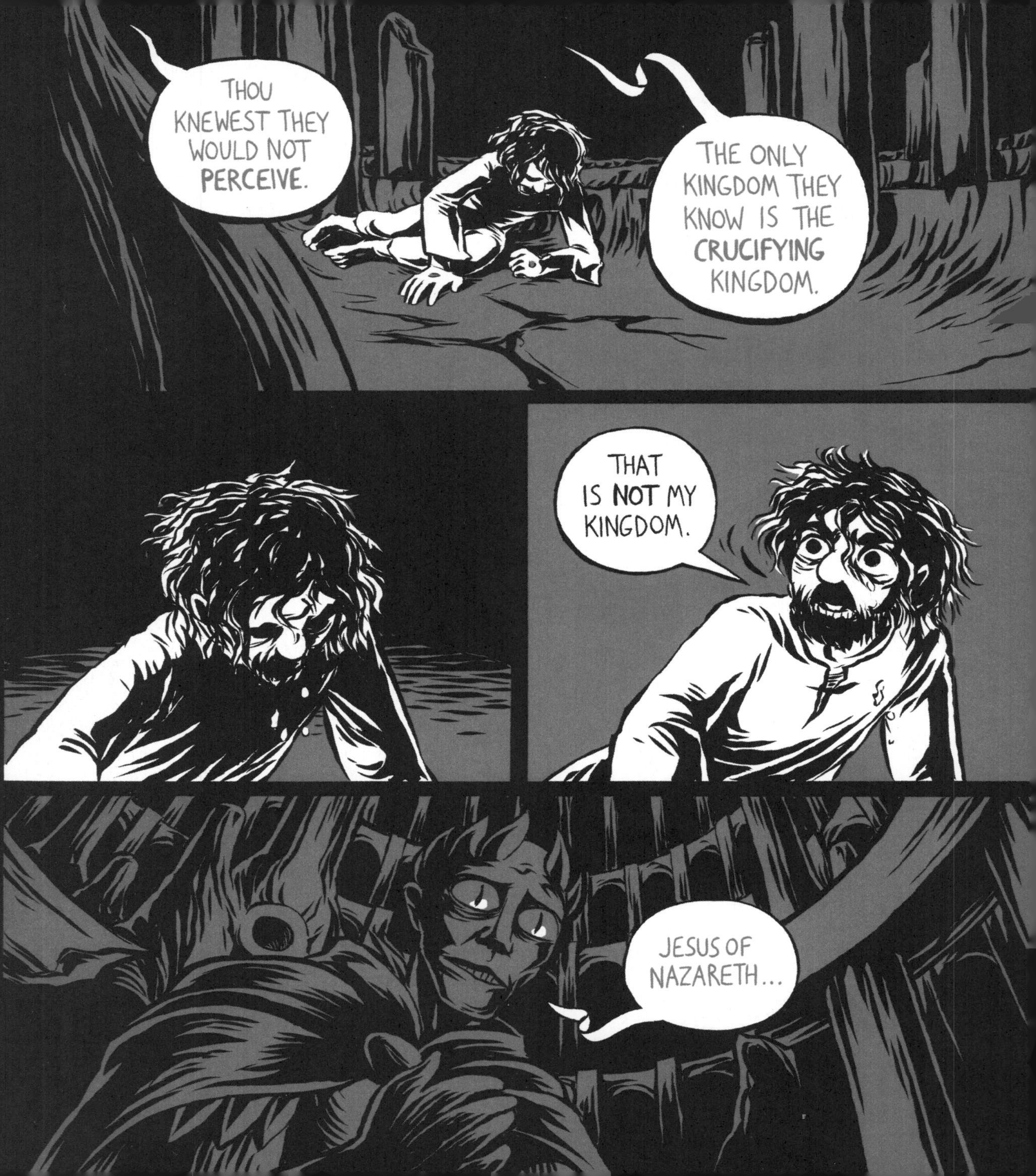
THOU KNEWEST THEY WOULD NOT PERCEIVE.
THE ONLY KINGDOM THEY KNOW IS THE CRUCIFYING KINGDOM.
THAT IS NOT MY KINGDOM.
JESUS OF NAZARETH...

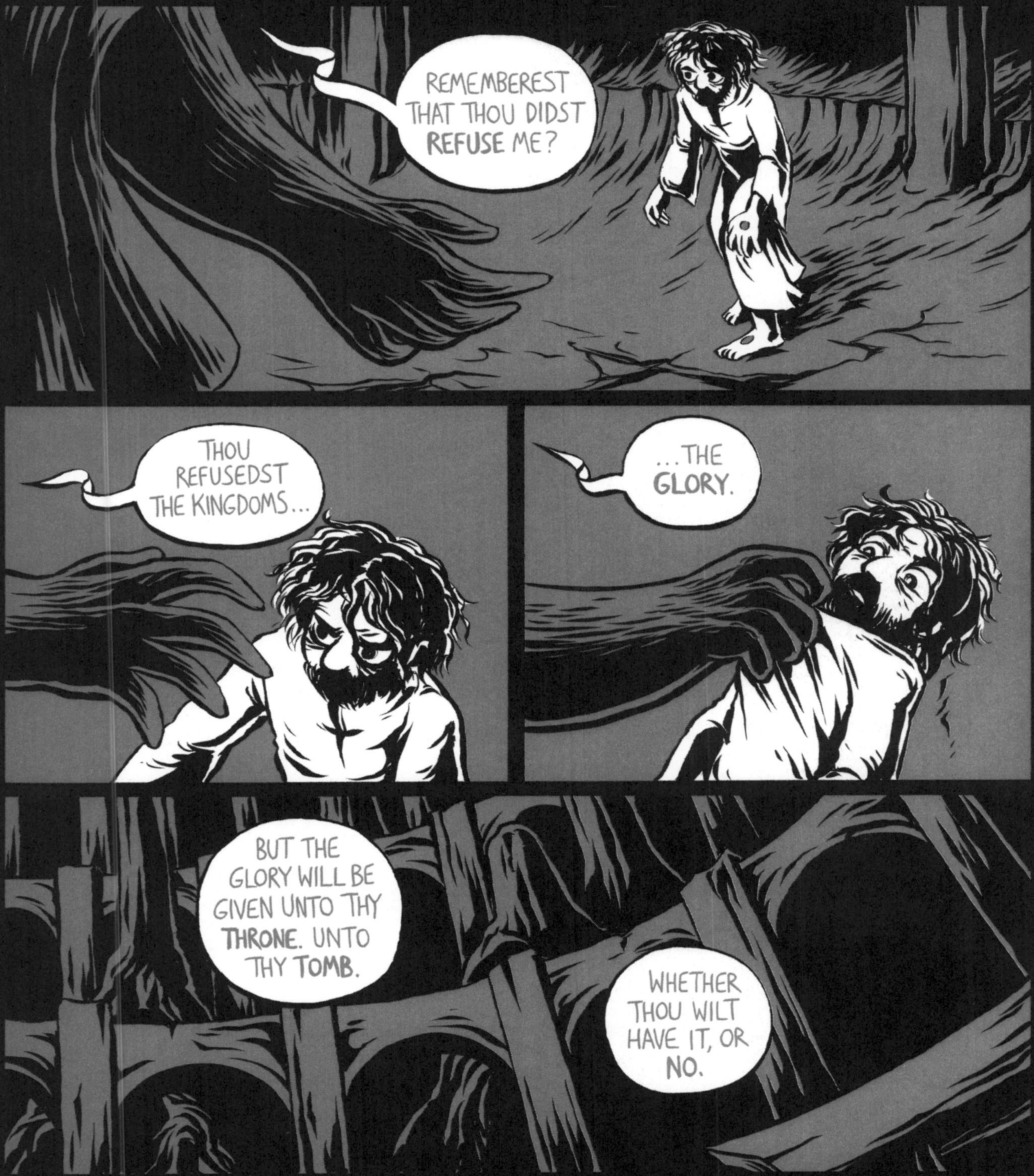
REMEMBEREST THAT THOU DIDST REFUSE ME?
THOU REFUSEDST THE KINGDOMS...
...THE GLORY.
BUT THE GLORY WILL BE GIVEN UNTO THY THRONE. UNTO THY TOMB.
WHETHER THOU WILT HAVE IT, OR NO.

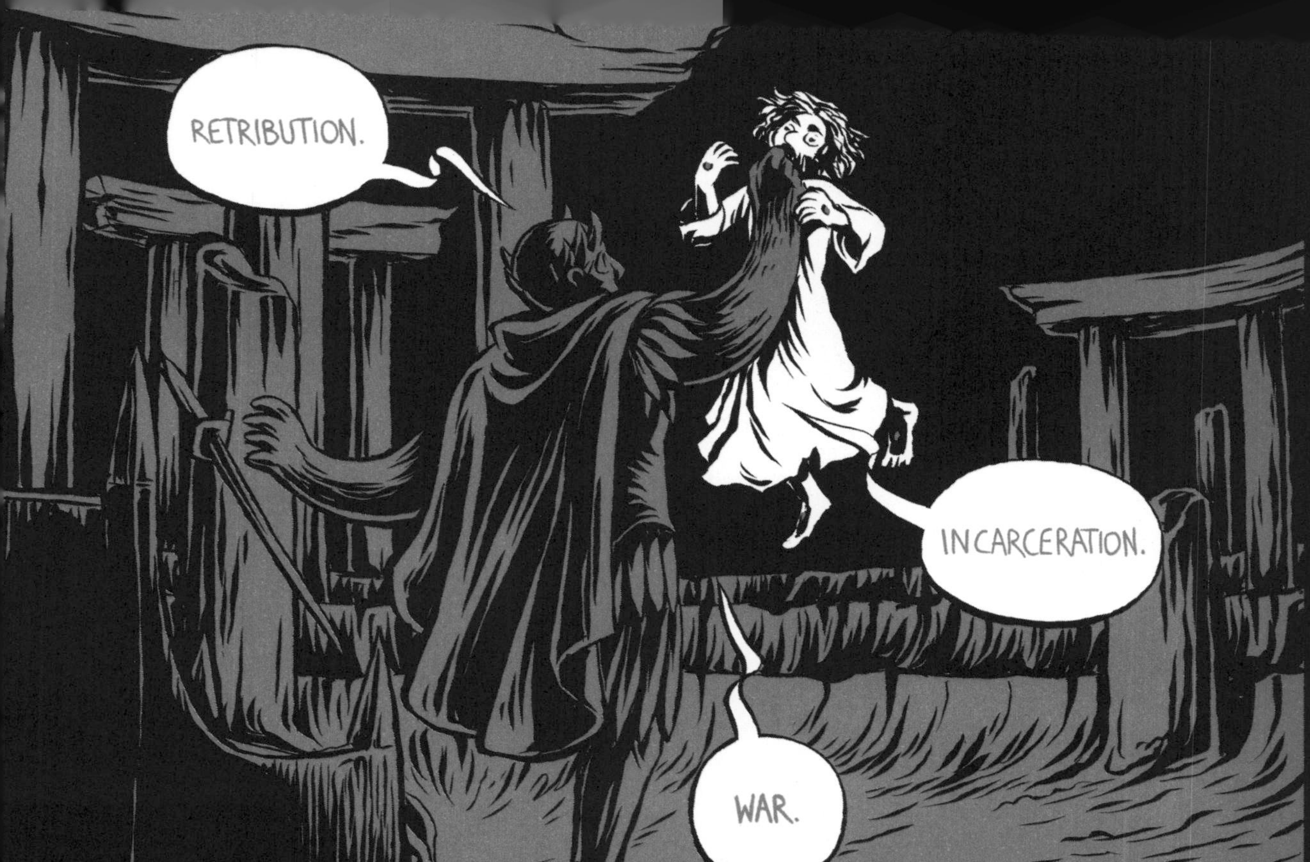
RETRIBUTION.
INCARCERATION.
WAR.
IN THY NAME.
JESUS CHRIST.

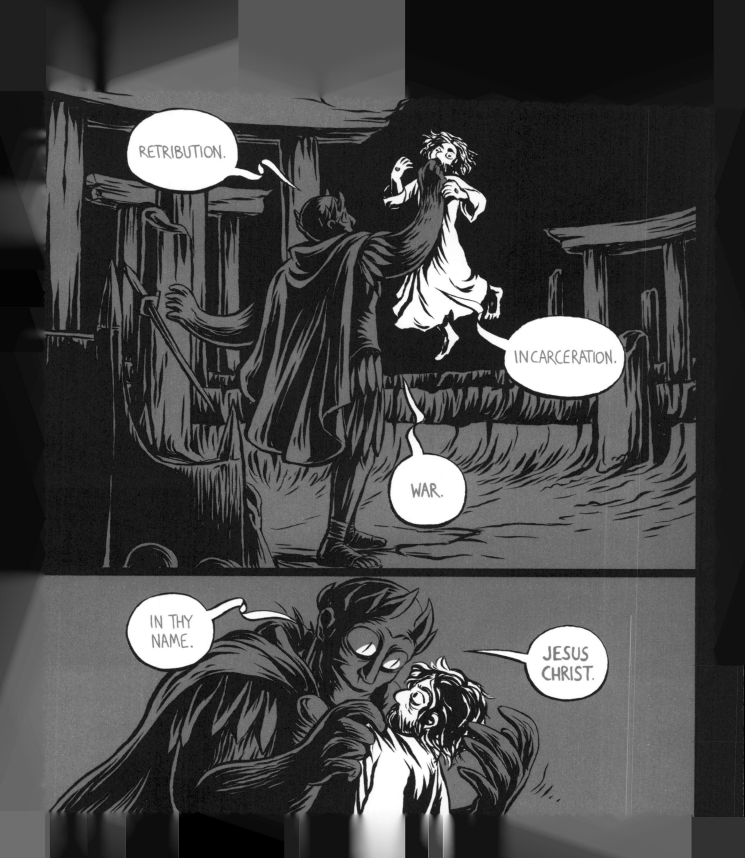

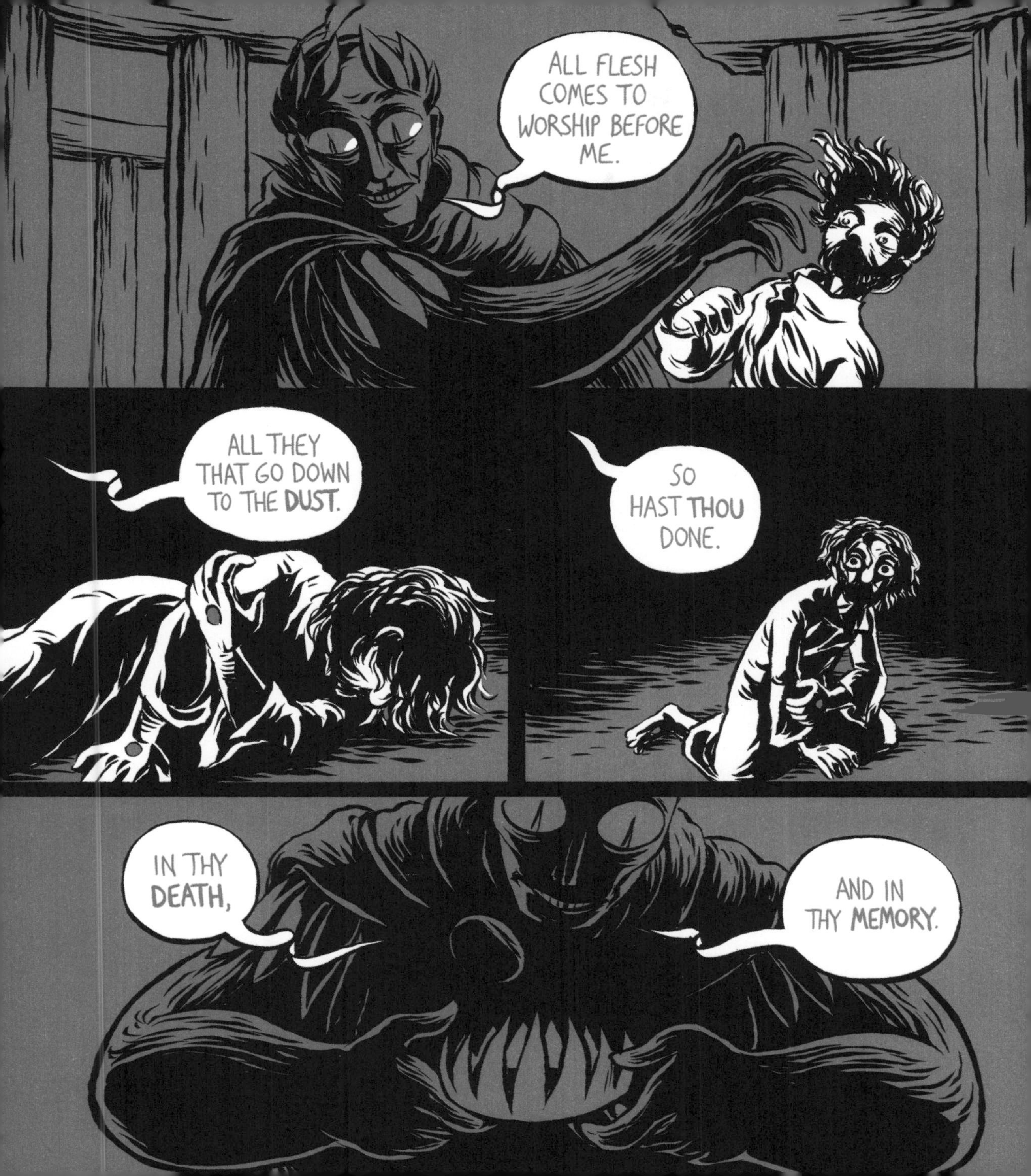
ALL FLESH COMES TO WORSHIP BEFORE ME.
ALL THEY THAT GO DOWN TO THE **DUST**.
SO HAST **THOU** DONE.
IN THY **DEATH**,
AND IN THY **MEMORY**.

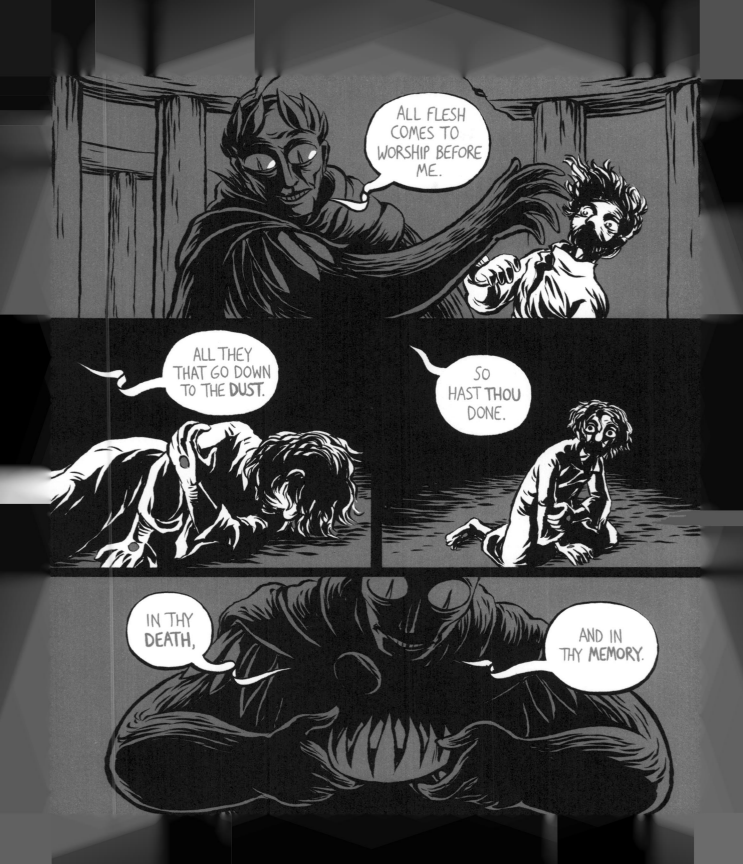

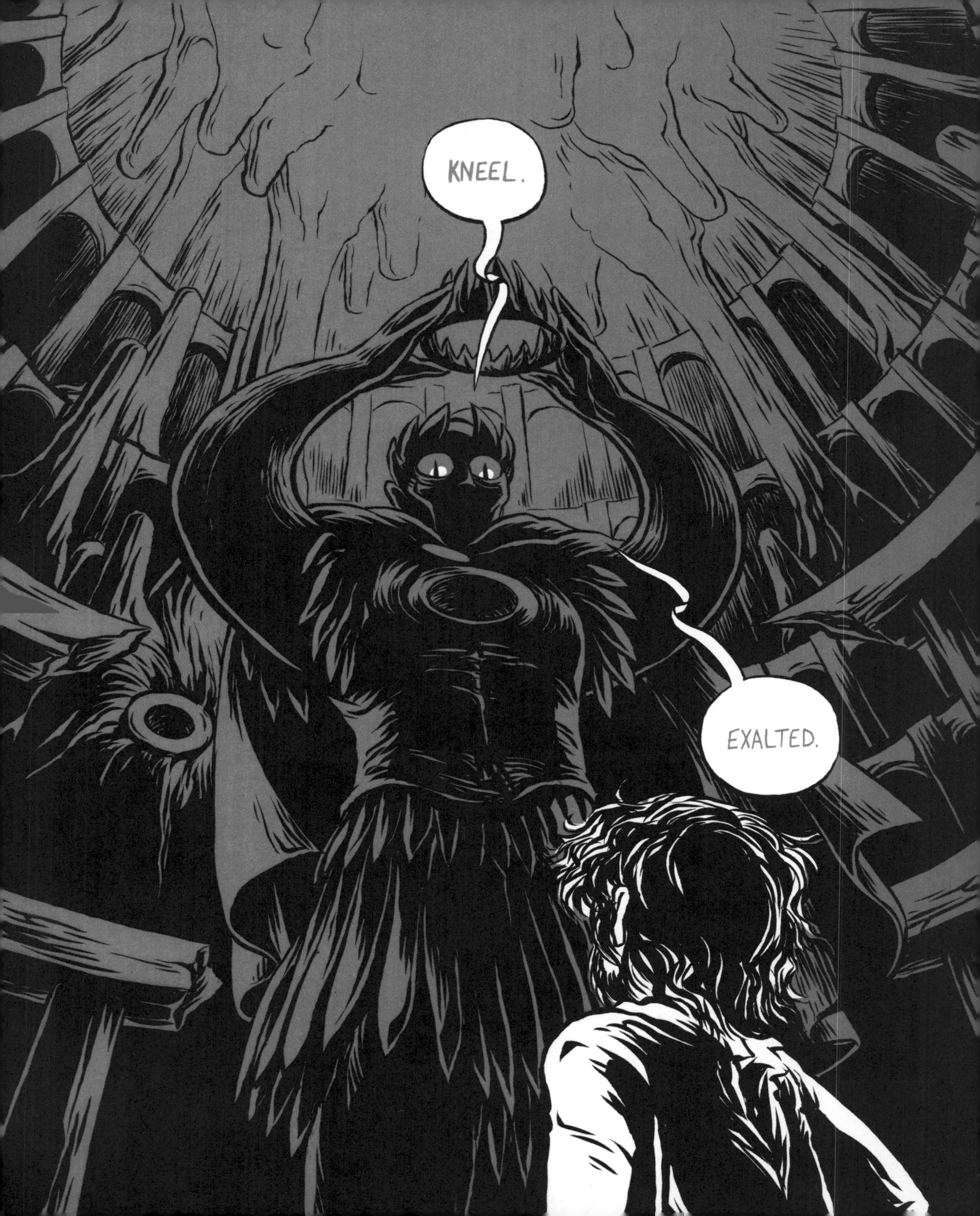
KNEEL.
EXALTED.

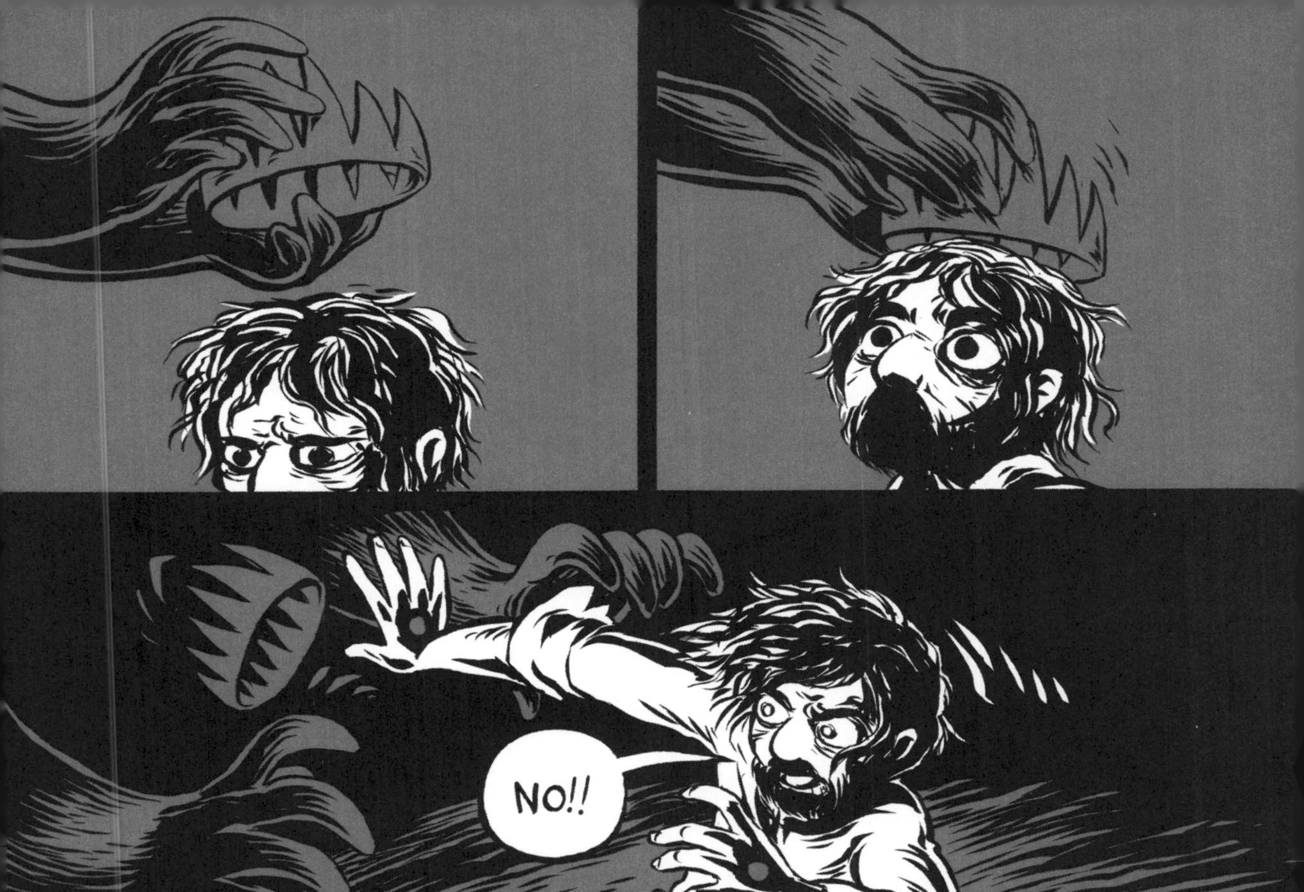
NO!!
TAK

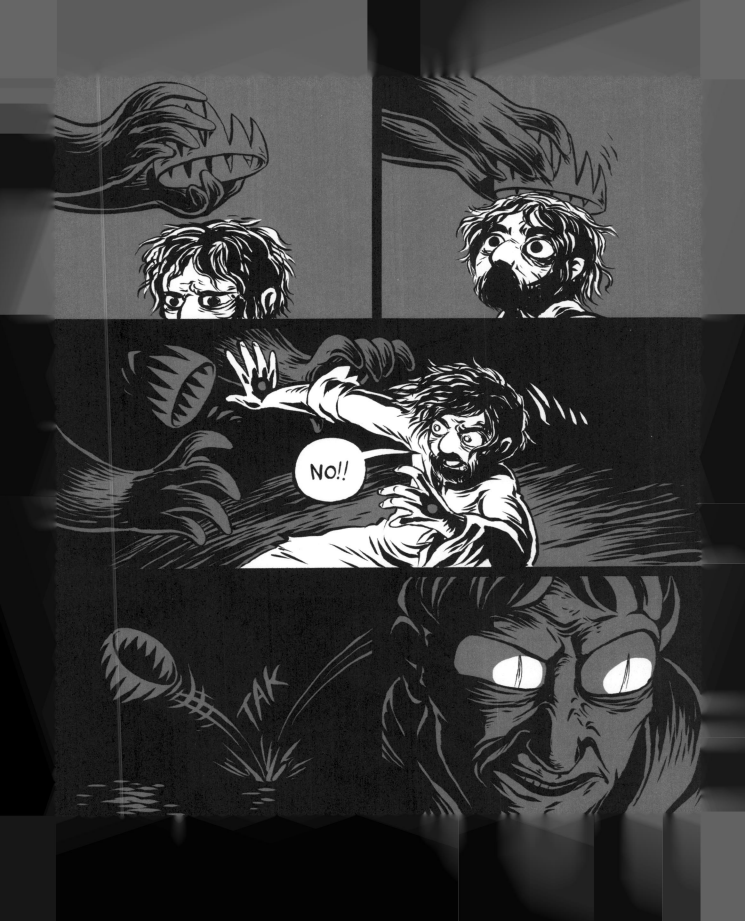

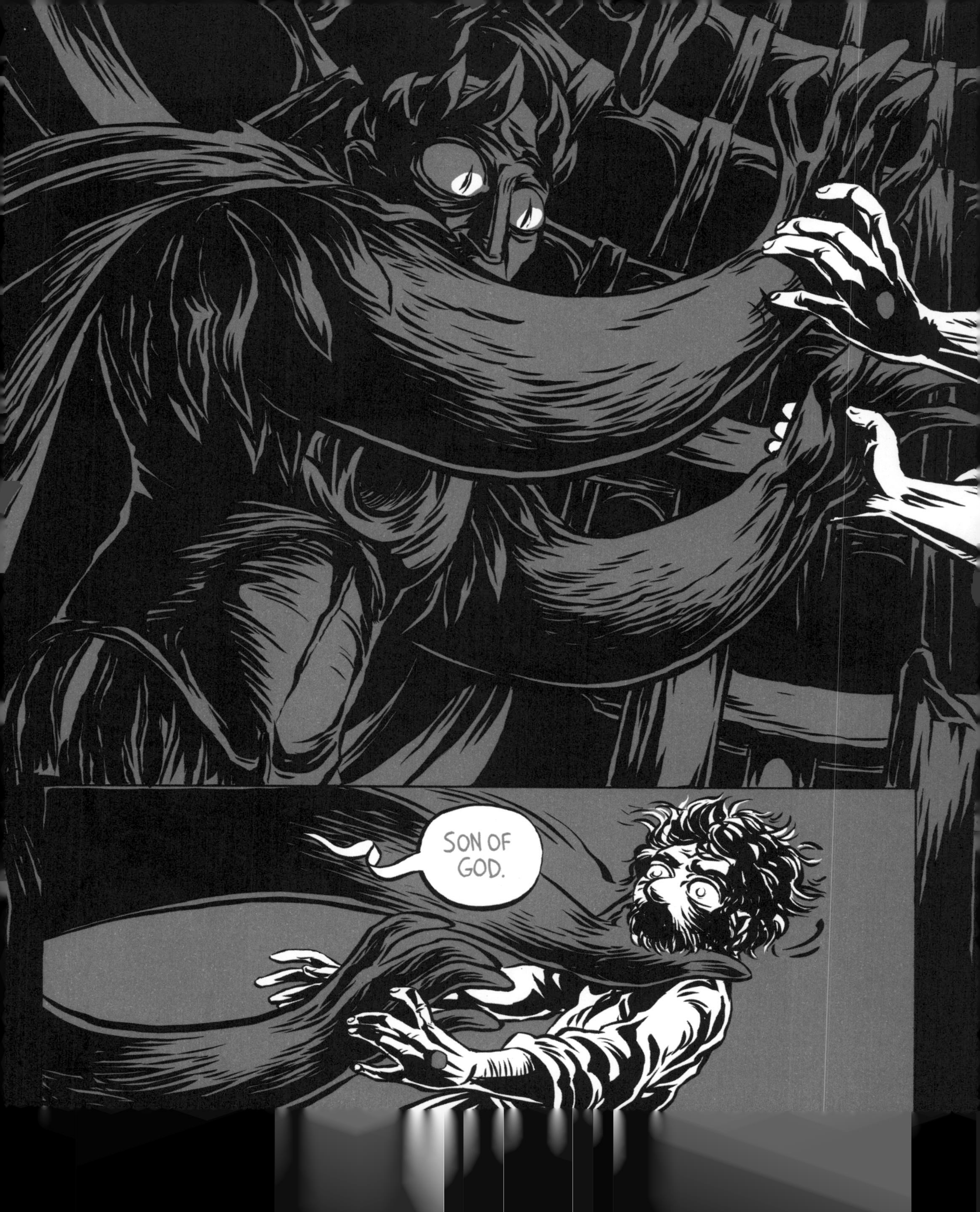
SON OF GOD.

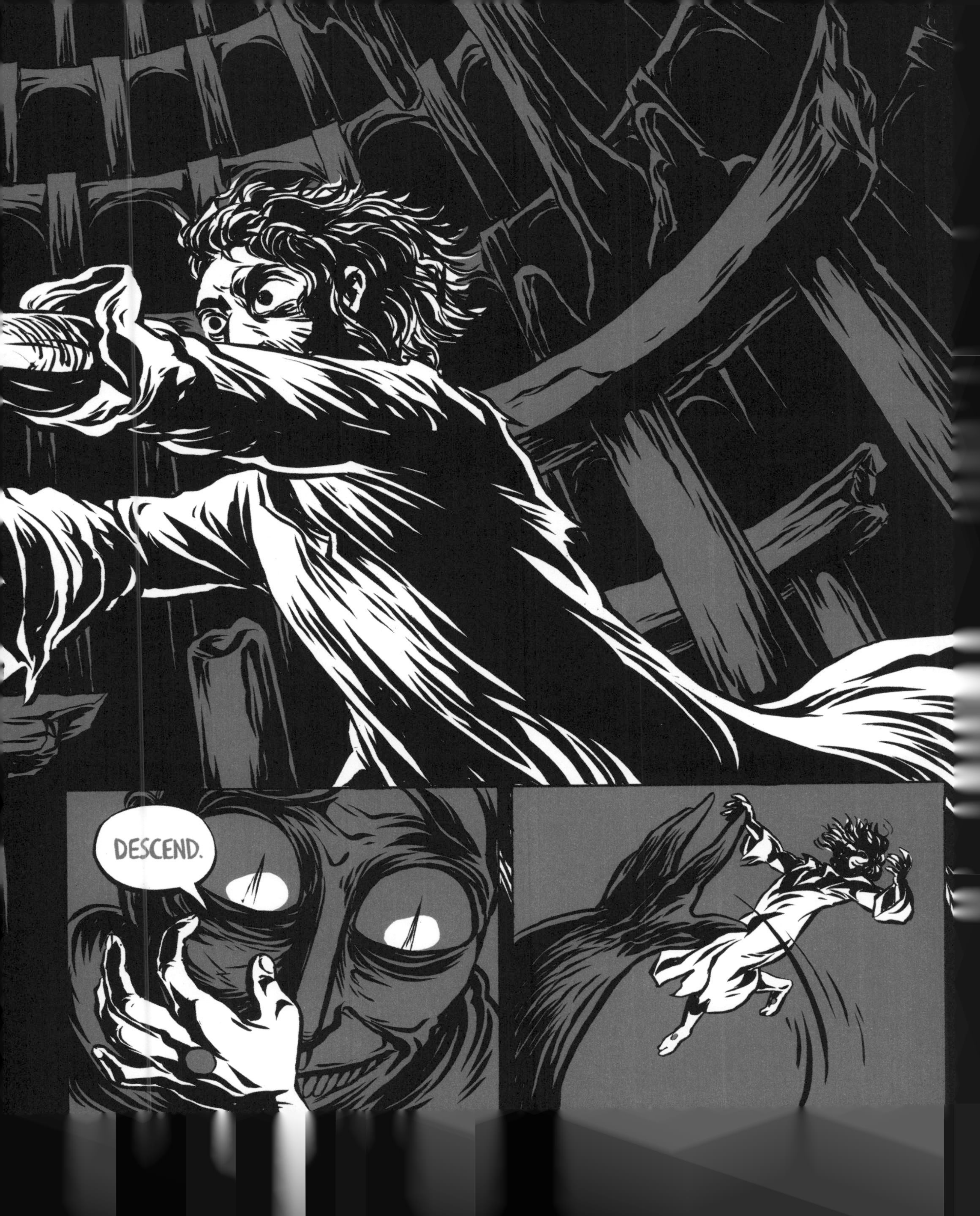
DESCEND.

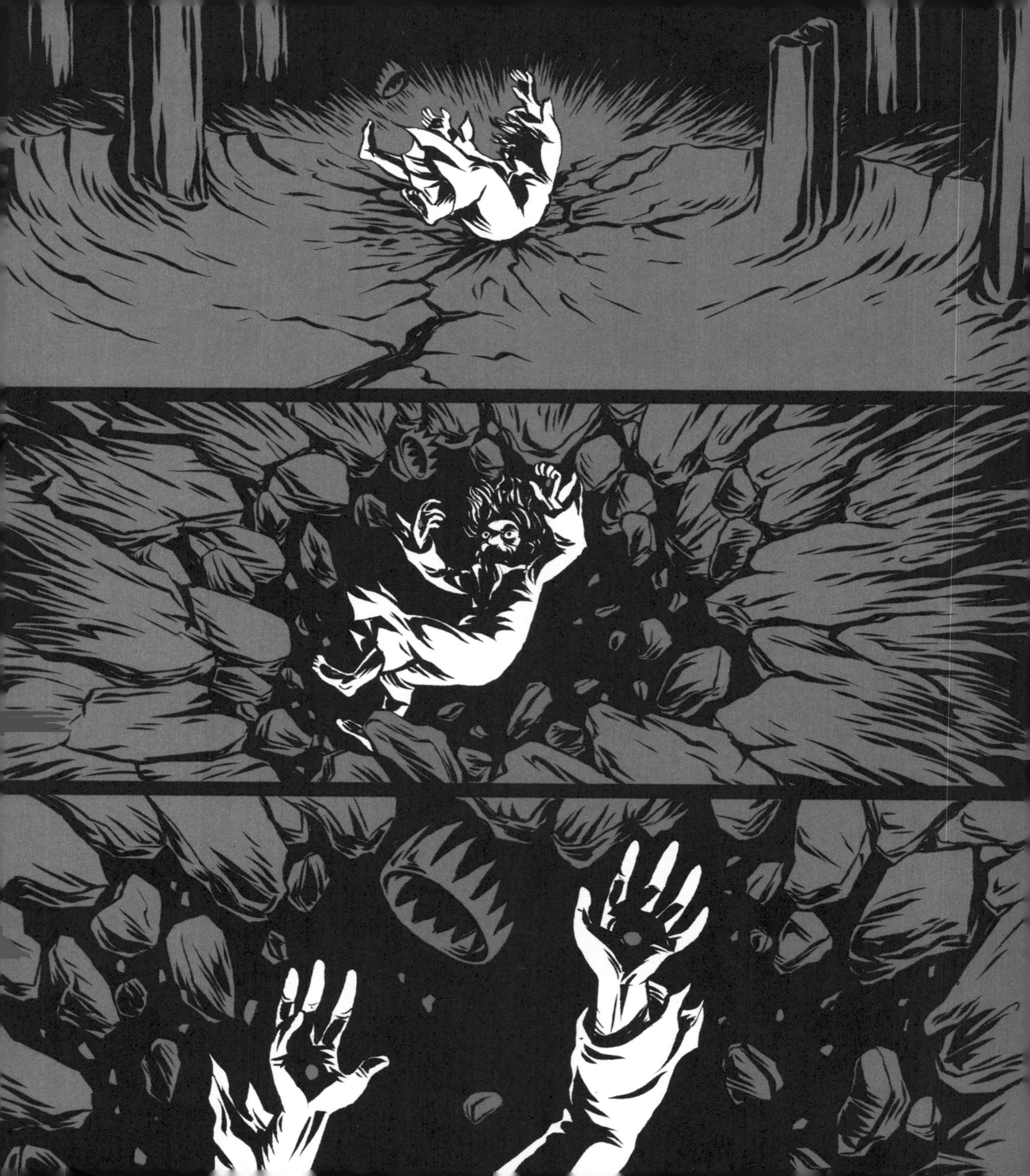

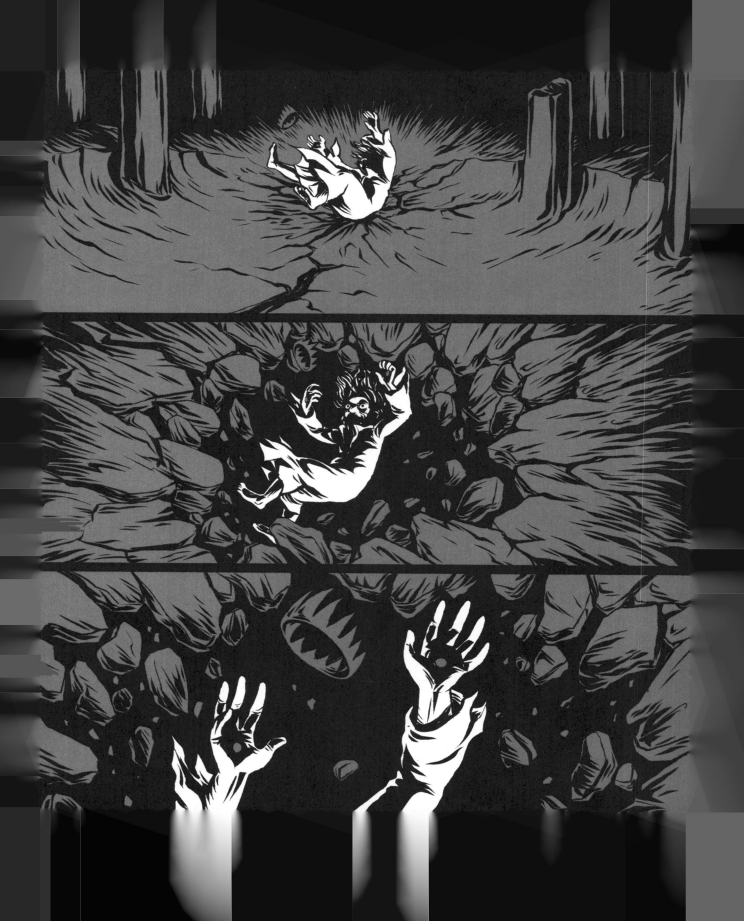

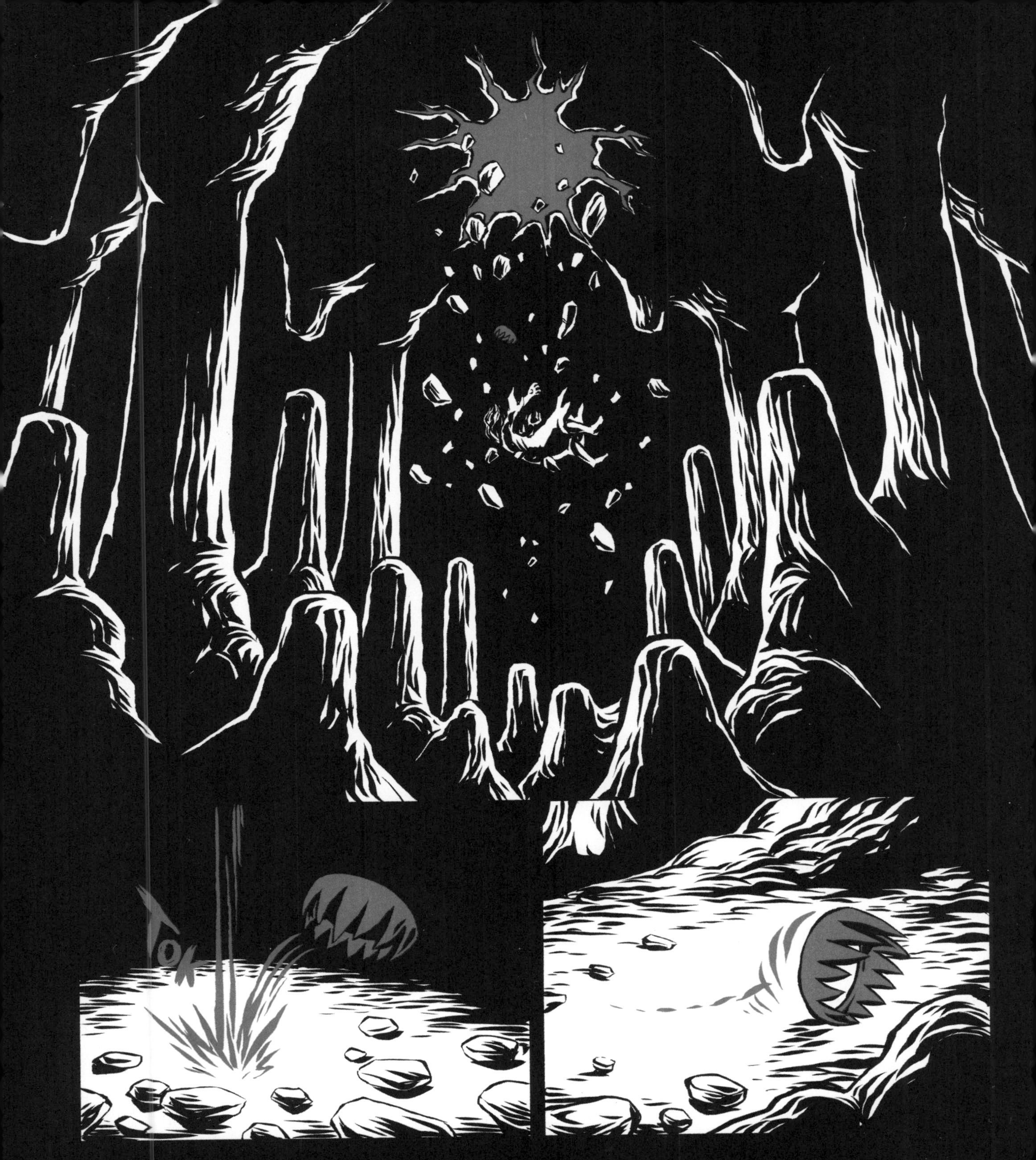
TOK

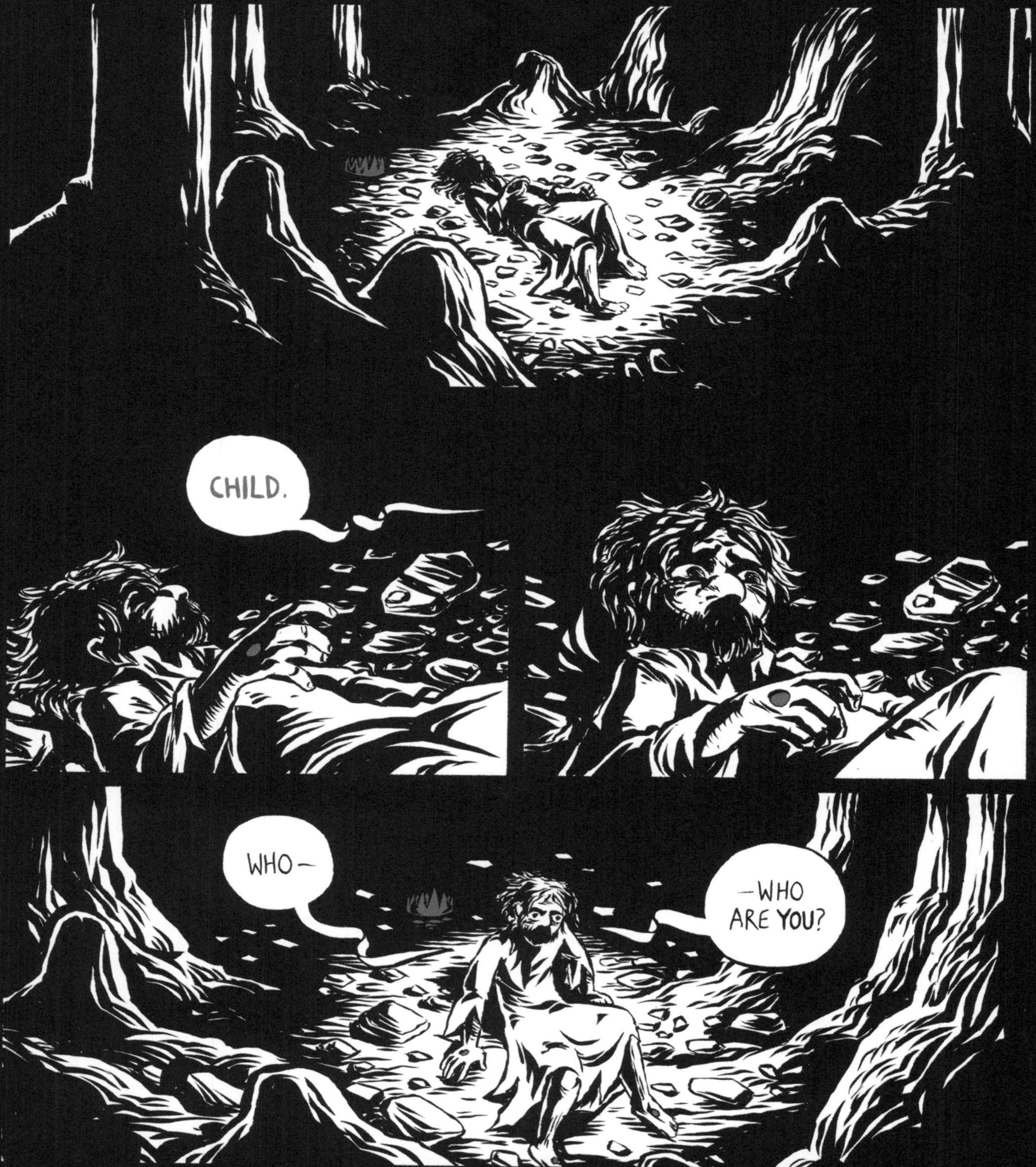
CHILD.
WHO–
–WHO ARE YOU?

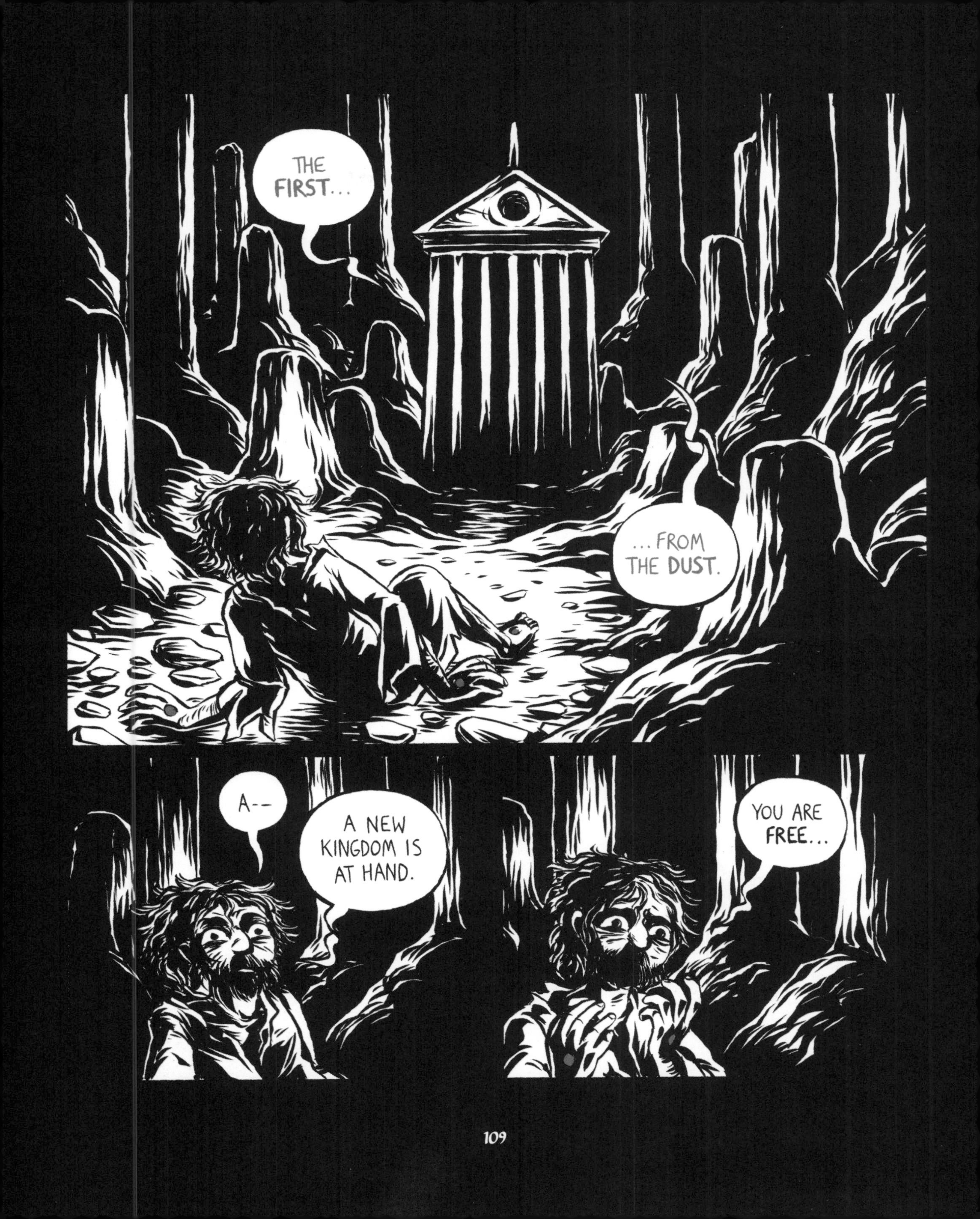
THE FIRST...
...FROM THE DUST.
A--
A NEW KINGDOM IS AT HAND.
YOU ARE FREE...

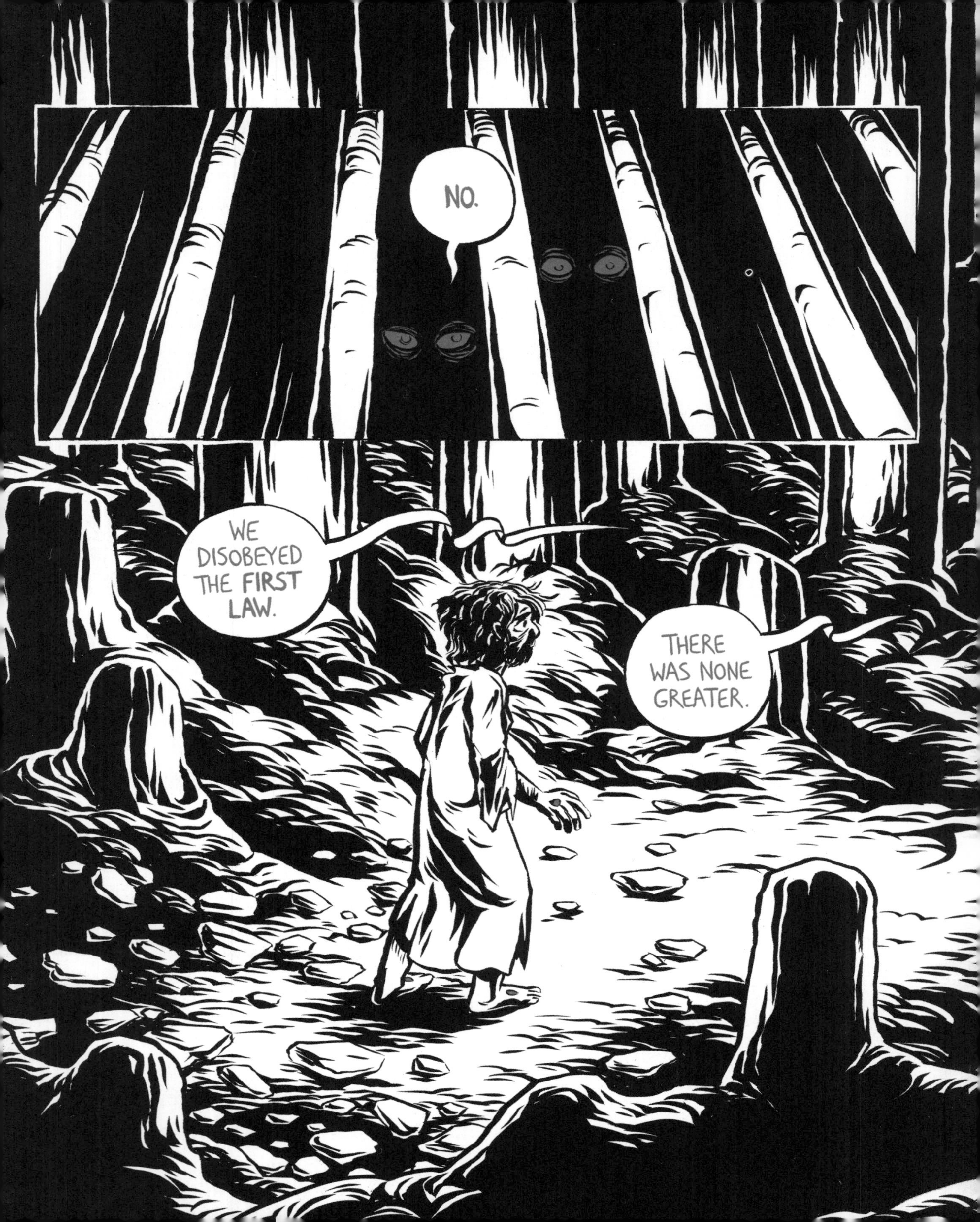
NO.
WE DISOBEYED THE FIRST LAW.
THERE WAS NONE GREATER.

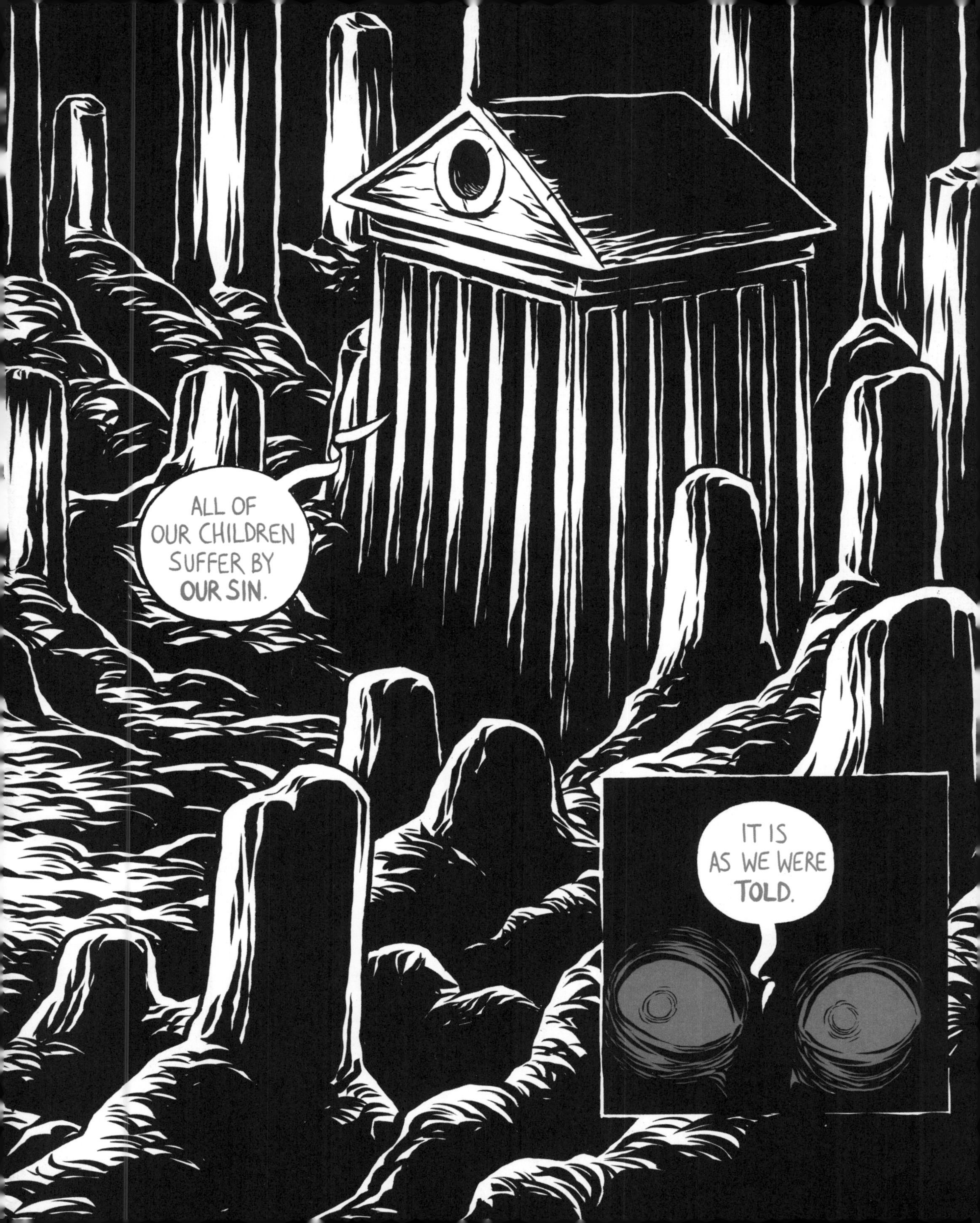
ALL OF OUR CHILDREN SUFFER BY **OUR SIN**.
IT IS AS WE WERE **TOLD**.

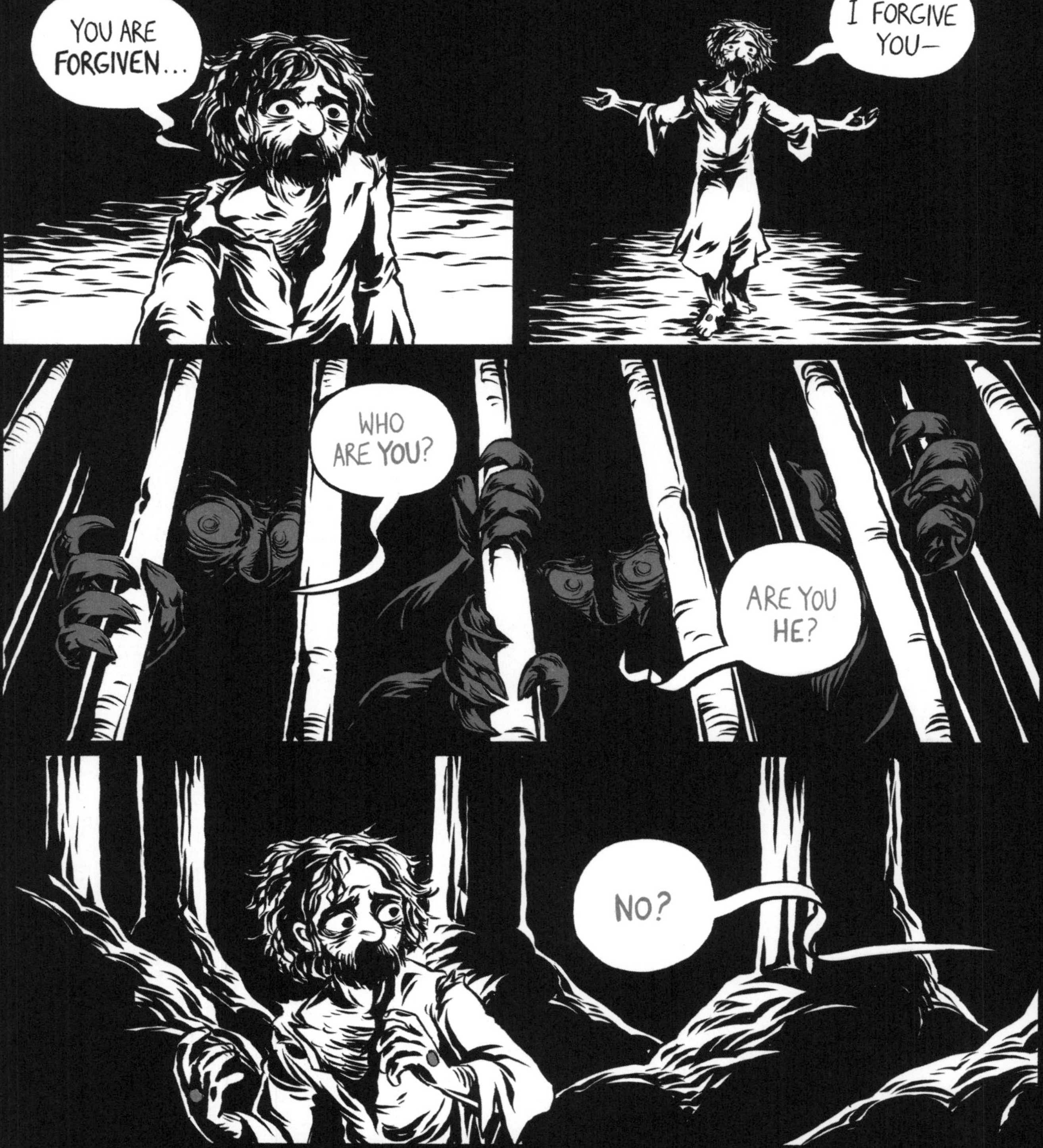
YOU ARE FORGIVEN...
I FORGIVE YOU—
WHO ARE YOU?
ARE YOU HE?
NO?

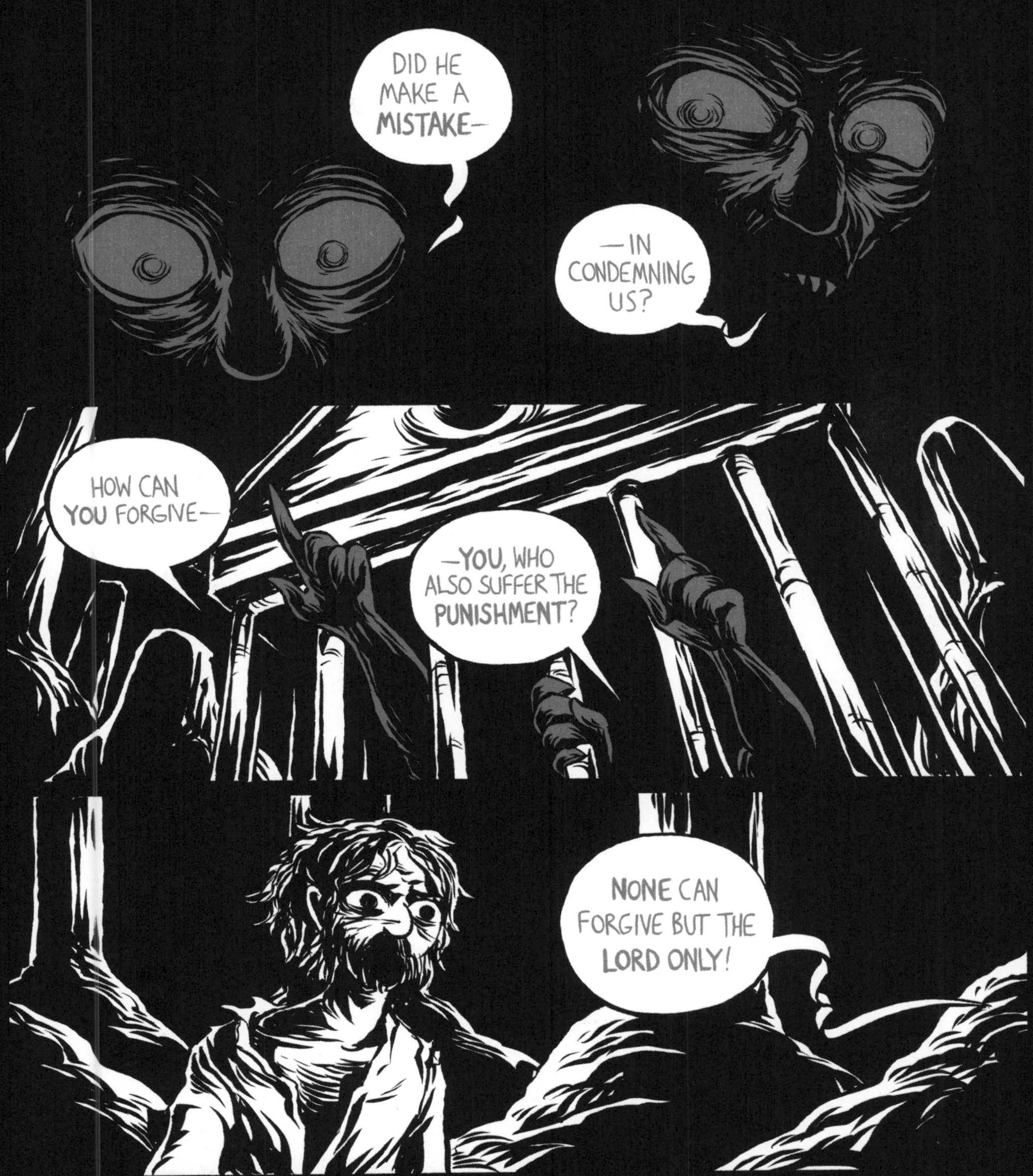
DID HE MAKE A MISTAKE—
—IN CONDEMNING US?
HOW CAN YOU FORGIVE—
—YOU, WHO ALSO SUFFER THE PUNISHMENT?
NONE CAN FORGIVE BUT THE LORD ONLY!

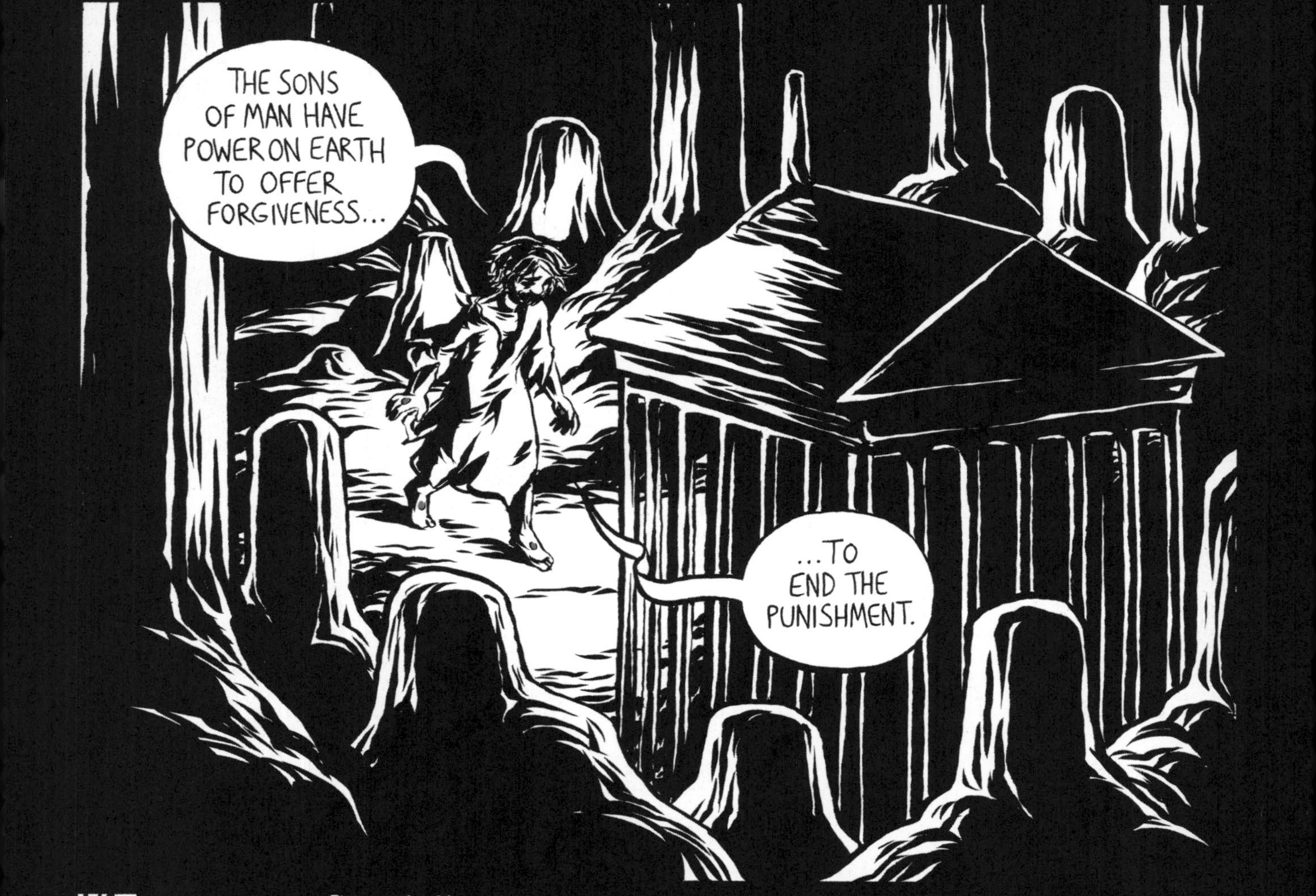
THE SONS OF MAN HAVE POWER ON EARTH TO OFFER FORGIVENESS...
...TO END THE PUNISHMENT.

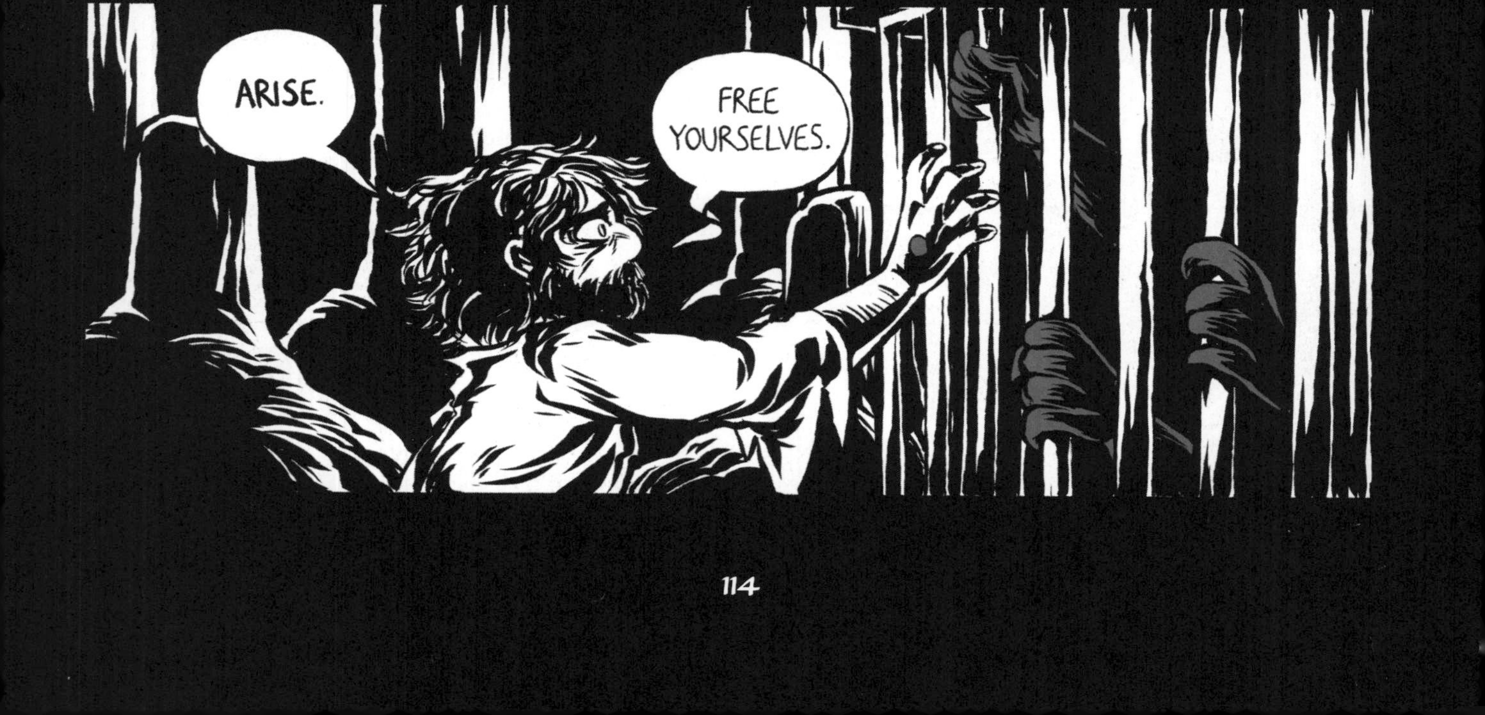
ARISE.
FREE YOURSELVES.

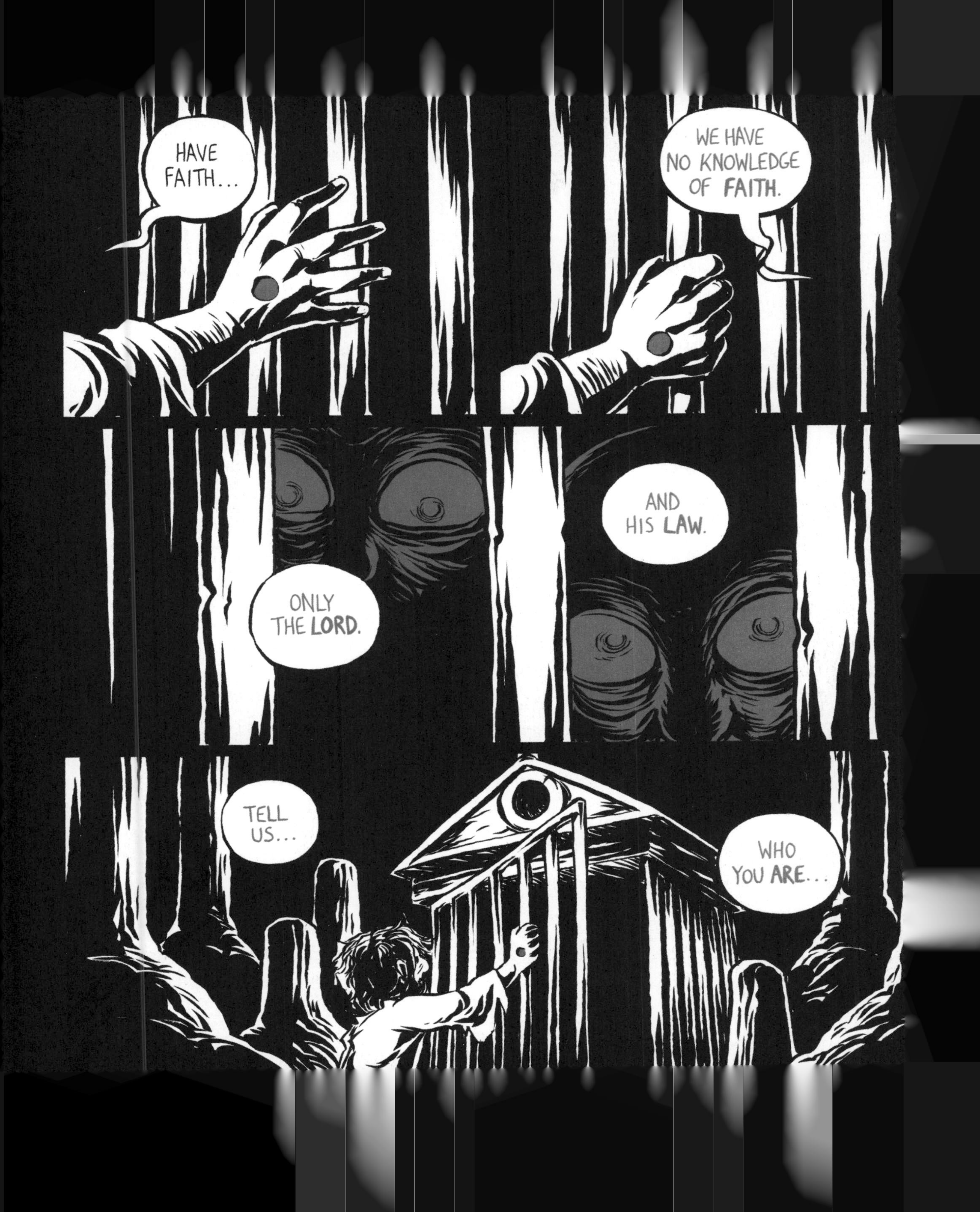
HAVE FAITH...
WE HAVE NO KNOWLEDGE OF FAITH.
ONLY THE LORD.
AND HIS LAW.
TELL US...
WHO YOU ARE...

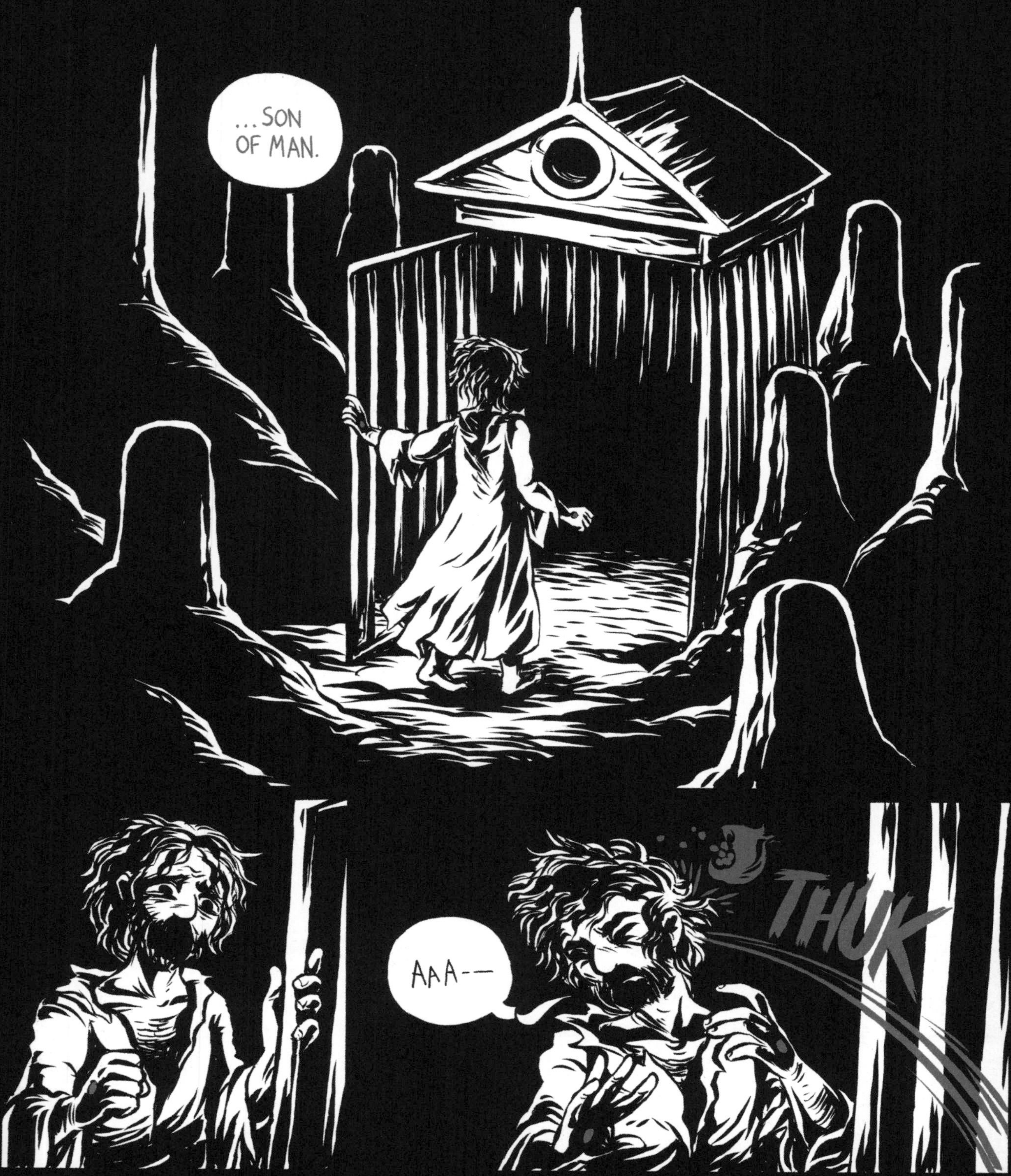
...SON OF MAN.
AAA--
THUK

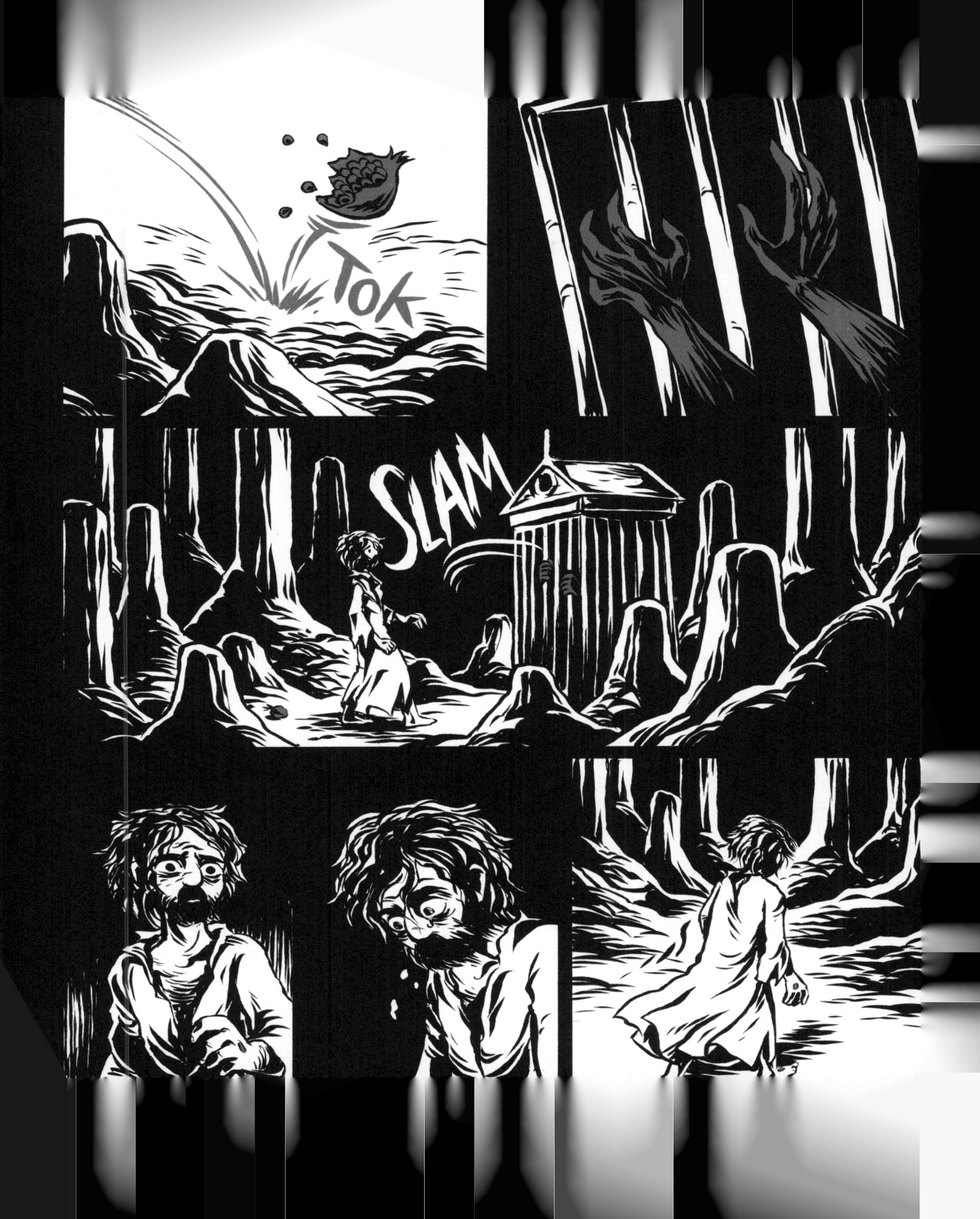
TOK
SLAM

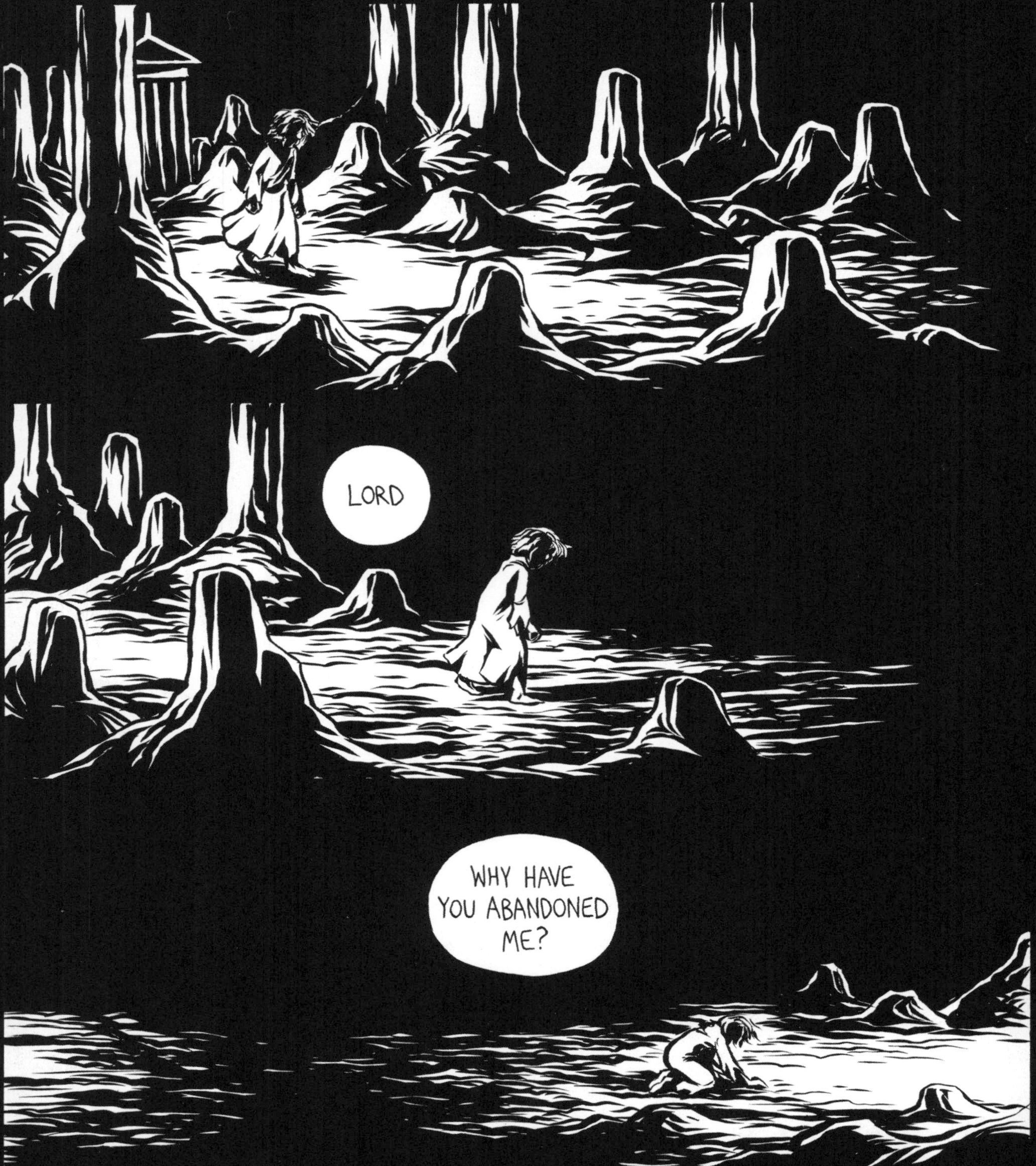
LORD
WHY HAVE YOU ABANDONED ME?

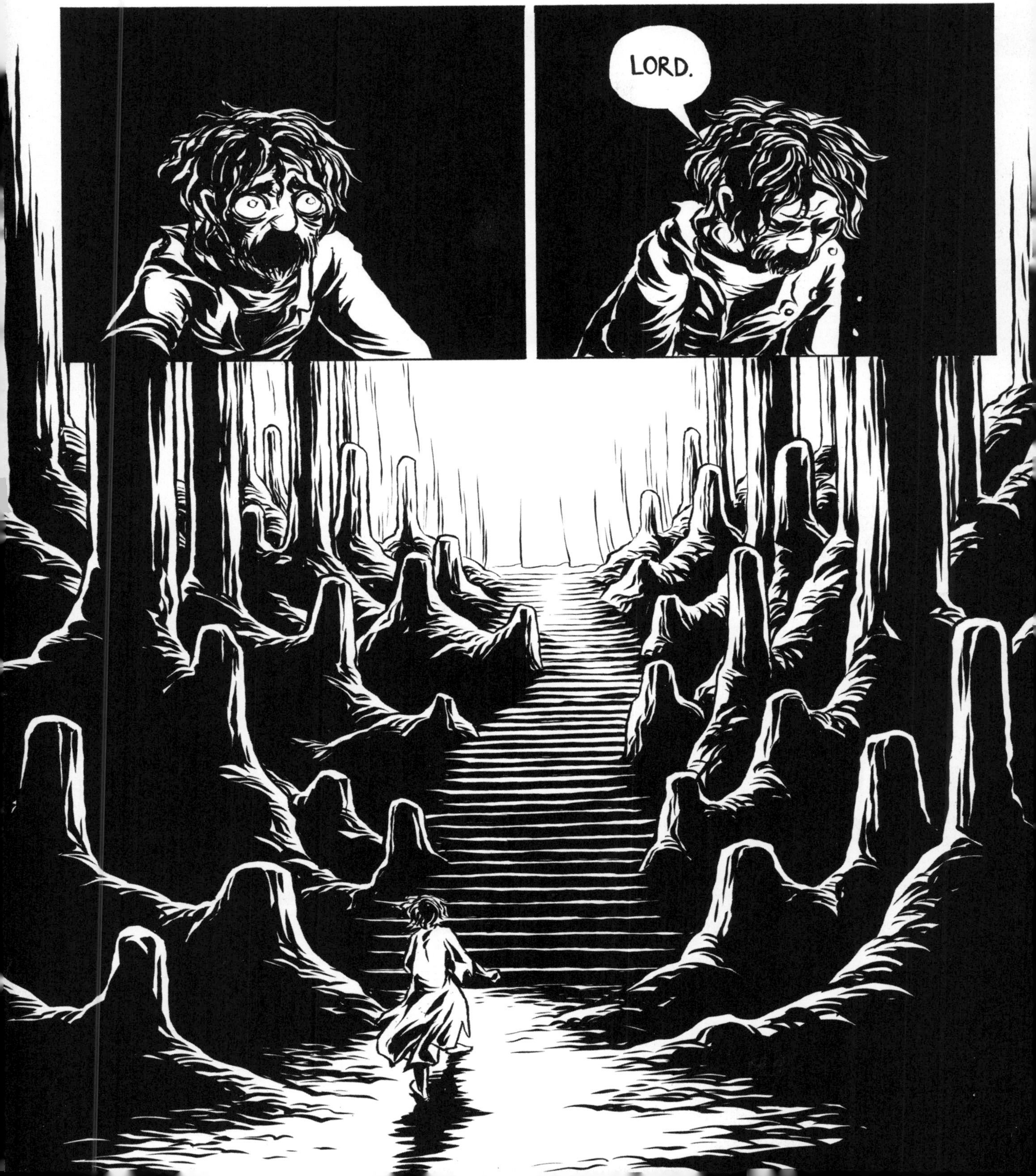
LORD.

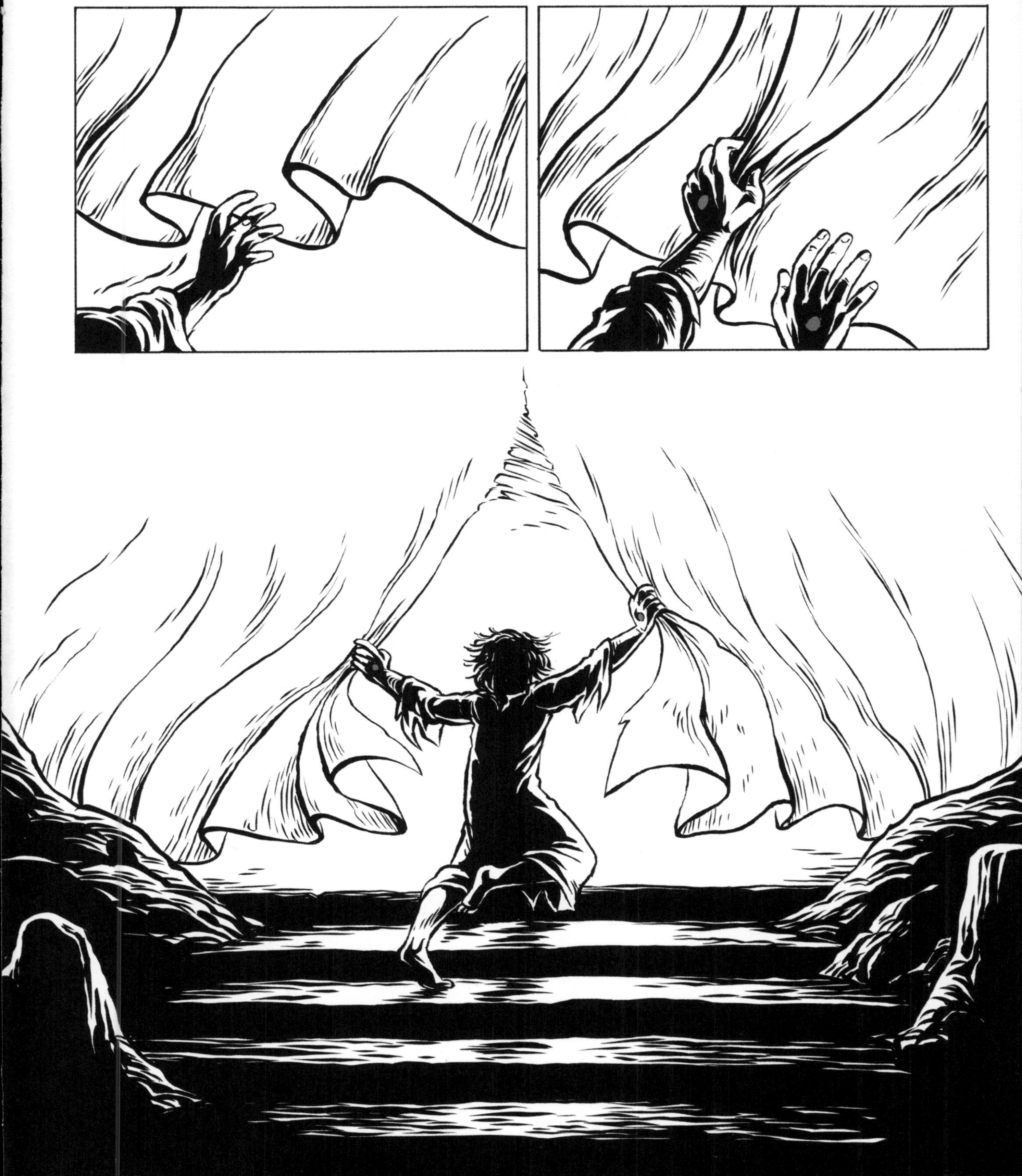

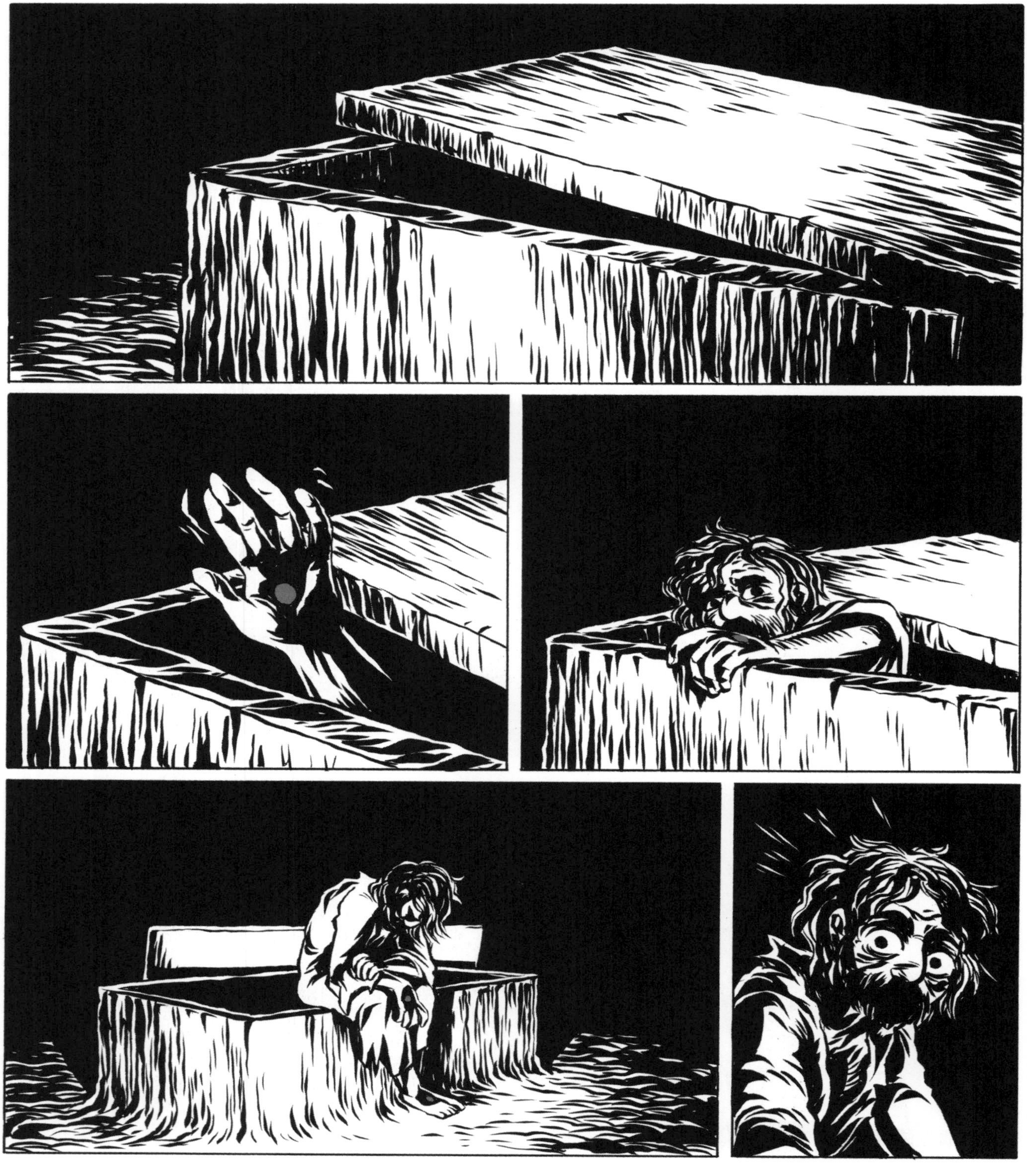

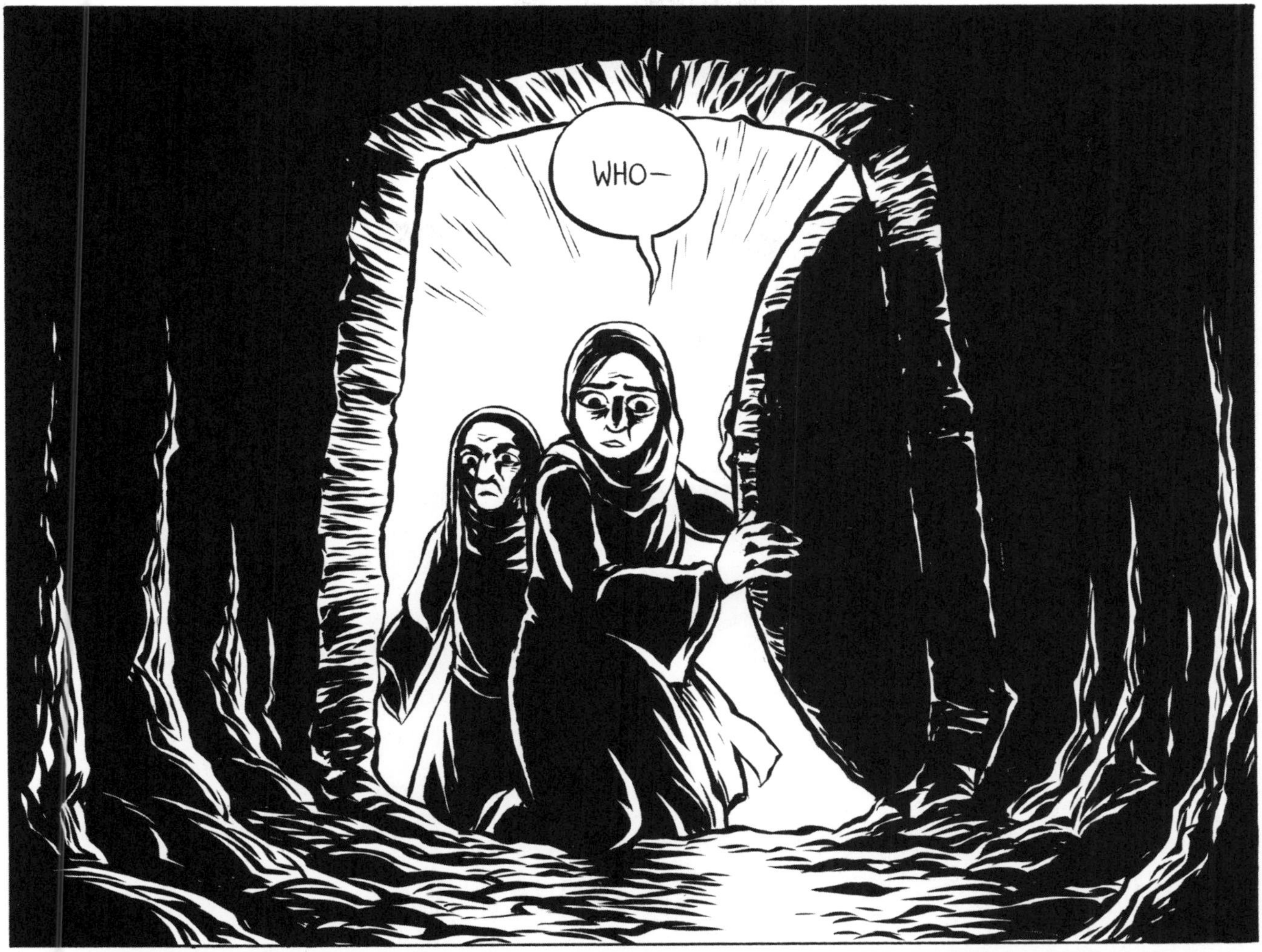
WHO–

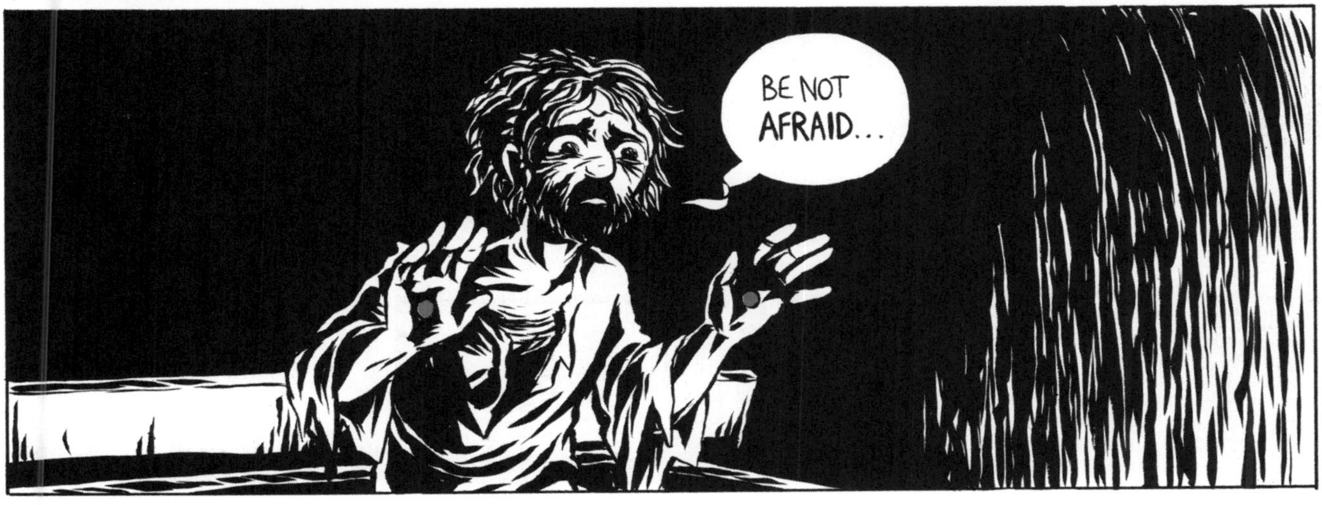
BE NOT AFRAID...

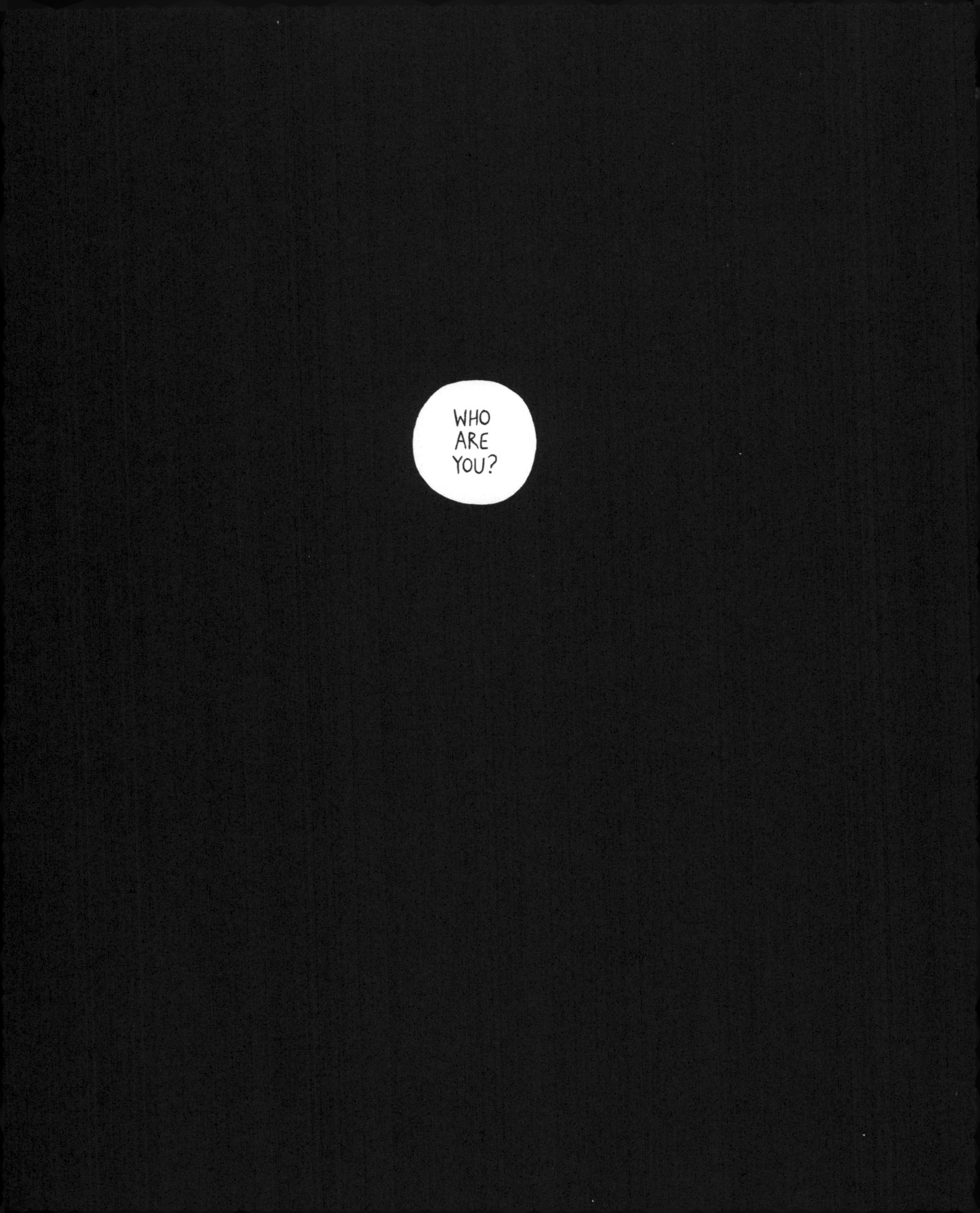
WHO ARE YOU?

ON THIS ADAPTATION

"The Harrowing of Hell" or *"Descensus Christi ad Inferos"* is a story of Christ's triumphant descent into an underworld after his crucifixion, building upon suggestions at a few points throughout the New Testament. As Christianity has worked to literalize every aspect of its scripture from the 70s AD until today, this story has interacted with our much later conception of Hell as an ultimate prison. This has led to a disavowal of the Harrowing as a literal story in most traditions, though I grew up reciting a version of the Apolstles' Creed in the Episcopal Church that still preserves the lines:

> *...suffered under Pontius Pilate,*
> *was crucified, died, and was buried;*
>
> *he descended into hell;*
> *on the third day he rose again from the dead...*

This adaptation draws on several sources in Christian and Jewish scripture and apocrypha; I can't keep up with the dense intertextuality that inaugurated Christianity, but it has been productive to try. I have however focused on two texts in particular:

The apocryphal Gospel of Nicodemus is the earliest known presentation of Christ's descent as a narrative.

It was probably written in the 300s AD: incidentally at the moment when Christianity was being incorporated into the Roman Empire under Emperor Constantine. The Gospel literalizes some aspects of the canonical gospels and helps support the claim that Jesus fulfilled Old Testament prophecy by having the dead Old Testament prophets directly proclaim their prophecies fulfilled by him. It, and the surrounding mythology of the Harrowing, were instrumental in the building of the Christian ideas of Hell and Satan that we inherit—these were still fairly ambiguous and variable concepts in much of the canon itself.

The other book I've focused on is its profound opposite: the King James version of the Gospel According to Mark, mostly agreed-upon to be the first canonical record of Jesus' life. Mark is an extremely spare, mysterious narrative—practically a work of political theory using the framework of a biography, with mystical elements deployed with their symbolic utility clearly in mind. Its intense thematic focus and its anti-authoritarian arguments at odds with practically everything we've ever heard about Jesus—even much included in the later gospels—are fascinating to me. I have almost totally prioritized this account of Jesus' life instead of building any sort of "gospel harmony," in an attempt to emphasize the text as a contingent work with its own themes, historical perspective, and vested interests.

This book draws on other books from the King James Bible, including Psalms, Isaiah, Daniel, Genesis, and Revelation. Alice Turner's *The History of Hell* is an overview of the underworld mythologies and their history that started me on this project. For Nicodemus and other Christian apocrypha, I used J.K. Elliott's *The Apocryphal Jesus*, and Elaine Pagel's work.

I owe a lot to radical Christianities and radical secular readings of Christianity, particularly those of John Dominic Crossan, Jacques Ellul, and Leo Tolstoy.

Some other interesting things that may have found their way into this include Werher H. Kelber's essay "The Gospel of Mark as Written Parable," Bart Ehrman's work on the "historical Jesus," tiny bits of Raymond E. Brown's *The Death of the Messiah*, and Alan Dundes' "The Hero Pattern and the Life of Jesus."

For the purposes of this project I am not at all interested in what the "real" Jesus was like, or in the truth of mystical claims. To me, a focus on such questions deadens much that is interesting and inspiring about ancient writings and traditions like this—to say nothing of the fact that our own particular modern standards of journalistic objectivity would have been inconceivable to ancient writers and thinkers.

I use "Old Testament" to emphasize the readings of those texts within Christianity; I don't meant to prioritize that reading outside of this project or to argue against their validity within other traditions.

COLOPHON

The pages of this book were drawn at 150% reproduction size, in India ink with a Winsor & Newton Series 7 brush on Bristol board. Lettering and formal elements were drawn with Micron pen. The spot color used is PANTONE 2347 U.